Force.com Enterprise Architecture

Blend industry best practices to architect and deliver packaged Force.com applications that cater to enterprise business needs

Andrew Fawcett

[PACKT] enterprise

PUBLISHING

professional expertise distilled

BIRMINGHAM - MUMBAI

Force.com Enterprise Architecture

First published: September 2014

Production reference: 1180914

Published by Packt Publishing Ltd.
Livery Place
35 Livery Street
Birmingham B3 2PB, UK.

ISBN 978-1-78217-299-4

www.packtpub.com

Cover image by Pratyush Mohanta (tysoncinematics@gmail.com)

Credits

Author

Andrew Fawcett

Reviewers

Matt Bingham

Steven Herod

John M. Daniel

Matt Lacey

Andrew Smith

Rohit Arora

Karanraj Sankaranarayanan

Jitendra Zaa

Commissioning Editor

Gregory Wild

Acquisition Editor

Gregory Wild

Content Development Editor

Neil Alexander

Technical Editors

Tanvi Bhatt

Neha Mankare

Copy Editors

Deepa Nambiar

Alfida Paiva

Project Coordinator

Sanchita Mandal

Proofreaders

Samuel Redman Birch

Stephen Copestake

Maria Gould

Paul Hindle

Indexers

Monica Ajmera Mehta

Rekha Nair

Graphics

Ronak Dhruv

Abhinash Sahu

Production Coordinator

Conidon Miranda

Cover Work

Conidon Miranda

Foreword

As a Developer Evangelist for salesforce.com, I've seen an ever-widening demand for the exact kind of material that Andrew brings to the table with this book. While I often get the joy of showing developers new features that are rolling out on Force.com, I am often also asked questions about daily challenges when it comes to leveraging those features and implementing solutions within the ecosystem required by enterprise developer teams. This book will go a long way in providing new reference material specifically for those concerns.

In 2007, I started developing at salesforce.com, and the landscape looked quite different than it is today. There was no Visualforce. Apex had just launched and lacked many of the interfaces it enjoys now, such as batchable and schedulable. Most custom interfaces were accomplished through extensive amounts of JavaScript embedded in S-Controls, which is a portion of the platform that is no longer supported. Communicating back to the platform could be done via the SOAP API using the AJAX toolkit. If you wanted truly fine-tuned business logic on the server side, you exposed it via a custom SOAP endpoint in Apex.

In 2014, the capabilities of the platform completely eclipse those days. With Standard Controllers, Visualforce provides basic business logic out of the box, without additional code required. For custom processing, a developer is not limited to just a single option, but various routes ranging from extending Visualforce's components library to exposing Apex methods directly to JavaScript—providing the flexibility from the old AJAX toolkit without ever needing to access the scope of the platform APIs. Apex can be scheduled, it can churn through records in the background, and it can be used to create completely custom REST endpoints. Developers now have access to powerful new APIs such as Streaming and Analytics as well as industrial strength identity services.

The platform continues to evolve. At Dreamforce, each year, we announce new tools, features, and functionality to the platform. Last year was Salesforce1 with a new mobile application that would make deploying interfaces to smartphones a simple and integrated process. This coming October, we will deliver new industry-changing innovations.

This pace of technical evolution combined with an ever increasing adoption of Force.com for enterprise applications poses a specific challenge for developers: to continually think of the platform not as just a solution for various use cases, but as a complete ecosystem that uses the platform efficiently. It is no longer sufficient to consider that a given application simply works on the platform; developers need to consider whether their applications are being designed in a way that leverages the correct features and that will co-exist efficiently and well. It takes the ability to view how the platform is being limited from a high level and with a clear direction.

I knew Andrew was the kind of architect with such an ability when we started discussing a new set of articles he was writing based on Martin Fowler's *Separation of Concerns* and how such design patterns could be used to develop Apex for enterprise solutions. Seven years ago, thinking about Apex in such layers of abstraction was certainly possible—it just wasn't really necessary. With all the potential tools and features in the hands of a Force.com developer now, not considering such concepts is begging for maintenance debt down the road.

Andrew being in a position to write this book should be a surprise to nobody familiar with his company's work. FinancialForce.com has created some of the most robust applications I've seen on Force.com, and as Chief Technical Officer, Andrew has been at the forefront of making them successful.

Hence, I'm delighted to see Andrew writing this book, and that at its core, we can see an expanded version of his previous design pattern articles. Actually, simply a printed copy of those articles would not be a bad addition to an architect's library, but here, we also see a more complete vision of what a developer should know before building applications on the platform that levels off from higher order considerations like interfacing Apex classes together down to the concrete tasks of properly leveraging Source Control software for Force.com.

I'm excited to see this book on my shelf, and hopefully yours—it will help you map out not only this generation of Force.com applications, but to move forward with future ones as well.

Joshua Birk
Salesforce Developer Evangelist

About the Author

Andrew Fawcett has over 20 years of experience, holding several software-development-related roles with increasing focus and responsibility around enterprise-level product architectures with major international accounting and ERP software vendors over the years. He is experienced in performing and managing all aspects of the software development life cycle across various technology platforms, frameworks, industry design patterns, and methodologies, more recently Salesforce's Force.com and Heroku.

He is currently a CTO, Force.com MVP, and Salesforce Certified Developer within a UNIT4 and salesforce.com-funded start-up company, FinancialForce.com. He is responsible for driving platform adoption, relationship, and technical strategy across the product suite. He is an avid blogger, a StackExchange junkie, an open source contributor and project owner, and an experienced speaker at various Salesforce and FinancialForce.com events. He loves watching Formula1 motor racing, movies, and building cloud-controlled Lego robots!

His Twitter handle is `@andyinthecloud`. His Lego robot Twitter handle and website is `@brickinthecloud`.

Acknowledgments

Work commitments are greater than ever these days and personal time is precious, so to give these things up and review my book deserves a huge, heartfelt show of appreciation and a thank you to the following people: Matt Bingham, Steven Herod, John M. Daniel, Matt Lacey, Andrew Smith, and Josh Birk, as well as the support from all the reviewers and technical editors at Packt.

I would also like to give thanks to FinancialForce.com for its commitment to the Salesforce community by sharing code through its public GitHub repositories, many of which are featured and leveraged in this book. Open source is nothing without contributors; these repositories continue to benefit from contributions made both in the past and present by developers both internal and external to FinancialForce.com. I also want to say thank you to those contributors!

Further, for all his understanding and help, I'd really like to say a massive thank you to Gregory Wild who has really supported me from start to finish through this exciting chapter in my career. Last but definitely not the least, I would like to thank my wife for her continued support.

About the Reviewers

Matt Bingham is a Force.com MVP and Sencha-certified specialist. He hails from Australia as an electronic designer. Matt works with BigAss Consulting (bigass.force.com), helping ISVs develop and transform their products on the Salesforce platform.

Steven Herod has 20 years of experience building web-based applications as a developer, architect, and in various technical leadership roles. His last 4 years have been focused on the Salesforce platform. He is a Salesforce MVP, Certified Technical Architect, and Certified Advanced Developer, and he also holds the Sales Cloud, Service Cloud, Administrator, and Advanced Administrator certifications. He co-leads the Sydney Salesforce Developer Group and regularly presents at conferences on cloud-based technologies. Currently, he is the Technical Director for the Asia Pacific and Japan region for Cloud Sherpas. He lives in Wollongong near Sydney, Australia.

> I'd like to thank my wife, Barbara, and children, Alex, Darcy, and Isabel, for their ongoing support.

John M. Daniel has been working in the technology sector for over 20 years. During that time, he has worked with a variety of technologies and project roles. Currently, John serves as a technical architect for Mavens Consulting, Chicago, Illinois, United States of America; a Salesforce partner with a focus on the Life Sciences space. He currently holds multiple certifications including the Service Cloud Consultant certification and the Advanced Developer certification. John is currently in the process of attaining the Certified Technical Architect certification as well. John's passions are spending time with his family, swimming, and working on various open source projects such as ApexUML.

He has also been a reviewer for *Learning Apex Development, Packt Publishing.*

> I would like to thank my wife, Allison, for always giving me the freedom to pursue my interests.

Matt Lacey is a Force.com MVP who has been developing on the platform for over 5 years. A passionate community advocate, Matt proposed and now moderates the Salesforce StackExchange site and co-hosts the Code Coverage podcast with Steven Herod. Matt is a co-founder at the S. P. Keasey Trading Co. and Proximity Insight, both Force.com ISV partners.

> I'd like to thank Andy for writing this excellent book; I only wish he'd done so several years ago.

Andrew Smith has over 12 years of experience in enterprise cloud apps and platforms. As Director of Product Management at salesforce.com for 8 years, he led the development of the Salesforce platform used by third parties to build, distribute, and sell their applications. He advised numerous startups built on Salesforce, helping them refine their offerings to grow their business'. He also designed many of the Salesforce platform development tools used by thousands of customers every day.

Rohit Arora is the founder/CEO at Raider Data Services Private Limited, with over 12 years of extensive experience in building enterprise applications. He is a postgraduate in Business Administration and also a technology enthusiast for cutting-edge technologies introduced in the cloud computing arena.

His company works with major industry leaders in services and product development for the cloud platform. Being actively involved in the design and execution of projects, they have positioned themselves in the market with an edge over similar consulting partners in both service and product development. Their consultants are extremely customer focused and keen learners and seek the opportunity to learn in every project, irrespective of size and scale.

I would like to thank the author of the book and Packt Publishing for bringing this up and collating the information into a powerful book.

Karanraj Sankaranarayanan, who likes to go by Karan, is a certified salesforce.com developer and works as a Salesforce consultant at HCL Technologies. Karan holds a Bachelor's degree in Engineering from Anna University with a specialization in Computer Science. He has more than 4 years of experience in the Salesforce platform and IT industry. He is passionate about the Salesforce platform and is an active member/contributor of the Salesforce community. He writes technical blogs too at `http://clicksandcode.blogspot.in/`.

He won second place in the Salesforce Summer of Hacks event in Bangalore. He is also the leader of the Chennai Salesforce platform Developer Group based in Chennai, India. He is one of the reviewers of *Force.com Tips and Tricks, Visualforce Development Cookbook*, and *Force.com Development Blueprints*, all by Packt Publishing. He can be reached via Twitter (`@karanrajs`) and through the Salesforce community at `https://success.salesforce.com/profile?u=00530000004fXkCAAU`.

Reviewing this book was a great experience. I would like to thank the author and Packt Publishing for presenting this opportunity to me.

Jitendra Zaa (@ilovenagpur) is a Force.com developer and owner of a well-known Salesforce blog, `blog.shivasoft.in`. He has extensively worked in many areas of Force.com such as integration, data loading, AppExchange, and application development. He is a Java and Salesforce Certified Advanced Developer, Administrator, and Consultant.

He has more than 7 years of experience in software development using Salesforce, Java, Node.Js, AngularJS, PHP, ORMB, J2ME, and ASP.NET technologies. He is currently working with Cognizant Technology Solutions in USA and graduated from RTM, Nagpur University.

Other than this book, he has also reviewed other Salesforce-related books by Packt Publishing, such as *Visualforce Cookbook*, *Developing Applications with Salesforce Chatter*, and many others.

I would like to thank my parents, family, friends, and especially my wife, for helping me in maintaining time for writing blogs and encouraging me. Also, I would like to thank the Packt Publishing team and the author of this book for giving me this unique opportunity.

www.PacktPub.com

Support files, eBooks, discount offers, and more

You might want to visit www.PacktPub.com for support files and downloads related to your book.

Did you know that Packt offers eBook versions of every book published, with PDF and ePub files available? You can upgrade to the eBook version at www.PacktPub.com and as a print book customer, you are entitled to a discount on the eBook copy. Get in touch with us at service@packtpub.com for more details.

At www.PacktPub.com, you can also read a collection of free technical articles, sign up for a range of free newsletters and receive exclusive discounts and offers on Packt books and eBooks.

http://PacktLib.PacktPub.com

Do you need instant solutions to your IT questions? PacktLib is Packt's online digital book library. Here, you can access, read and search across Packt's entire library of books.

Why subscribe?

- Fully searchable across every book published by Packt
- Copy and paste, print and bookmark content
- On demand and accessible via web browser

Free access for Packt account holders

If you have an account with Packt at www.PacktPub.com, you can use this to access PacktLib today and view nine entirely free books. Simply use your login credentials for immediate access.

Instant updates on new Packt books

Get notified! Find out when new books are published by following @PacktEnterprise on Twitter, or the *Packt Enterprise* Facebook page.

Table of Contents

Preface   **1**

Chapter 1: Building, Publishing, and Supporting Your Application   **9**

Required organizations   **10**
Introducing the book's sample application   **12**
Package types and benefits   **13**
    Features and benefits of managed packages   14
Creating your first managed package   **15**
    Setting your package namespace   15
    Creating the package and assigning it to the namespace   17
    Adding components to the package   18
    Extension packages   19
Package dependencies and uploading   **19**
    Uploading the release and beta packages   20
    Optional package dependencies   22
        Dynamic Apex and Visualforce   22
        Extension packages   22
Introduction to AppExchange and listings   **23**
Installing and testing your package   **24**
    Automating package installation   26
Becoming a Salesforce partner and benefits   **28**
    Security review and benefits   29
Licensing   **31**
    The Licenses tab and managing customer licenses   33
    The Subscribers tab   34
    The Subscriber Overview page   35
    How licensing is enforced in the subscriber org   36
Providing support   **36**
Customer metrics   **38**

Trialforce and Test Drive	**38**
Summary	**39**
Chapter 2: Leveraging Platform Features	**41**
Packaging and upgradable components	**42**
Custom field – picklist values	43
Automating upgrades with the Salesforce Metadata API	44
Understanding the custom field features	**45**
Default field values	45
Encrypted fields	46
Lookup options, filters, and layouts	47
Rollup summaries and limits	50
Understanding the available security features	**53**
Functional security	53
Your code and security review considerations	56
Data security	57
Your code and security review considerations	60
Platform APIs	**60**
Considerations when naming objects and fields	62
Localization and translation	**63**
Localization	63
Translation	64
Building customizable user interfaces	**65**
Layouts	66
Visualforce	66
E-mail customization with e-mail templates	**66**
Workflow and Flow	**67**
Social features and mobile	**68**
Summary	**72**
Chapter 3: Application Storage	**73**
Mapping out end user storage requirements	**74**
Understanding the different storage types	**75**
Data storage	76
Columns versus rows	76
Visualizing your object model	78
Custom settings storage	79
File storage	81
Record identification, uniqueness, and auto numbering	81
Unique and external ID fields	82
Auto Number fields	82
Record relationships	85

Reusing the existing Standard Objects   **87**
Importing and exporting data   **87**
Options for replicating and archiving data   **90**
External data sources   **91**
Summary   **91**

Chapter 4: Apex Execution and Separation of Concerns   **93**
Execution contexts   **94**
Exploring execution contexts   94
Execution context and state   96
Execution context and security   97
Execution context transaction management   98
Apex governors and namespaces   **99**
The namespaces and governor scope   99
Deterministic and non-deterministic governors   101
Key governors for Apex package developers   102
Where is Apex used?   **103**
Separation of Concerns   **106**
Apex code evolution   106
Separating concerns in Apex   107
Execution context logic versus application logic concerns   108
Improving incremental code reuse   110
Patterns of Enterprise Application Architecture   **112**
The Service layer   113
The Domain Model layer   113
The Data Mapper (Selector) layer   114
Introducing the FinancialForce.com Apex Commons library   114
Unit testing versus system testing   **115**
The packaging code   **116**
Summary   **117**

Chapter 5: Application Service Layer   **119**
Introducing the Service layer pattern   **120**
Implementation of design guidelines   **121**
Naming conventions   121
Bulkification   125
Defining and passing data   126
Considerations when using SObjects in the Service layer interface   128
Transaction management   129
Compound services   129
A quick guideline checklist   131

Handling DML with the Unit Of Work pattern   **132**
Without a Unit Of Work   134
With Unit Of Work   136
The Unit Of Work scope   140
Unit Of Work special considerations   140
Services calling services   **141**
Contract Driven Development   **146**
Testing the Service layer   **149**
Mocking the Service layer   150
Calling the Service layer   **150**
Updating the FormulaForce package   152
Summary   **154**

Chapter 6: Application Domain Layer   **155**
Introducing the Domain layer pattern   **156**
Encapsulating an object's behavior in code   157
Interpreting the Domain layer in Force.com   157
Domain classes in Apex compared to other platforms   158
Implementation design guidelines   **159**
Naming conventions   159
Bulkification   161
Defining and passing data   162
Transaction management   162
Domain class template   **162**
Implementing Domain Trigger logic   **164**
Routing trigger events to Domain class methods   164
Enforcing object security   166
Apex Trigger event handling   166
Defaulting field values on insert   167
Validation on insert   167
Validation on update   168
Implementing custom Domain logic   **169**
Object-oriented programming   **170**
Creating a compliance application framework   170
An Apex Interface example   171
Step 5 – defining a generic service   172
Step 6 – implementing the Domain class interface   173
Step 7 – the domain class factory pattern   175
Step 8 – implementing a generic service   176
Step 9 – using the generic service from a generic controller   177
Summarizing compliance framework implementation   179

Testing the Domain layer   **180**
  Unit testing   181
  Test methods using DML and SOQL   181
  Test methods using the Domain class methods   183
Calling the Domain layer   **184**
  Service layer interactions   185
  Domain layer interactions   187
Updating the FormulaForce package   **190**
Summary   **191**

Chapter 7: Application Selector Layer   **193**
Introducing the Selector layer pattern   **194**
Implementing design guidelines   **195**
  Naming conventions   195
  Bulkification   196
  Record order consistency   196
  Querying fields consistently   197
The Selector class template   **198**
Implementing the standard query logic   **201**
  Standard features of the selectSObjectsById method   201
    Security   202
    Ordering   202
    Field Sets   203
    Multi-Currency   204
Implementing the custom query logic   **205**
  A basic custom Selector method   206
  A custom Selector method with sub-select   207
  A custom Selector method with related fields   209
  A custom Selector method with a custom data set   210
    Combining Apex data types with SObject types   213
  SOSL and Aggregate SOQL queries   214
Introducing the Selector factory   **215**
  SelectorFactory methods   216
    Usage and reasons for the newInstance method   216
    Writing tests and the Selector layer   218
  Mocking Selectors   219
    Step 1 – using the Application.Selector.newInstance approach   219
    Step 2 – applying virtual and @TestVisible   220
    Step 3 – creating a mock Selector class   221
    Step 4 – writing a test with Application.Selector.setMock   222
    Which type of Selector methods cannot be mocked?   223
Updating the FormulaForce package   **223**
Summary   **224**

Chapter 8: User Interface   225
What devices should you target?   226
Leveraging the Salesforce standard UI   226
Overriding the standard Salesforce UI   227
Hybrid standard and Visualforce UIs   228
Custom Buttons and Related lists   230
Rendering the standard UI within a Visualforce page   232
Translation and localization   232
Client communication layers   233
Client communication options   233
API governors and availability   235
Database transaction scope and client calls   236
Visualforce   236
What can I do within a Visualforce page?   237
Executing the code on page load with the action attribute   237
Caching content with the cache and the expires attributes   238
Creating a Download button with the contentType attribute   239
Overriding the language of the page with the language attribute 240
HTML5 and the docType attribute   241
Offline Visualforce pages with the manifest attribute   241
Generating PDF content with the renderAs attribute   241
Visualforce SOQL, iterator limits, and the readOnly attribute   242
Field-level security   242
Page response time and components   247
Demonstrating a large component tree   248
Considerations for managing large component trees   250
Client-managed state versus server-managed state   251
Action methods versus JavaScript Remoting   252
Mixing the use of action methods and JavaScript Remoting   255
Applying JavaScript Remoting to the Service layer   256
Considerations for client-side logic and Service layer logic   256
When should I use JavaScript Remote Objects?   257
Client-side alternatives to Visualforce UI components   258
Salesforce Aura   259
Custom Publisher Actions   260
Creating websites   260
Mobile strategy   261
Custom Reporting and the Analytics API   261
Updating the FormulaForce package   262
Summary   262

Chapter 9: Providing Integration and Extensibility — 265

Reviewing your integration and extensibility needs — 266
Defining the Developer X persona — 266
Versioning — 267
Versioning the API definition — 267
Versioning application access through the Salesforce APIs — 268
Versioning the API functionality — 269
Translation and localization — 270
Terminology and platform alignment — 272
What are your application's integration needs? — 272
Developer X calling your APIs on-platform — 273
Developer X calling your APIs off-platform — 274
What are your applications extensibility needs? — 275
Force.com platform APIs for integration — 276
Application integration APIs — 277
Providing Apex application APIs — 277
Calling an application API from Apex — 279
Modifying and depreciating the application API — 281
Versioning Apex API definitions — 282
Versioning Apex API behavior — 285
Providing RESTful application APIs — 286
Key aspects of being RESTful — 287
What are your application resources? — 287
Mapping HTTP methods — 289
Providing REST application APIs — 290
Calling your REST application APIs — 291
Versioning REST APIs — 292
Is it worth versioning Apex REST APIs? — 294
Alignment with Force.com extensibility features — 294
Extending the application logic with Apex Interfaces — 295
Summary — 298
Chapter 10: Asynchronous Processing and Big Data Volumes — 299
Creating test data for volume testing — 300
Using the Apex script to create the Race Data object — 301
Indexes, being selective, and query optimization — 303
Standard and custom indexes — 303
Ensuring queries leverage indexes — 305
Factors affecting the use of indexes — 305
Profiling queries — 307
Skinny tables — 313
Handling large result sets — 313
Processing unlimited result sets in Apex — 315

Asynchronous execution contexts	**318**
General async design considerations	319
Running Apex in the asynchronous mode	321
@future	322
Batch Apex	323
Volume testing	**328**
Summary	**329**
Chapter 11: Source Control and Continuous Integration	**331**
Development workflow and infrastructure	**332**
Packaging org versus sandbox versus developer org	332
Creating and preparing your developer orgs	333
The developer workflow	334
Developing with Source Control	**337**
Populating your Source Control repository	338
The Ant build script to clean and build your application	344
Developing in developer orgs versus packaging orgs	346
Leveraging the Metadata API and Tooling APIs from Ant	347
Updating your Source Control repository	348
Browser-based development and Source Control	349
Desktop-based development and Source Control	350
Hooking up Continuous Integration	**352**
The Continuous Integration process	353
Updating the Ant build script for CI	354
Installing, configuring, and testing the Jenkins CI server	355
Exploring Jenkins and CI further	357
Releasing from Source Control	**359**
Automated regression testing	**360**
Summary	**361**
Index	**363**

Preface

Enterprise organizations have complex processes and integration requirements that typically span multiple locations around the world. They seek out the best in class applications that support their needs today and in the future. The ability to adapt an application to their practices, terminology, and integrations with other existing applications or processes is key to them. They invest as much in your application as they do in you as the vendor capable of delivering an application strategy that will grow with them.

Throughout this book, you will be shown how to architect and support enduring applications for enterprise clients with Salesforce by exploring how to identify architecture needs and design solutions based on industry-standard patterns. Large-scale applications require careful coding practices to keep the code base scalable. You'll learn advanced coding patterns based on industry-standard enterprise patterns and reconceive them for Force.com, allowing you to get the most out of the platform and build in best practices from the start of your project.

As your development team grows, managing the development cycle with more robust application life cycle tools and using approaches such as Continuous Integration become increasingly important. There are many ways to build solutions on Force.com; this book cuts a logical path through the steps and considerations for building packaged solutions from start to finish, covering all aspects from engineering to getting it into the hands of your customers and beyond, ensuring they get the best value possible from your Force.com application.

What this book covers

Chapter 1, Building, Publishing, and Supporting Your Application, gets your application out to your prospects and customers using packages, AppExchange, and subscriber support.

Chapter 2, Leveraging Platform Features, ensures that your application is aligned with the platform features and uses them whenever possible, which is great for productivity when building your application, but perhaps more importantly, it ensures whether your customers are also able to extend and integrate with your application further.

Chapter 3, Application Storage, teaches you how to model your application's data to make effective use of storage space, which can make a big difference to your customer's ongoing costs and initial decision-making when choosing your application.

Chapter 4, Apex Execution and Separation of Concerns, explains how the platform handles requests and at what point Apex code is invoked. This is important to understand how to design your code for maximum reuse and durability.

Chapter 5, Application Service Layer, focuses on understanding the real heart of your application: how to design it, make it durable, and future proofing around a rapidly evolving platform using Martin Fowler's Service pattern as a template.

Chapter 6, Application Domain Layer, aligns Apex code typically locked away in Apex Triggers into classes more aligned with the functional purpose and behavior of your objects, using object-orientated programming (OOP) to increase reuse and streamline code and leveraging Martin Fowler's Domain pattern as a template.

Chapter 7, Application Selector Layer, leverages SOQL to make the most out of the query engine, which can make queries complex. Using Martin Fowler's Mapping pattern as a template, this chapter illustrates a means to encapsulate queries, making them more accessible and reusable, and their results more predictable and robust across your code base.

Chapter 8, User Interface, covers the concerns of an enterprise application user interface with respect to translation, localization, and customization, as well as the pros and cons of the various UI options available in the platform.

Chapter 9, Providing Integration and Extensibility, explains that enterprise-scale applications require you to carefully consider integration with existing applications and business needs while looking into the future, by designing the application with extensibility in mind.

Chapter 10, Asynchronous Processing and Big Data Volumes, shows that designing an application that processes massive volumes of data either interactively or asynchronously requires consideration in understanding your customer's volume requirements and leveraging the latest platform tools and features, such as understanding the query optimizer and when to create indexes.

Chapter 11, Source Control and Continuous Integration, shows that maintaining a consistent code base across applications of scale requires careful consideration of Source Control and a planned approach to integration as the application is developed and implemented.

What you need for this book

In order to follow the practical examples in this book, you will need to install the Salesforce Force.com IDE, Apache Ant v1.6 or later, Java v1.6 or later, and the Salesforce Developer Edition Orgs.

The following is the list:

- Salesforce Developer Edition Orgs
- Java v1.6 (or later)
- Apache Ant v1.6 (or later)
- GitHub Client (optional for chapters 1 - 10)
- Salesforce Force.com IDE (optional)
- MavensMate (optional for chapters 1 - 10)
- Salesforce Developer Console (optional)

Who this book is for

This book is aimed at Force.com developers who are looking to push past Force.com basics, and learn how to truly discover its potential. You will be looking to expand your knowledge of developing packaged ISV software and complex, scalable applications for use in enterprise businesses with the Salesforce platform. You will know your way around Force.com's non programmatic functionality as well as Apex, and are looking to learn how to architect powerful solutions for enterprise-scale demands. If you have a background in developing inside other enterprise software ecosystems you will find this book an invaluable resource for adopting Force.com.

Conventions

In this book, you will find a number of styles of text that distinguish between different kinds of information. Here are some examples of these styles, and an explanation of their meaning.

Code words in text, database table names, folder names, filenames, file extensions, pathnames, dummy URLs, user input, and Twitter handles are shown as follows: "This example utilizes read and write member variables in the `RaceRetirement` class, indicating both are required."

A block of code is set as follows:

```
try
{
  Set<Id> seasons = new Set<Id> { seasonId };

  SeasonService.updateStandings(seasons);

  SeasonService.issueNewsLetters(seasons);
}
catch (Exception e)
{
  ApexPages.addMessage(e);
}
```

When we wish to draw your attention to a particular part of a code block, the relevant lines or items are set in bold:

```
public PageReference awardPoints()
{
  try
  {
    ContestantService.awardChampionshipPoints(
      new Set<Id> { standardController.getId() });
  }
  catch (Exception e)
  {
    ApexPages.addMessages(e);
  }
  return null;
}
```

Any command-line input or output is written as follows:

```
ant package.installdemo

  -Dsf.username=testorgusername

  -Dsf.password=testorgpasswordtestorgtoken
```

New terms and **important words** are shown in bold. Words that you see on the screen, in menus or dialog boxes for example, appear in the text like this: "The **Developer Console** option provides some excellent tools to profile the consumption of governors."

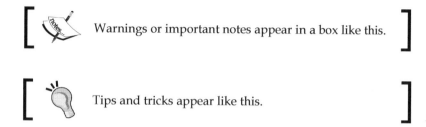

Warnings or important notes appear in a box like this.

Tips and tricks appear like this.

Reader feedback

Feedback from our readers is always welcome. Let us know what you think about this book—what you liked or may have disliked. Reader feedback is important for us to develop titles that you really get the most out of.

To send us general feedback, simply send an e-mail to feedback@packtpub.com, and mention the book title via the subject of your message.

If there is a topic that you have expertise in and you are interested in either writing or contributing to a book, see our author guide on www.packtpub.com/authors.

Customer support

Now that you are the proud owner of a Packt book, we have a number of things to help you to get the most from your purchase.

Downloading the example code

The source code for this book has been provided through the cloud-based source control repository known as GitHub. The collective source code for the application built throughout the book is available in the `main` branch. For each chapter, a branch has been provided containing the code added during that chapter building from the previous one, for example, branch `chapter-02` will contain code from `chapter-01`.

The repository for this book can be found at `https://github.com/afawcett/forcedotcom-enterprise-architecture`.

Downloading the source code

You can download the example code files for all Packt books you have purchased from your account at `http://www.packtpub.com`. If you purchased this book elsewhere, you can visit `http://www.packtpub.com/support` and register to have the files e-mailed directly to you.

An alternate way to **download the source code** is to navigate to `www.github.com` in your browser using the link given in the preceding section, locate the repository and branch you want to download, either the `main` branch or a specific chapter branch, and then click on the **Download Zip** button in the sidebar on the right.

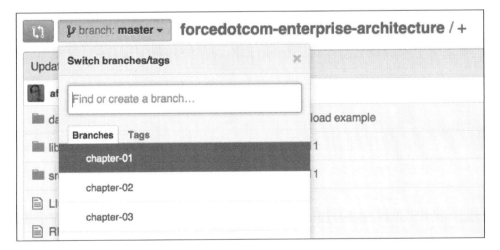

Alternatively, you can download the GitHub desktop clients as listed above and click on the **Clone in Desktop** button.

Of course, if you are familiar with Git, you are free to use the tool of your choice.

Deploying the source code

Once you have the source code downloaded for your chosen chapter, you should execute the **Ant build script** to deploy the code into your chosen **Salesforce Developer Edition** org (as described in *Chapter 1, Building, Publishing, and Supporting Your Application*).

Open a command line and navigate to the root folder where you downloaded the source code (this should be the folder with the `build.xml` file in it). To deploy the code, execute the following command, all on one line:

```
# ant deploy
  -Dsf.username=myapp@packaging.andyinthecloud.com
  -Dsf.password=mypasswordmytoken
```

Remember that the password and token are concatenated together.

Keep in mind that each chapter branch builds incrementally from the last and will overlay new files as well as changes into your chosen DE org. So, each branch may overwrite changes you make to existing files as you have been exploring that chapter. If you are concerned about this, it is best to use one of the desktop development tools listed earlier, and prior to running the previous command, download the code from the server for safe keeping.

Downloading the color images of this book

We also provide you a PDF file that has color images of the screenshots/diagrams used in this book. The color images will help you better understand the changes in the output. You can download this file from `https://www.packtpub.com/sites/default/files/downloads/2994EN_GraphicsBundle.pdf`.

Errata

Although we have taken every care to ensure the accuracy of our content, mistakes do happen. If you find a mistake in one of our books — maybe a mistake in the text or the code — we would be grateful if you would report this to us. By doing so, you can save other readers from frustration and help us improve subsequent versions of this book. If you find any errata, please report them by visiting `http://www.packtpub.com/submit-errata`, selecting your book, clicking on the **errata submission form** link, and entering the details of your errata. Once your errata are verified, your submission will be accepted and the errata will be uploaded on our website, or added to any list of existing errata, under the Errata section of that title. Any existing errata can be viewed by selecting your title from `http://www.packtpub.com/support`.

Piracy

Piracy of copyright material on the Internet is an ongoing problem across all media. At Packt, we take the protection of our copyright and licenses very seriously. If you come across any illegal copies of our works, in any form, on the Internet, please provide us with the location address or website name immediately so that we can pursue a remedy.

Please contact us at `copyright@packtpub.com` with a link to the suspected pirated material.

We appreciate your help in protecting our authors, and our ability to bring you valuable content.

Questions

You can contact us at `questions@packtpub.com` if you are having a problem with any aspect of the book, and we will do our best to address it.

1
Building, Publishing, and Supporting Your Application

The key for turning an idea into reality lies in its execution. From having the inception of an idea to getting it implemented as an application and into the hands of users is an exciting journey, and is one that constantly develops and evolves between you and your users. One of the great things about developing on **Force.com** is the support you get from the platform beyond the core engineering phase of the production process.

In this first chapter, we will use the declarative aspects of the platform to quickly build an initial version of an application that we will use throughout this book, which will give you an opportunity to get some hands-on experience with some of the packaging and installation features that are needed to *release applications* to subscribers. We will also take a look at the facilities available to *publish* your application through **Salesforce AppExchange** (equivalent to the Apple App Store) and finally provide end user support.

We will then use this application as a basis for incrementally releasing new versions of the application throughout the chapters of this book to build our understanding of Enterprise Application Development. The following topics outline what we will achieve in this chapter:

- Required organizations
- Introducing the book's sample application
- Package types and benefits
- Creating your first managed package
- Package dependencies and uploading
- Introduction to AppExchange and creating listings

- Installing and testing your package
- Becoming a Salesforce partner and its benefits
- Licensing
- Supporting your application
- Customer metrics
- Trialforce and Test Drive

Required organizations

Several Salesforce organizations are required to develop, package, and test your application. You can sign up for these organizations at `https://developer.salesforce.com/`, though in due course, as your relationship with Salesforce becomes more formal, you will have the option of accessing their **Partner Portal** website to create organizations of different types and capabilities. We will discuss more on this later.

It's a good idea to have some kind of naming convention to keep track of the different organizations and logins. Use the following table as a guide and create the following organizations via `https://developer.salesforce.com/`. As stated earlier, these organizations will be used only for the purposes of learning and exploring throughout this book:

Username	Usage	Purpose
`myapp@packaging.my.com`	Packaging	Though we will perform initial work in this org, it will eventually be reserved solely for assembling and uploading a release.
`myapp@testing.my.com`	Testing	In this org, we will install the application and test upgrades. You may want to create several of these in practice, via the Partner Portal website described later in this chapter.
`myapp@dev.my.com`	Developing	In a later chapter, we will shift development of the application into this org, leaving the packaging org to focus only on packaging.

You will have to substitute myapp and my.com (perhaps by reusing your company domain name to avoid naming conflicts) with your own values. Take time to take note of andyapp@packaging.andyinthecloud.com.

The following are other organization types that you will eventually need in order to manage the publication and licensing of your application. However, they are not needed to complete the chapters in this book.

Usage	Purpose
Production / CRM Org	Your organization may already be using this org for managing contacts, leads, opportunities, cases, and other CRM objects. Make sure that you have the complete authority to make changes, if any, to this org since this is where you run your business. If you do not have such an org, you can request one via the Partner Program website described later in this chapter, by requesting (via a case) a CRM ISV org. Even if you choose to not fully adopt Salesforce for this part of your business, such an org is still required when it comes to utilizing the licensing aspects of the platform.
AppExchange Publishing Org (APO)	This org is used to manage your use of AppExchange. We will discuss this a little later in this chapter. This org is actually the same Salesforce org you designate as your production org, where you conduct your sales and support activities from.
License Management Org (LMO)	Within this organization, you can track who installs your application (as leads), the licenses you grant to them, and for how long. It is recommended that this is the same org as the APO described earlier.
Trialforce Management Org (TMO) **Trialforce Source Org (TSO)**	Trialforce is a way to provide orgs with your preconfigured application data for prospective customers to try out your application before buying. It will be discussed later in this chapter.

 Typically, the LMO and APO can be the same as your primary Salesforce production org, which allows you to track all your leads and future opportunities in the same place. This leads to the rule of *APO = LMO = production org*. Though neither of them should be your actual developer or test orgs, you can work with Salesforce support and your Salesforce account manager to plan and assign these orgs.

Introducing the book's sample application

For this book, we will use the world of **Formula1** motor car racing as the basis for a packaged application that we will build together. Formula1 is for me the motor sport that is equivalent to **Enterprise** applications software, due to its scale and complexity. It is also a sport that I follow, both of which helped me when building the examples that we will use.

We will refer to this application as **FormulaForce** throughout this book, though please keep in mind Salesforce's branding policies when naming your own application, as they prevent the use of the word "Force" in the company or product titles.

This application will focus on the data collection aspects of the races, drivers, and their many statistics, utilizing platform features to structure, visualize, and process this data in both historic and current contexts.

For this chapter, we will create some initial **Custom Objects** as detailed in the following table. Do not worry about creating any custom tabs just yet. You can use your preferred approach for creating these initial objects. Ensure that you are logged in to your **packaging org** (we will use the development org later in this book).

Object	Field name and type
Season__c	Name (text)
Race__c	Name (text)
	Season__c (Master-Detail to Season__c)
Driver__c	Name
Contestant__c	Name (Auto Number, CONTESTANT-{00000000})
	Race__c (Master-Detail to Race__c)
	Driver__c (Lookup to Driver__c)

The following screenshot shows the preceding objects within the **Schema Builder** tool, available under the **Setup** menu:

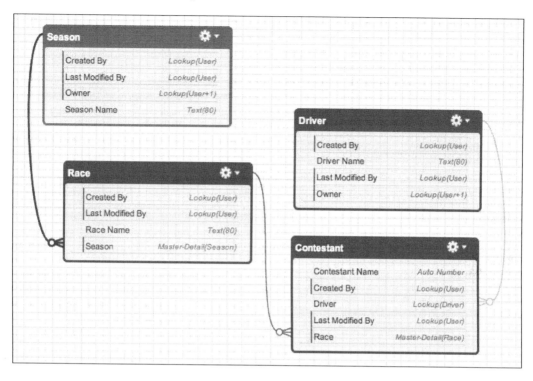

Package types and benefits

A **package** is a container that holds your application components such as Custom Objects, Apex code, Apex triggers, **Visualforce** pages, and so on. This makes up your application. While there are other ways to move components between Salesforce orgs, a package provides a container that you can use for your entire application or deliver optional features by leveraging the so-called **extension packages**.

There are two types of packages, **managed** and **unmanaged**. Unmanaged packages result in the transfer of components from one org to another; however, the result is as if those components had been originally created in the destination org, meaning that they can be readily modified or even deleted by the administrator of that org. They are also not upgradable and are not particularly ideal from a support perspective. Moreover, the Apex code that you write is also visible for all to see, so your Intellectual Property is at risk.

Unmanaged packages can be used for sharing template components that are intended to be changed by the subscriber. If you are not using GitHub and the GitHub Salesforce Deployment Tool (`https://github.com/afawcett/githubsfdeploy`), they can also provide a means to share open source libraries to developers.

Features and benefits of managed packages

This book focuses solely on managed packages. Managed packages have the following features that are ideal for distributing your application. The org where your application package is installed is referred to as a **subscriber org**, since users of this org are subscribing to the services your application provides:

- **Intellectual Property (IP) protection**: Users in the subscriber org cannot see your Apex source code, although they can see your Visualforce pages code and static resources. While the Apex code is hidden, JavaScript code is not, so you may want to consider using a minify process to partially obscure such code.

- **The naming scope**: Your component names are unique to your package throughout the utilization of a namespace. This means that even if you have object *X* in your application, and the subscriber has an object of the same name, they remain distinct. You will define a namespace later in this chapter.

- **The governor scope**: Code in your application executes within its own governor limit scope (such as DML and SOQL governors that are subject to passing Salesforce Security Review) and is not affected by other applications or code within the subscriber org. Note that some governors such as the CPU time governor are shared by the whole execution context (discussed in a later chapter) regardless of the namespace.

- **Upgrades and versioning**: Once the subscribers have started using your application, creating data, making configurations, and so on, you will want to provide upgrades and patches with new versions of your application.

There are other benefits to managed packages, but these are only accessible after becoming a **Salesforce Partner** and completing the security review process; these benefits are described later in this chapter. Salesforce provides *ISVForce Guide* (otherwise known as the **Packaging Guide**) in which these topics are discussed in depth; bookmark it now! The following is the URL for *ISVForce Guide*:

`http://login.salesforce.com/help/pdfs/en/salesforce_packaging_guide.pdf`.

Creating your first managed package

Packages are created in your **packaging org**. There can be only one managed package being developed in your packaging org (though additional unmanaged packages are supported, it is not recommended to mix your packaging org with them). You can also install other dependent managed packages and reference their components from your application. The steps to be performed are discussed in the following sections:

- Setting your package namespace
- Creating the package and assigning it to the namespace
- Adding components to the package

Setting your package namespace

An important decision when creating a managed package is the **namespace**; this is a prefix applied to all your components (Custom Objects, Visualforce pages, and so on) and is used by developers in subscriber orgs to uniquely qualify between your packaged components and others, even those from other packages. The namespace prefix is an important part of the branding of the application since it is implicitly attached to any Apex code or other components that you include in your package.

It can be up to 15 characters, though I personally recommend that you keep it less than this, as it becomes hard to remember and leads to frustrating typos if you make it too complicated. I would also avoid underscore characters as well. It is a good idea to have a naming convention if you are likely to create more managed packages in the future (in different packaging orgs). The following is the format of an example naming convention:

```
[company acronym - 1 to 4 characters][package prefix 1 to 4 characters]
```

For example, the *ACME Corporation's Road Runner* application might be named acmerr.

When the namespace has not been set, the **Packages** page (accessed under the **Setup** menu under the **Create** submenu) indicates that only unmanaged packages can be created. Click on the **Edit** button to begin a small wizard to enter your desired namespace. This can only be done once and must be globally unique (meaning it cannot be set in any other org), much like a website domain name.

Assigning namespaces

For the purposes of following this book, please feel free to make up any namespace you desire, for example, `fforce{yourinitials}`. Do not use one that you may plan to use in the future, since once it has been assigned, it cannot be changed or reused.

The following screenshot shows the **Packages** page:

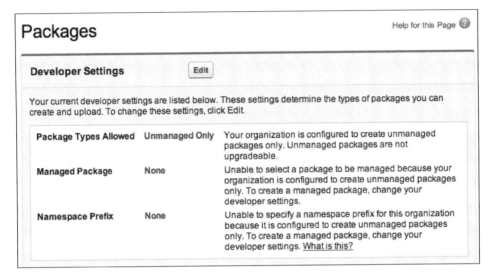

Once you have set the namespace, the preceding page should look like the following screenshot, with the only difference being the namespace prefix that you have used. You are now ready to create a managed package and assign it to the namespace.

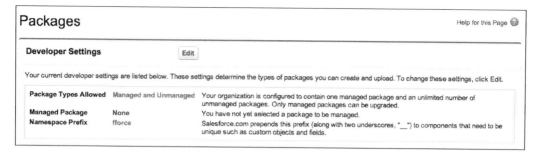

Creating the package and assigning it to the namespace

Click on the **New** button on the **Packages** page and give your package a name (it can be changed later). Make sure to tick the **Managed** checkbox as well. Click on **Save** and return to the **Packages** page, which should now look like the following:

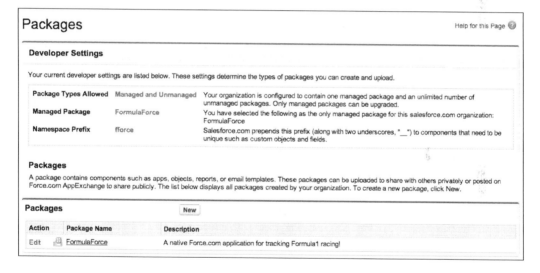

Adding components to the package

In the **Packages** page, click on the link to your package in order to view its details. From this page, you can manage the contents of your package and upload it. Click on the **Add** button to add the Custom Objects created earlier in this chapter. Note that you do not need to add any custom fields; these are added automatically. The following screenshot shows broadly what your Package Details page should look like at this stage:

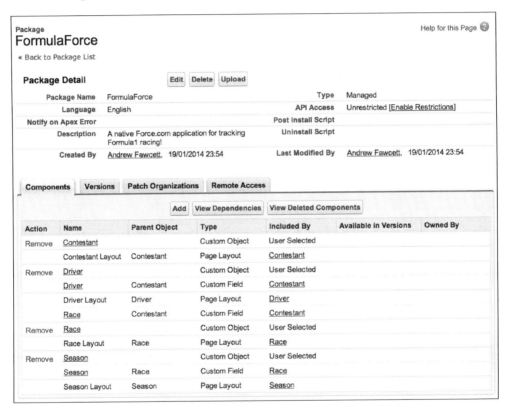

When you review the components added to the package, you will see that some components can be removed while other components cannot be removed. This is because the platform implicitly adds some components for you as they are dependencies. As we progress through this book, adding different component types, you will see this list automatically grow in some cases, and in others, we must explicitly add them.

Extension packages

As the name suggests, **extension packages** extend or add to the functionality delivered by the existing packages they are based on, though they cannot change the base package contents. They can extend one or more base packages, and you can even have several layers of extension packages, though you may want to keep an eye on how extensively you use this feature, as managing inter-package dependency can get quite complex to manage, especially during development.

Extension packages are created in pretty much the same way as the process you've just completed (including requiring their own packaging org), except that the packaging org must also have the dependent packages installed in it.

As code and Visualforce pages contained within extension packages make reference to other Custom Objects, fields, Apex code, and Visualforce pages present in base packages. The platform tracks these dependencies and the version of the base package present at the time the reference was made.

When an extension package is installed, this dependency information ensures that the subscriber org must have the correct version (minimum) of the base packages installed before permitting the installation to complete.

You can also manage the dependencies between extension packages and base packages yourself through the **Versions** tab or **XML metadata** for applicable components (we will revisit versioning in Apex in a later chapter while discussing API integration).

Package dependencies and uploading

Packages can have dependencies on platform features and/or other packages. You can review and manage these dependencies through the usage of the **Package detail** page and the use of dynamic coding conventions as described here.

While some features of Salesforce are common, customers can purchase different editions and features according to their needs. Developer Edition organizations have access to most of these features for free. This means that as you develop your application, it is important to understand when and when not to use those features.

By default, when referencing a certain Standard Object, field, or component type, you will generate a prerequisite dependency on your package, which your customers will need to have before they can complete the installation. Some Salesforce features, for example Multi-Currency or Chatter, have either a configuration or, in some cases, a cost impact to your users (different org editions). Carefully consider which features your package is dependent on.

Most of the feature dependencies, though not all, are visible via the **View Dependencies** button on the **Package** details page (this information is also available on the **Upload** page, allowing you to make a final check). It is a good practice to add this check into your packaging procedures to ensure that no unwanted dependencies have crept in. Clicking on this button, for the package that we have been building in this chapter so far, confirms that there are no dependencies.

Show Dependencies
No Dependency Information for Package FormulaForce

« Back to Package: FormulaForce

There are no dependencies.

Uploading the release and beta packages

Once you have checked your dependencies, click on the **Upload** button. You will be prompted to give a name and version to your package. The version will be managed for you in subsequent releases. Packages are uploaded in one of two modes (beta or release). We will perform a **release** upload by selecting the **Managed - Released** option from the **Release Type** field, so make sure you are happy with the objects created in the earlier section of this chapter, as they cannot easily be changed after this point.

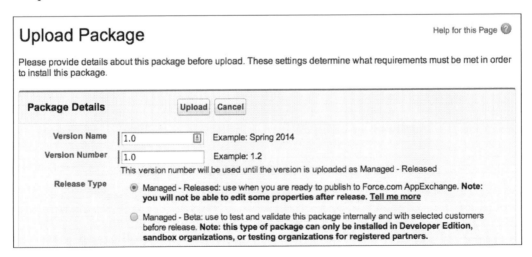

Once you are happy with the information on the screen, click on the **Upload** button once again to begin the packaging process. Once the upload process completes, you will see a confirmation page as follows:

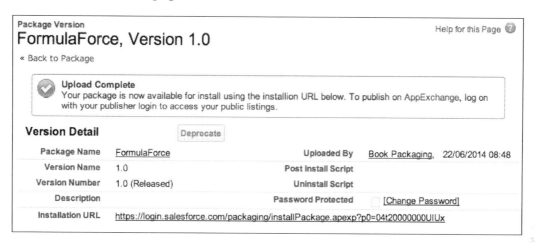

Packages can be uploaded in one of two states as described here:

- **Release** packages can be installed into subscriber production orgs and also provide an upgrade path from previous releases. The downside is that you cannot delete the previously released components and change certain things such as a field's type. Changes to the components that are marked **global**, such as Apex Code and Visualforce components, are also restricted. While Salesforce is gradually enhancing the platform to provide the ability to modify certain released aspects, you need to be certain that your application release is stable before selecting this option.

- **Beta** packages cannot be installed into subscriber production orgs; you can install only into Developer Edition (such as your testing org), **sandbox**, or **Partner Portal** created orgs. Also, Beta packages cannot be upgraded once installed; hence, this is the reason why Salesforce does not permit their installation into production orgs. The key benefit is in the ability to continue to change new components of the release, to address bugs and features relating to user feedback.

 The ability to *delete* previously-published components (uploaded within a release package) is, at the time of writing this book, in pilot. It can be enabled through raising a support case with Salesforce Support. Once you have understood the full implications, they will enable it.

At this stage in the book, we have simply added some Custom Objects. So, the upload should complete reasonably quickly. Note that what you're actually uploading to is **AppExchange**, which will be covered in the following sections.

> If you want to protect your package, you can provide a password (this can be changed afterwards). The user performing the installation will be prompted for it during the installation process.

Optional package dependencies

It is possible to make some Salesforce features and/or base package component references (Custom Objects and fields) an optional aspect of your application. There are two approaches to this, depending on the type of the feature.

Dynamic Apex and Visualforce

For example, the Multi-Currency feature adds a **CurrencyIsoCode** field to the standard and Custom Objects. If you explicitly reference this field, for example in your Apex or Visualforce pages, you will incur a hard dependency on your package. If you want to avoid this and make it a configuration option (for example) in your application, you can utilize dynamic Apex and Visualforce.

Extension packages

If you wish to package component types that are only available in subscriber orgs of certain editions, you can choose to include these in extension packages. For example, you may wish to support Professional Edition, which does not support record types. In this case, create an Enterprise Edition extension package for your application's functionality, which leverages the functionality from this edition.

> Note that you will need multiple testing organizations for each combination of features that you utilize in this way to effectively test the configuration options or installation options that your application requires.

Introduction to AppExchange and listings

Salesforce provides a website referred to as **AppExchange**, which lets prospective customers find, try out, and install applications built using Force.com. Applications listed here can also receive ratings and feedback. You can also list your mobile applications on this site as well.

 In this section, I will be using an AppExchange package that I already own. The package has already gone through the process to help illustrate the steps that are involved. For this reason, you do not need to perform these steps at this stage in the book; they can be revisited at a later phase in your development once you're happy to start promoting your application.

Once your package is known to AppExchange, each time you click on the **Upload** button on your released package (as described previously), you effectively create a **private listing**. Private listings are not visible to the public until you decide to make them so. It gives you the chance to prepare any relevant marketing details and pricing information while final testing is completed. Note that you can still distribute your package to other Salesforce users or even early beta or pilot customers without having to make your listing public.

In order to start building a listing, you need to log in to AppExchange using the login details you designated to your **AppExchange Publishing Org (APO)**. Go to www. appexchange.com and click on **Login** in the banner at the top-right corner. This will present you with the usual Salesforce login screen. Once logged in, you should see something like this:

Select the **Publishing Console** option from the menu, then click on the **Create New Listing** button and complete the steps shown in the wizard to associate the packaging org with AppExchange; once completed, you should see it listed.

It's really important that you consistently log in to AppExchange using your APO user credentials. Salesforce will let you log in with other users. To make it easy to confirm, consider changing the user's display name to something like `MyCompany Packaging`.

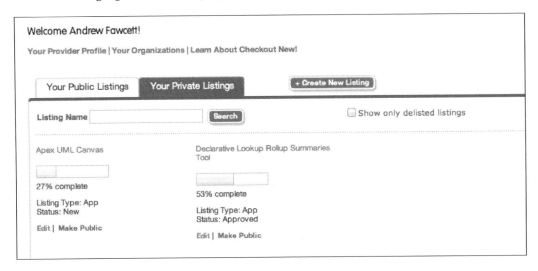

Though it is not a requirement to complete the listing steps, unless you want to try out the process yourself a little further to see the type of information required, you can delete any private listings that you created after you complete this book.

Downloading the example code

You can download the example code files for all Packt books you have purchased from your account at `http://www.packtpub.com`. If you purchased this book elsewhere, you can visit `http://www.packtpub.com/support` and register to have the files e-mailed directly to you.

Installing and testing your package

When you uploaded your package earlier in this chapter, you will receive an e-mail with a link to install the package. If not, review the **Versions** tab on the **Package** detail page in your packaging org. Ensure that you're logged out and click on the link. When prompted, log in to your testing org. The installation process will start. A reduced screenshot of the initial installation page is shown in the following screenshot; click on the **Continue** button and follow the default installation prompts to complete the installation:

Package installation covers the following aspects (once the user has entered the package password if one was set):

- **Package overview**: The platform provides an overview of the components that will be added or updated (if this is an upgrade) to the user. Note that due to the namespace assigned to your package, these will not overwrite existing components in the subscriber org created by the subscriber.

- **Connected App and Remote Access**: If the package contains components that represent connections to the services outside of the Salesforce services, the user is prompted to approve these.

- **Approve Package API Access**: If the package contains components that make use of the client API (such as JavaScript code), the user is prompted to confirm and/or configure this. Such components will generally not be called much; features such as **JavaScript Remoting** are preferred, and they leverage the Apex runtime security configured post install.

- **Security configuration**: In this step, you can determine the initial visibility of the components being installed (objects, pages, and so on). Selecting admin only or the ability to select Profiles to be updated. This option predates the introduction of **permission sets**, which permit post installation configuration.

If you package profiles in your application, the user will need to remember to map these to the existing profiles in the subscriber org as per step 2. This is a one-time option, as the profiles in the package are not actually installed, only merged. I recommend that you utilize permission sets to provide security configurations for your application. These are installed and are much more granular in nature.

When the installation is complete, navigate to the **Installed Packages** menu option under the **Setup** menu. Here, you can see confirmation of some of your package details such as namespace and version, as well as any licensing details, which will be discussed later in this chapter.

It is also possible to provide a **Configure** link for your package, which will be displayed next to the package when installed and listed on the **Installed Packages** page in the subscriber org. Here, you can provide a Visualforce page to access configuration options and processes for example. If you have enabled **Seat based licensing**, there will also be a **Manage Licenses** link to determine which users in the subscriber org have access to your package components such as tabs, objects, and Visualforce pages. Licensing, in general, is discussed in more detail later in this chapter.

Automating package installation

It is possible to automate some of the processes using the **Salesforce Metadata API** and associated tools, such as the **Salesforce Migration Toolkit** (available from the **Tools** menu under **Setup**), which can be run from the popular Apache Ant scripting environment. This can be useful if you want to automate the deployment of your packages to customers or test orgs. In the final chapter of this book, we will study Ant scripts in more detail.

Options that require a user response such as the security configuration are not covered by automation. However, password-protected managed packages are supported. You can find more details on this by looking up the Installed Package component in the online help for the Salesforce Metadata API at https://www.salesforce.com/us/developer/docs/api_meta/.

As an aid to performing this from Ant, a custom Ant task can be found in the sample code related to this chapter (see /lib/antsalesforce.xml). The following is a /build.xml Ant script (also included in the chapter code) to uninstall and reinstall the package. Note that the installation will also upgrade a package if the package is already installed. The following is the Ant script:

```xml
<project name="FormulaForce"
    xmlns:sf="antlib:com.salesforce" basedir=".">

  <!-- Downloaded from Salesforce Tools page under Setup -->
  <typedef
    uri="antlib:com.salesforce"
    resource="com/salesforce/antlib.xml"
    classpath="${basedir}/lib/ant-salesforce.jar"/>

  <!-- Import macros to install/uninstall packages -->
  <import file="${basedir}/lib/ant-salesforce.xml"/>
  <target name="package.installdemo">

    <uninstallPackage
        namespace="yournamespace"
        username="${sf.username}"
        password="${sf.password}"/>
    <installPackage
        namespace="yournamespace"
        version="1.0"
        username="${sf.username}"
        password="${sf.password}"/>
  </target>
</project>
```

You can try the preceding example with your testing org by replacing the namespace attribute values with the namespace you entered earlier in this chapter. Enter the following commands, all on one line, from the folder that contains the build.xml file:

```
ant package.installdemo
  -Dsf.username=testorgusername
  -Dsf.password=testorgpasswordtestorgtoken
```

You can also use the Salesforce Metadata API to list packages installed in an org, for example, if you wanted to determine whether a dependent package needs to be installed or upgraded before sending an installation request. Finally, you can also uninstall packages if you wish.

Becoming a Salesforce partner and benefits

The **Salesforce Partner Program** has many advantages. The first place to visit is `http://www.salesforce.com/partners/overview`. You will want to focus on the areas of the site relating to being an **Independent Software Vendor (ISV)** partner. From here, you can click on **Join**. It is free to join, though you will want to read through the various agreements carefully of course.

Once you wish to start listing a package and charging users for it, you will need to arrange billing details for Salesforce to take the various fees involved. While this book is not equipped to go into the details, do pay careful attention to the Standard Objects used in your package, as this will determine the license type required by your users and the overall cost to them in addition to your charges.

Obviously, Salesforce would prefer your application to use as many features of the CRM application as possible, which may also be beneficial to you as a feature of your application, since it's an appealing immediate integration not found on other platforms, such as the ability to instantly integrate with accounts and contacts.

If you're planning on using Standard Objects and are in doubt about the costs (as they do vary depending on the type), you can request a conversation with Salesforce to discuss this; this is something to keep in mind in the early stages.

Once you have completed the signup process, you will gain access to the Partner Portal (your user will end with `@partnerforce.com`). You must log in to the specific site as opposed to the standard Salesforce login; currently, the URL is `https://www.salesforce.com/partners/login`.

Starting from July 2014, the `http://partners.salesforce.com` URL provides access to the Partner Community. Logging in to this service using your production org user credentials is recommended.

The following screenshot shows what the current **Partner Portal** home page looks like. Here you can see some of its key features:

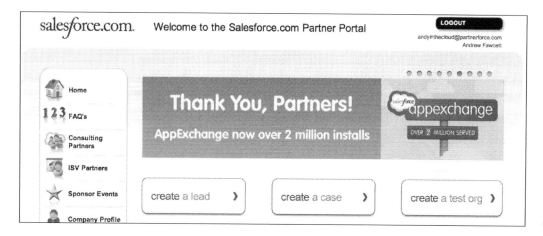

This is your primary place to communicate with Salesforce and also to access additional materials and announcements relevant to ISVs, so do keep checking often. You can raise cases and provide additional logins to other users in your organization, such as other developers who may wish to report issues or ask questions.

There is also the facility to create test or developer orgs; here, you can choose the appropriate edition (Professional, Group, Enterprise, and others) you want to test against. You can also create **Partner Developer Edition** orgs from this option as well. These carry additional licenses and limits over the public's so-called **Single Developer Editions** orgs and are thus recommended for use only once you start using the Partner Portal.

Note, however, that these orgs do expire, subject to either continued activity over 6 months or renewing the security review process (described in the following section) each year. Once you click on the **create a test org** button, there is a link on the page displayed that navigates to a table that describes the benefits, processes, and the expiry rules.

Security review and benefits

The following features require that a completed package release goes through a Salesforce-driven process known as the **security review**, which is initiated via your listing when logged into AppExchange. Unless you plan to give your package away for free, there is a charge involved in putting your package through this process.

However, the review is optional. There is nothing stopping you from distributing your package installation URL directly. However, you will not be able to benefit from the ability to list your new application on AppExchange for others to see and review. More importantly, you will also not have access to the following features to help you deploy, license, and support your application. The following is a list of the benefits you get once your package has passed the security review:

- **Bypass subscriber org setup limits**: Limits such as the number of tabs and Custom Objects are bypassed. This means that if the subscriber org has reached its maximum number of Custom Objects, your package will still install. This feature is sometimes referred to as **Aloha**. Without this, your package installation may fail. You can determine whether Aloha has been enabled via the **Subscriber Overview** page that comes with the LMA application, which is discussed in the next section.

- **Licensing**: You are able to utilize the Salesforce-provided License Management Application in your LMO (License Management Org as described previously).

- **Subscriber support**: With this feature, the users in the subscriber org can enable, for a specific period, a means for you to log in to their org (without exchanging passwords), reproduce issues, and enable much more detailed debug information such as Apex stack traces. In this mode, you can also see custom settings that you have declared as protected in your package, which are useful for enabling additional debug or advanced features.

- **Push upgrade**: Using this feature, you can automatically apply upgrades to your subscribers without their manual intervention, either directly by you or on a scheduled basis. You may use this for applying either smaller bug fixes that don't affect the Custom Objects or APIs or deploy full upgrades. The latter requires careful coordination and planning with your subscribers to ensure that changes and new features are adopted properly.

 Salesforce asks you to perform an automated security scan of your software via a web page (`http://security.force.com/security/tools/forcecom/scanner`). This service can be quite slow depending on how many scans are in the queue. Another option is to obtain the Eclipse plugin from the actual vendor CheckMarx at `http://www.checkmarx.com`, which runs the same scan but allows you to control it locally. Finally, for the ultimate confidence as you develop your application, Salesforce can provide a license to integrate it into your **Continuous Integration (CI)** build system. CI is covered in the final chapter of this book.

This book focuses on building a fully native application, as such additional work involved with so-called "hybrid" applications (where parts of your application have been implemented on your own servers, for example) are not considered here. However, keep in mind that if you make any callouts to external services, Salesforce will also most likely ask you and/or the service provider to run a BURP scanner, to check for security flaws.

Make sure you plan a reasonable amount of time (at least 2–3 weeks, in my experience) to go through the security review process; it is a must to initially list your package, though if it becomes an issue, you have the option of issuing your package install URL directly to initial customers and early adopters.

Licensing

Once you have completed the security review, you are able to request through raising support cases via the Partner Portal to have access to the **LMA**. Once this is provided by Salesforce, use the installation URL to install it like any other package into your LMO.

 If you have requested a CRM for ISV's org (through a case raised within the Partner Portal), you may find the LMA already installed.

The following screenshot shows the main tabs of the **License Management Application** once installed:

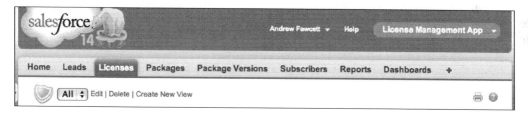

In this section, I will use a package that I already own and have already taken through the process to help illustrate the steps that are involved. For this reason, you do not need to perform these steps.

After completing the installation, return to AppExchange and log in. Then, locate your listing in **Publisher Console** under **Uploaded Packages**. Next to your package, there will be a **Manage Licenses** link. The first time after clicking on this link, you will be asked to connect your package to your LMO org. Once this is done, you will be able to define the license requirements for your package.

The following example shows the license for a free package, with an immediately active license for all users in the subscriber org:

Default License Settings

What organization do you use to manage your licenses (LMO)?
andyinthecloud.com (00D70000000JlxzEAG)

What type of default license does your application have?
◯ Default license is a free trial
◉ Default license is active

What is the length of your default license?
◉ License does not expire
◯ License length:

How many seats are available with your default license?
◉ License is site-wide
◯ Default number of seats:

In most cases, for packages that you intend to charge for, you would select a free trial rather than setting the license default to active immediately. For paid packages, select a license length, unless perhaps it's a one-off charge, and then select the license that does not expire. Finally, if you're providing a trial license, you need to consider carefully the default number of seats (users); users may need to be able to assign themselves different roles in your application to get the full experience.

While licensing is expressed at a package level currently, it is very likely that more granular licensing around the modules or features in your package will be provided by Salesforce in the future. This will likely be driven by the Permission Sets feature. As such, keep in mind a functional orientation to your Permission Set design.

The **Manage Licenses** link is shown on the **Installed Packages** page next to your package if you configure a number of seats against the license. The administrator in the subscriber org can use this page to assign applicable users to your package. The following screenshot shows how your installed package looks to the administrator when the package has licensing enabled:

Note that you do not need to keep reapplying the license requirements for each version you upload; the last details you defined will be carried forward to new versions of your package until you change them. Either way, these details can also be completely overridden on the **License** page of the LMA application as well.

 You may want to apply a site-wide (org-wide) active license to extensions or add-on packages. This allows you to at least track who has installed such packages even though you don't intend to manage any licenses around them, since you are addressing licensing on the main package.

The Licenses tab and managing customer licenses

The **Licenses** tab provides a list of individual license records that are automatically generated when the users install your package into their orgs. Salesforce captures this action and creates the relevant details, including **Lead** information, and also contains contact details of the organization and person who performed the install, as shown in the following screenshot:

From each of these records, you can modify the current license details to extend the expiry period or disable the application completely. If you do this, the package will remain installed with all of its data. However, none of the users will be able to access the objects, Apex code, or pages, not even the administrator. You can also re-enable the license at any time. The following screenshot shows the **License Edit** section:

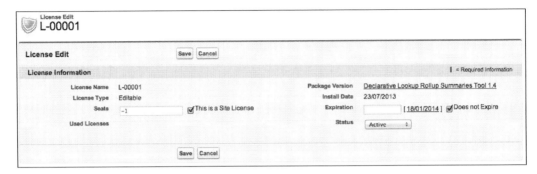

The Subscribers tab

The Subscribers tab lists all your customers or subscribers (it shows their **Organization Name** from the company profile) that have your packages installed (only those linked via AppExchange). This includes their organization ID, edition (Developer, Enterprise, or others), and also the type of instance (sandbox or production).

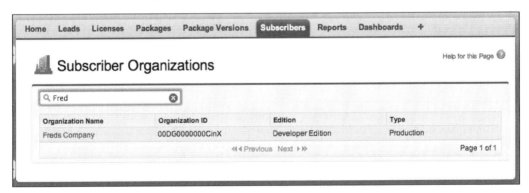

The Subscriber Overview page

When you click on **Organization Name** from the list in this tab, you are taken to the **Subscriber Overview** page. This page is sometimes known as the **Partner Black Tab**. This page is packed with useful information such as the contact details (also seen via the **Leads** tab) and the login access that may have been granted (we will discuss this in more detail in the next section), as well as which of your packages they have installed, its current licensed status, and when it was installed. The following is a screenshot of the **Subscriber Overview** page:

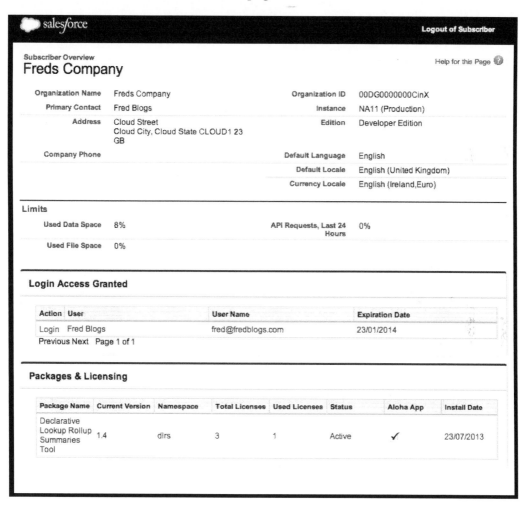

How licensing is enforced in the subscriber org

Licensing is enforced in one of two ways, depending on the execution context in which your packaged Custom Objects, fields, and Apex code are being accessed from.

The first context is where a user is interacting directly with your objects, fields, tabs, and pages via the user interface or via the Salesforce APIs (Partner and Enterprise). If the user or the organization is not licensed for your package, these will simply be hidden from view, and in the case of the API, return an error. Note that administrators can still see packaged components under the **Setup** menu.

The second context is the type of access made from Apex code, such as an Apex trigger or controller, written by the customers themselves or from within another package. This indirect way of accessing your package components is permitted if the license is site (org) wide or there is at least one user in the organization that is allocated a seat.

This condition means that even if the current user has not been assigned a seat (via the **Manage Licenses** link), they are still accessing your application's objects and code, although indirectly, for example, via a customer-specific utility page or Apex trigger, which automates the creation of some records or defaulting of fields in your package.

 Your application's Apex triggers (for example, the ones you might add to Standard Objects) will always execute even if the user does not have a seat license, as long as there is just one user seat license assigned in the subscriber org to your package. However, if that license expires, the Apex trigger will no longer be executed by the platform, until the license expiry is extended.

Providing support

Once your package has completed the security review, additional functionality for supporting your customers is enabled. Specifically, this includes the ability to log in securely (without exchanging passwords) to their environments and debug your application. When logged in this way, you can see everything the user sees in addition to extended Debug Logs that contain the same level of detail as they would in a developer org.

First, your customer enables access via the **Grant Account Login** page. This time however, your organization (note that this is the **Company Name** as defined in the packaging org under **Company Profile**) will be listed as one of those available in addition to Salesforce Support. The following screenshot shows the **Grant Account Login** page:

Next, you log in to your LMO and navigate to the **Subscribers** tab as described. Open **Subscriber Overview** for the customer, and you should now see the link to **Login** as that user. From this point on, you can follow the steps given to you by your customer and utilize the standard Debug Log and Developer Console tools to capture the debug information you need. The following screenshot shows a user who has been granted login access via your package to their org:

 This mode of access also permits you to see protected custom settings if you have included any of those in your package. If you have not encountered these before, it's well worth researching them as they provide an ideal way to enable and disable debug, diagnostic, or advanced configurations that you don't want your customers to normally see.

Customer metrics

Salesforce has started to expose information relating to the usage of your package components in the subscriber orgs since the Spring '14 release of the platform. This enables you to report what Custom Objects and Visualforce pages your customers are using and more importantly those they are not. This information is provided by Salesforce and cannot be opted out by the customer.

At the time of writing, this facility is in pilot and needs to be enabled by **Salesforce Support**. Once enabled, the `MetricsDataFile` object is available in your production org and will receive a data file periodically that contains the metrics records. The **Usage Metrics Visualization** application can be found by searching on AppExchange and can help with visualizing this information.

Trialforce and Test Drive

Large enterprise applications often require some consultation with customers to tune and customize to their needs after the initial package installation. If you wish to provide trial versions of your application, Salesforce provides a means to take snapshots of the results of this installation and setup process, including sample data.

You can then allow prospects that visit your AppExchange listing or your website to sign up to receive a personalized instance of a Salesforce org based on the snapshot you made. The potential customers can then use this to fully explore the application for a limited duration until they sign up to be a paid customer from the trial version. Such orgs will eventually expire when the Salesforce trial period ends for the org created (typically 14 days). Thus, you should keep this in mind when setting the default expiry on your package licensing.

The standard approach is to offer a web form for the prospect to complete in order to obtain the trial. Review the *Providing a Free Trial on your Website* and *Providing a Free Trial on AppExchange* sections of the *ISVForce Guide* for more on this. You can also consider utilizing the **Signup Request API**, which gives you more control over how the process is started and the ability to monitor it, such that you can create the lead records yourself. You can find out more about this in the *Creating Signups using the API* section in the *ISVForce Guide*.

Alternatively, if the prospect wishes to try your package in their sandbox environment for example, you can permit them to install the package directly either from AppExchange or from your website. In this case, ensure that you have defined a default expiry on your package license as described earlier. In this scenario, you or the prospect will have to perform the setup steps after installation.

Finally, there is a third option called **Test Drive**, which does not create a new org for the prospect on request, but does require you to set up an org with your application, preconfigure it, and then link it to your listing via AppExchange. Instead of the users completing a signup page, they click on the **Test Drive** button on your AppExchange listing. This logs them into your test drive org as a read-only user. Because this is a shared org, the user experience and features you can offer to users is limited to those that mainly read information. I recommend that you consider Trialforce over this option unless there is some really compelling reason to use it.

When defining your listing in AppExchange, the **Leads** tab can be used to configure the creation of lead records for trials, test drives, and other activities on your listing. Enabling this will result in a form being presented to the user before accessing these features on your listing. If you provide access to trials through signup forms on your website for example, lead information will not be captured.

Summary

This chapter has given you a practical overview of the initial package creation process through installing it into another Salesforce organization. While some of the features discussed cannot be fully exercised until you're close to your first release phase, you can now head to development with a good understanding of how early decisions such as references to Standard Objects are critical to your licensing and cost decisions.

It is also important to keep in mind that while tools such as Trialforce help automate the setup, this does not apply to installing and configuring your customer environments. Thus, when making choices regarding configurations and defaults in your design, keep in mind the costs to the customer during the implementation cycle.

Make sure you plan for the security review process in your release cycle (the free online version has a limited bandwidth) and ideally integrate it into your CI build system (a paid facility) as early as possible, since the tool not only monitors security flaws but also helps report breaches in best practices such as lack of test asserts and SOQL or DML statements in loops.

In the following chapters, we will start exploring the engineering aspects of building an enterprise application, as we build upgrades on the package created in this chapter, allowing us to better explore how the platform supports incremental growth of your application.

 As you revisit the tools covered in this chapter, be sure to reference the excellent *ISVForce Guide* at `http://www.salesforce.com/us/developer/docs/packagingGuide/index.htm` for the latest detailed steps and instructions on how to access, configure, and use these features.

Leveraging Platform Features

2

In this chapter, we will explore some key features of the Force.com platform that enable developers to build the application more rapidly, but also provide key features to the end users of the application. Using these features in a balanced way is the key to ensuring that you and your users not only get the best out of the platform today but continue to do so in the future as the platform evolves.

A key requirement for an enterprise application is the ability to customize and extend its functionality, as enterprise customers have varied and complex businesses. You should also keep in mind that as your ecosystem grows, you should ensure that your partner relationships are empowered with the correct level of integration options and that they need to interface their solutions with yours; the platform also plays a key role here as well.

As we expand our FormulaForce package, we will explore the following to better understand some of the decision making around platform alignment:

- Packaging and upgradable components
- Custom field features
- Security features
- Platform APIs
- Localization and translation
- Building customizable user interfaces
- E-mail customization with e-mail templates
- Workflow and flow
- Social features and mobile

Packaging and upgradable components

The time it takes to install your application and get it prepared for live usage by your customers is a critical phase in your customer relationship. They are obviously keen to get their hands on your new and improved releases as quickly as possible. Careful planning and awareness of which components you are using are packable and upgradeable are important to monitor the effort involved at this stage.

When exploring the various platform features available to you, it is important to check whether the related component type can be packaged or not. For a full list of components that can be packaged, search for the *Available Components* section in *ISVforce Guide* referenced in the previous chapter.

If a component type relating to a feature you wish to use cannot be packaged, it does not necessarily mean it is of no use to you or your users, as it may well be something you can promote in your consulting team and to your end user admins to take advantage after installation. Though keep in mind how often you recommend this, especially if it starts to become a required post-installation task; this will increase the time it takes for your users to go live on your application.

Another aspect to consider is if the component type is upgradeable, that is, if you define and include one release of your package, then modify it in a subsequent release, it will be updated in the subscriber (customer) organization. The table in the *Available Components* section in *ISVforce Guide* will also give you the latest information on this. Some component types that are not upgradeable are as follows:

- Layouts
- E-mail templates
- List view

These features are the key to your application design and are covered in more detail later in this chapter. It is also important that end users can customize these; hence, Salesforce allows them to be edited. Unfortunately, this means they are not upgradable, that is, any new fields you add to your Custom Objects do not appear by default after an upgrade is available for your users. However, new installations of your package will receive the latest versions of these components from your package.

This also applies to some attributes of components that are flagged as upgradeable in the table referenced previously, but have certain attributes that are then not upgradeable. Refer to the *Editing Components and Attributes After Installation* section in *ISVforce Guide* for the latest details on this. Some common attributes that are packable and not upgradable and hence end user modifiable are as follows:

- Custom field: Picklist values
- Validation Rule: Active
- Custom Object: Action overrides

> The active status of the Validation Rule is quite a surprising one; while the user cannot modify your packaged Validation Rule, they can disable it. For most purposes, this means that this platform feature becomes a post-install optional activity left to the end user where they should wish to implement rules unique to them. For validations you wish to implement these in **Apex**, you can utilize a protected Custom Setting to control activation if desired (such settings are only visible to your support teams via subscriber support).

Custom field – picklist values

Probably the most surprising of the non-upgradable attributes of the custom field is the list of picklist values. These are completely modifiable by end users; they can be added, modified, or deleted. This means that you need to be very careful about how you reference these in your Apex code, and consequently, you provide guidelines to your end users about editing and applying changes post upgrade.

> The Salesforce Translation Workbench tool, under the **Setup** menu, can be used to effectively relabel a pick list value by editing the users' current language without having to rename its value on the field definition. This can be done after installation of the tool by the end user admin.

Also, remember that the platform treats picklist fields mostly as if they were text fields; as such, you can query and even update a picklist field with any value you like. Also, keep in mind that you can upgrade customer data (if you change or delete a picklist value) through an Apex post-install script.

Automating upgrades with the Salesforce Metadata API

Salesforce as ever is great at providing APIs; the **Metadata API** is no exception, as it provides a pretty broad coverage of most things that can be done under the **Setup** menu. This means that it is feasible to consider the development of upgrade tools to assist in upgrading components, such as layouts or picklist values. Such tools will have to handle the logic of merging and confirming the changes with the user of, for example, providing a means to merge new fields into layouts, which the user selects from a UI prompt.

Currently, the Metadata API is not directly accessible from Apex (though I remain hopeful that it will be accessible in the future). However, it can be invoked via an Apex HTTP callout, as it is available as a SOAP API.

The Apex Metadata API library has provided an Apex wrapper at `https://github.com/financialforcedev/apex-mdapi` to make it easier to use. The following Apex code shows the library being used to programmatically update a layout to add a new custom button. This code can be used as part of a tool you provide with your application or separately by your consultants. For more information, you can refer to the README file in the Github repository.

```
// Read the layout
MetadataService.Layout layout =
   (MetadataService.Layout) service.readMetadata(
     'Layout', new String[]
     { 'Test__c-Test Layout' }).getRecords()[0];

// Add a button to the layout
layout.customButtons.add('anewbutton');

// Update the layout
List<MetadataService.SaveResult> result =
service.updateMetadata(
  new MetadataService.Metadata[] { layout });
```

 It is feasible to consider invoking this logic from a package post-install script. However, Salesforce currently requires that you define a remote site in order to authorize the callout, even to their own servers. As the end point differs for this API, based on the subscriber orgs Salesforce instance, it is hard to predefine and thus preinstall this configuration as part of your package. As such, unless you are confident that the remote site has been set up before an upgrade, it might be best to guide the user to a Visualforce page (perhaps via an e-mail from the post-install script), where you can prompt the user.

Understanding the custom field features

Custom fields carry many more features than you might think; they are much more than simple field definitions you find on other platforms. Having a good understanding of a custom field is the key to reducing the amount of code you have written and improving the user experience and reporting of your application's data.

Default field values

Adding default values to your fields improves the usability of your application and can reduce the number of fields needed on the screen, as users can remove fields with acceptable defaults from the layouts.

Default values defined on custom fields apply in the native user interfaces and Visualforce UIs (providing the `apex:inputField` component is used) and in some cases, through the APIs. You can define a default value based on a formula using either literal values and/or variables such as $User, $Organization, and $Setup.

Let's try this out. Create a **Year** text field on the **Season** object as per the following screenshot. Make sure that you select the **External ID** checkbox as this cannot be changed on the field once the package is uploaded at the end of this chapter. This will become important in the next chapter.

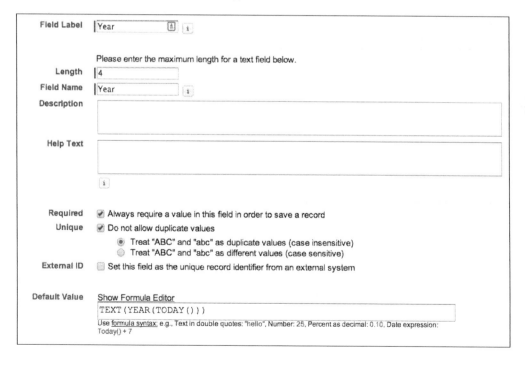

The default value you define cannot be overridden through a customization in the subscriber org, however, you can reference a Custom Setting (hierarchy type only) in a default value formula using a $Setup reference. This allows for some customization through editing the Custom Setting at an organization, profile, or individual user level.

To create a record in the **Season** object, we need to first create a tab for it. Perform the following steps in the package org to try out this process:

1. Create a tab for the **Season** object.

2. Go to the **Season** tab and click on **New**.

3. This results in the current year being displayed in the **Year** field as shown in the following screenshot:

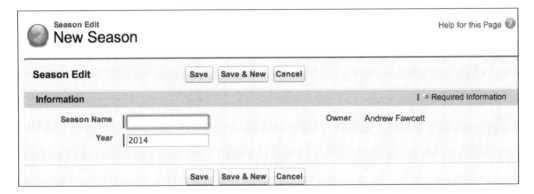

Unfortunately, by default, the Apex code does not apply default values when you construct an SObject in the direct manner via new Season(); however, if you utilize the SObjectType.newSObject method, you can request for defaults to be applied as follows:

```
Season__c season = (Season__c)
    Season__c.SObjectType.newSObject(null, true);
System.assertEquals('2014', season.Year__c);
```

Encrypted fields

Encrypted fields leverage 128-bit master keys and use the **Advanced Encryption Standard** (**AES**) algorithm to store values; they are displayed using a character mask (currently not developer definable).

However, they are visible to those who have the **View Encrypted Data** permission, which is a facility that may not be something your requirements tolerate. This also includes users whom you grant the login access to, such as through subscriber support. Apex and Validation Rule logic can see the unencrypted values. Finally, note that they cannot be queried or filtered, though they do appear in reports and e-mail output.

Lookup options, filters, and layouts

The standard lookup UI from Salesforce can be configured to make it easier for users to recognize the correct record to select, filter out those that are not relevant, and if necessary, prevent them from deleting records that are in use elsewhere in your application, all without writing any code.

Perform the following steps in the package org to try out this process:

1. Create **Tabs** for the `Driver` and `Race` objects.
2. Add an **Active** checkbox field to the `Driver` Custom Object; ensure that the default is **checked**.
3. Create a driver record, for example, `Lewis Hamilton`.
4. From the **Season** record created in the previous section, create a **Race** record, for example, `Spa`.
5. Associate `Lewis Hamilton` with the `Spa` race via the **Contestants** relationship.

First, let's ensure that drivers cannot be deleted if they are associated with a `Contestant` record (meaning they have or are taking part in a race). Edit the **Driver** field on the **Contestant** object and enable **Don't allow deletion of the lookup record that's part of a lookup relationship**. This is similar to expressing a **referential integrity** rule in other database platforms.

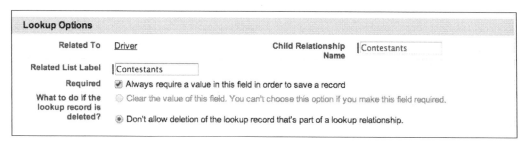

Now if you try to delete **Lewis Hamilton**, you should receive a message as shown in the following screenshot. This also applies if you attempt to delete via Apex DML or the Salesforce API.

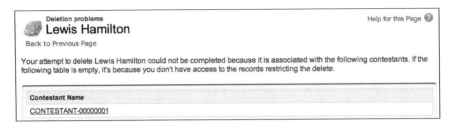

You've just saved yourself some Apex Trigger code and used a platform feature.

Let's take a look at another lookup feature, known as **lookup filters**. Formula 1 drivers come and go all the time; let's ensure when selecting drivers to be in races, via the `Driver` lookup on the `Contestant` record, that only the active drivers are shown and are permitted when entered directly.

Perform the following steps in the packaging org to try out the steps:

1. Create a **Driver** record, for example, `Rubens Barrichello` and ensure that the **Active** field is unchecked.

2. Edit the **Driver** field on the **Contestant** object and complete the **Lookup Filter** section as shown in the following screenshot, entering the suggested messages in the **If it doesn't, display this error message on save** and **Add this informational message to the lookup window** fields, and click on **Save**:

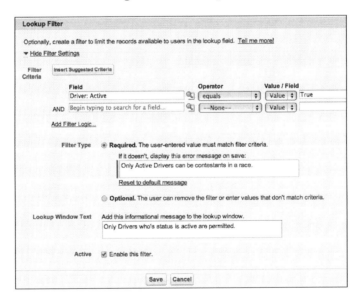

You can have up to five active lookup filters per object. This is not a limit that is set by your package namespace. So, use them sparingly to give your end users room to create their own lookup filters. If you don't have a strong need for filtering, consider implementing it as an Apex Trigger validation.

Test the filter by attempting to create a `Contestant` child record for the `Spa` record. First, by using the lookup dialog, you will see the informational message entered previously and will be unable to select `Rubens Barrichello`, as shown in the following screenshot:

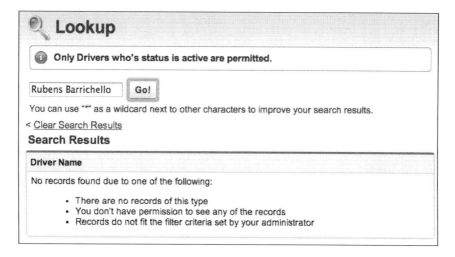

If you attempt to enter an inactive driver's name directly, this is also blocked as shown in the following screenshot:

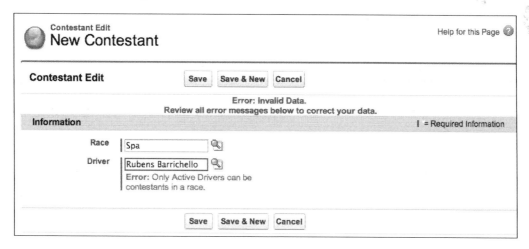

This validation is also enforced through Apex DML and Salesforce APIs. Unlike Validation Rules, it cannot be disabled by the end user. However, changes related to records, such as making the Driver subsequently inactive, is permitted by the platform. In this case, the next time the **Contestant** record is edited, the error given in the preceding screenshot will occur.

Finally, you are also able to display additional columns on the lookup dialogs, which help the user identify the correct record based on other fields. The following steps describe how to do this:

1. Add a **Nationality** field to the **Driver** object of the **Picklist** type, and enter the following values: British, Spanish, Brazilian, Finnish, and Mexican.

2. Edit the existing **Driver** records and set an appropriate value in the **Nationality** field.

3. Locate the **Search Layouts** section of the **Driver** object, edit the **Lookup Dialogs** layout, add the **Nationality** field created in step 1, and save the layout. When selecting a driver, the lookup should now show this additional field, as follows:

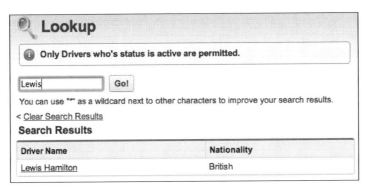

Lookups are a hugely powerful declarative feature of the platform; they are not just used to express the application data model relationships, but they actually enforce the integrity of the data as well, thereby making the user's job of entering data much easier.

Rollup summaries and limits

When it comes to performing calculations on your data, the platform provides a number of options: reports, Analytics API, dashboards, Apex Triggers, Visualforce, and Rollup summaries. The Rollup summary option provides a code-free solution with the ability to apply some condition filtering. Rollup summary fields can then also be referenced and combined with other features such as formula fields and Validation Rules.

The key requirement is that there is a Master-Detail relationship between the detail records being summarized on the field being added to the master records, such as that between **Race** and **Contestant**. The following example will total the number of competitors that did not finish a given race (or DNF in Formula 1 terms).

Perform the following steps in the package org to try out this process:

1. Create a **DNF** field on the **Contestant** object using the **Checkbox** field type.

2. Create a **Driver** record for `Charles Pic` and add him to the `Spa` race via the **Contestant** object, checking the **DNF** field.

3. Create a **Total DNFs** field on the **Race** object using a **Rollup Summary** field type. Select the **Contestants** object from the **Summarized Object** dropdown and **COUNT** as **Rollup-Up Type** and apply the **Filter Criteria** field as shown in the following screenshot, to select only **Contestant** records with the **DNF** field checked:

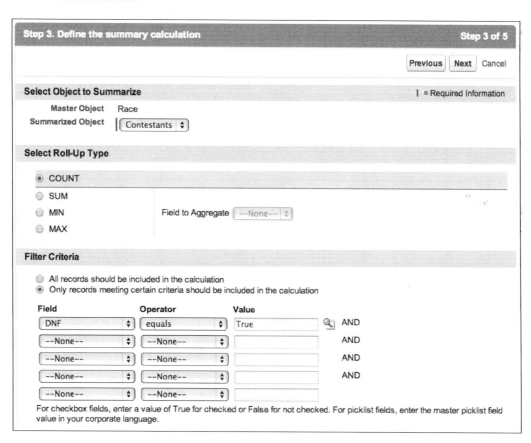

Navigate to the Spa record and note that the Total DNFs shows the value 1. Experiment by changing the status of the **DNF** field on the **Driver** records to see the value recalculate.

Rollup summaries provide a real-time calculation once configured. However, when creating or changing rollups, Salesforce states that it can take up to 30 minutes. You can read more about them by searching for *About Roll-Up Summary Fields* in the documentation and by reviewing the *Roll Up Summary Field Technology Overview* knowledge base article at `http://help.salesforce.com/apex/HTViewSolution?id=000004281`.

You can combine the use of Rollup summary fields in your Apex Trigger logic, for example, you can add the Apex logic to check the number of DNFs in the `after` phase of the trigger on the **Race** object. Your users can also apply Validation Rules on the **Race** object that references its Rollup summary fields. Any changes to **Contestant** detail records that cause this Validation Rule to be invalid will prevent updates to the related **Contestant** record.

As you can imagine, calculating Rollup summaries can be quite an intensive job for the Salesforce servers. As such, Salesforce limits the total number of Rollup summaries to 10 per object, though this can be increased to 25 by contacting Salesforce Support with a valid business case. Keep in mind that as a packaged application provider, this limit is not scoped by your namespace, unlike other limits. This means that if you use all 10, your end users will not be able to add their own post-installation. Similarly, if they have created their own post-installation and an upgrade causes the limit to be breached, the install will fail.

While this can be a powerful feature, carefully consider other summarization options listed in the previous paragraph and if your users really need this information real-time or accessible from formulas and Validation Rules. If not, a good compromise is a Visualforce page that can be added inline into the **Page Layout** objects. The Visualforce page can utilize the `readonly=true` attribute in which the Apex Controller logic can utilize aggregate SOQL queries to aggregate up to 5 million records (subject to appropriate indexes and within standard timeout tolerance). This page can then display when the user reviews the record in the UI and is thus calculated on demand. Enhancing the Salesforce standard pages with Visualforce is discussed in more detail later in this chapter.

Understanding the available security features

The platform provides security controls to manage the accessibility of functionalities in your application and also the visibility of the individual records it creates. As an application provider, your code has a responsibility to enforce security rules as well as provided integrations that help administrators configure security easily. This section is not aimed at taking a deep dive into the security features of the platform, but is more an aid in understanding the options, best practices, and packaging implications.

One of the key checks the security review process described in the previous chapter makes is to scan the code to ensure whether it is using the appropriate Apex conventions to enforce the security rules administrators of your application configure, as not all security checks are enforced automatically for you.

This chapter discusses the following two categories of security as provided by the platform:

- Security that applies to application objects and some code entry points (providing APIs) and also Visualforce pages that deliver the features of the application is referred to here as **functional security**

- In contrast to security applied to individual record data created and maintained by the application, this type of security is referred to as **data security**

Functional security

Both **profiles** and **Permission Sets** can be created and packaged in your application to help administrators of your application control access to your objects, fields, tabs, and pages. Fundamentally, profiles have been historically used to prepackage the roles, such as *team principle,* you envisage users when using your application. In contrast, Permission Sets can be used to express the functionality in your application such as *the ability to assign a driver to a race.*

By now, most people are familiar with configuring profiles to control security. The issue is that they can eventually lead to a proliferation of profiles; as small differences in needs between users arise, profiles are then cloned and thus increases the administration overhead when performing common changes. To manage this, Salesforce created Permission Sets, which is a much more granular way of expressing security controls.

From an application perspective, you can package Permission Sets and even have them upgraded automatically as they change in accordance with the new or updated functionality in your application. They can also assign them after installation, in contrast to profiles, which can only be done during the installation. Also unlike profiles, administrators cannot edit them though they can clone them if there is a need (this is not possible in Professional and Group Editions of Salesforce). Because of these benefits, it is recommended that Permission Sets be used over profiles when packaging security information about your application.

It is important to plan your use of Permission Sets from the start so that your development team keeps them updated and their usage remains consistent throughout. Consider the following when designing your Permission Set strategy:

- **Think features not roles**: Do not be tempted to fall back to expressing the roles you envisage your application users being assigned. Enterprise organizations are large and complex; rarely does one size fit all. For example, a **team principle** can have many different responsibilities across your application from one installation to another. If you get this wrong, the administrator will be forced to clone the Permission Set, resulting in the start of proliferation of unmanaged Permission Sets that do not track with the new or changed functionality as your package is upgraded.

- **Granularity**: As you design the functionality of your application, modules are defined (you can use **Application** under **Setup** to indicate these), and within these objects, tabs, or pages, each has distinct operations. For example, the **Contestant** object might describe the ability to indicate that a driver has crashed out of the race and update the appropriate **DNF** field, which is **Update DNF Status**. For example, this permission might be assigned to the race controller user. In contrast, you might have a less granular Permission Set called **Race Management**, which encompasses the **Update DNF Status** permission plus others. Considering this approach to design your Permission Sets means that administrators have less work to assign to users, while at the same time, they have the power to be more selective should they wish to.

- **Naming convention**: When the administrator is viewing your Permission Sets in the Salesforce UI ensure they are grouped according to the functional aspects of your application by considering a naming convention, for example, `FormulaForce - Race Management` and `FormulaForce - Race Management - Update DNF Status`.

One of the limitations of the **License Management Application (LMA)** described in the previous chapter is that it is not very granular; you can only effectively grant user licenses to the whole package and not modules or key features within it. With the introduction of Permission Set licenses, Salesforce looks to be heading down the path of providing a means to define your licensing requirements with respect to Permission Sets. At the time of writing this, there was no support for developers to create their own; this looks like the next obvious step. This is something to consider when designing your Permission Sets for use as license control, for example, one day you may be able to use this to enforce a pricing model for high-priced licenses associated with the Race Management permission.

Perform the following steps in the package org to try out this process:

1. Create a `Race Management` custom application (under **Setup | Create**) and add the **Driver, Season**, and **Race** tabs created earlier to it; make the **Race** tab the default.

2. Create a `Race Analytics` custom application and add the **Race** and **Reports** tabs to it; make the **Reports** tab the default.

3. Create the Permission Sets for the **FormulaForce** application as shown in the following table. Leave the **User License** field set to **None**.

4. Finally, add the following Permission Sets to the **FormulaForce** package.

Permission Set	Permissions
FormulaForce - Race Management	Race Management (Custom Application)
	Race Analytics (Custom Application)
	Season tab (Custom Tab)
	Race tab (Custom Tab)
	Driver tab (Custom Tab)
	Object (Custom Object, Full Access)
	Race object (Custom Object, Full Access)
	Driver object (Custom Object, Full Access)
	Contestant object (Custom Object, Full Access)
FormulaForce - Race Management - Update DNF Status	Contestant object (Custom Object, Read, Edit)
	DNF (Custom Field, Read, Edit)
FormulaForce - Race Analytics	Race Analytics (Custom Application)
	Race object (Custom Object, Read Only, Read DNF)

Here, Full Access means it gives access to read, create, edit, and delete all custom fields. Also, at the time of writing this, the Custom Application and Custom Tab components within Permission Sets are not packable. Until they become packable, it is recommended that you still maintain this information in the Permission Sets.

Your code and security review considerations

Not all code you write will automatically be subjected to enforcement by the platform through the object- and field-level security defined by the Permission Sets or profiles assigned to users. While certain Visualforce components such as `apex:inputField` and `apex:outputField` enforce security, other ways in which you obtain or display information to users will not enforce security, such as `apex:inputText` and `apex:outputText`. The differences will be discussed in more detail in a later chapter.

When your code is performing calculations or transformations on fields in the controller, expose this data indirectly via Apex bindings or remote action methods on your controller; for this, you need to add additional checks yourself. This also applies to any customer facing the Apex code such as `global` methods or Apex REST APIs you build.

In these cases, you can use the **Apex Describe** facility to specifically check the user's profile or Permission Set assignment for access and prevent further execution by returning errors or throwing exceptions. The formal reference information for implementing this can be found in the following two Salesforce articles:

- **Enforcing CRUD and FLS**: `https://developer.salesforce.com/page/Enforcing_CRUD_and_FLS`
- **Testing CRUD and FLS Enforcement**: `https://developer.salesforce.com/page/Testing_CRUD_and_FLS_Enforcement`

The Salesforce security review scanner and team insist that you check Custom Object level security (CRUD security for short) and include checking for every field that is accessed (**field-level security** or FLS for short).

Implementing code to check both needs careful consideration, planning, and monitoring. Implementing FLS is especially complex with multiple use cases and contexts applying different usage patterns within your code base. For some functionalities, you may wish the application to access certain objects and/or fields on the users' behalf without checking security; document these cases well as you might need to present them to Salesforce.

Implementing CRUD security is something we will revisit in later chapters on the Domain and Selector layers of your Apex code, where some automated support within the library used to support these patterns has been provided.

> It's best to review and document your approach and use the CRUD and FLS checking as a part of defining your coding conventions, and if in doubt, discuss with your Salesforce **Technical Account Manager (TAM)** or by raising a support case in Partner Portal. This way, you will also have some reference decisions and conversations to use when providing input and background to the security review team. Meanwhile, the Salesforce community, including myself, is looking at ways of creating generic ways to enforce CRUD and field-level security without having to see hardcoded checks throughout the code base.

Note that it is a common misconception that applying the `with sharing` keyword to your Apex classes will automatically enforce CRUD or FLS security, but it does not. This keyword solely controls the records returned when querying objects, so is in fact related only to data security.

Data security

Regardless as to which Custom Objects or fields are accessible to the end user through their profile or Permission Set assignments, there may still be a requirement to filter which records certain users can see, for example, certain race data during and after the race can only be visible to the owning teams.

Salesforce allows this level of security to be controlled through the **Owner** field on each record and optionally a facility known as sharing. This is defined via the **Sharing Settings** page (under **Security Controls | Setup**), in the packaging org for the FormulaForce application. This page is shown in the following screenshot:

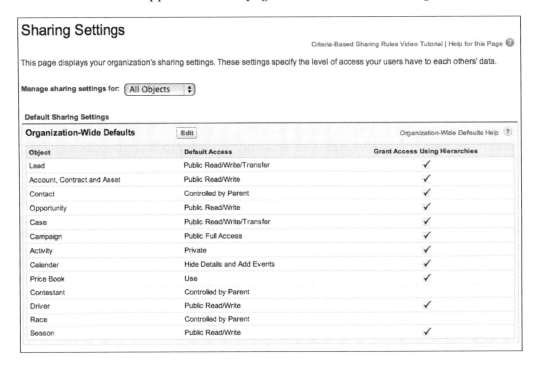

You can see the Standard Objects and also the Custom Objects we have created so far listed here. When you click on **Edit**, **Default Access** shows that the access options vary based on whether the object is a standard or Custom Object, as Salesforce has some special access modes for certain Standard Objects such as **Price Book**.

Notice that where an object is in a child relationship with a parent record, in the case of **Race** and **Session**, there is no facility to control the security of this object. Thus, when you are designing your application object schema, make sure that you consider whether you or your users will need to utilize sharing on this object; if so, it might be better to consider a standard lookup relationship.

For the Custom Objects that exist as a part of the FormulaForce application, you can define **Public Read/Write**, **Public Read Only**, and **Private**. The default value is always **Public Read/Write**.

The default access defines the starting position for the platform to determine the visibility of a given record using the **Owner** field and the object's **sharing rules**. In other words, you cannot use these features to hide records from a given user if the object has **Public Read** or **Public Read/Write** default access.

 Although this setting is packaged with Custom Objects, it is editable in the subscriber org and is thus not upgradable. If you decide to change this in a later release, this will need to be done manually as a post-install task.

If you set the **Private** default access and do nothing, the **Owner** field determines the visibility of the records. By default, the owner is the user that created the record. Thus, users can only see records they create or records created by other users below them in the **role hierarchy** (if enabled). A record owner can be a user or a group (known as **Queue** within the API), for example, members of a specific racing team. Users can choose to manually share a record they own with other users or groups also.

Sometimes, a more sophisticated and dynamic logic is required; in these cases, sharing rules can be added and they can be created either declaratively (from the **Sharing Settings** page) or programmatically. Regardless of the approach used, the platform creates a `Share` object (for example, for a `RaceData__c` object, this would be `RaceData__Share`) that contains records resulting from the evaluation of sharing rules; these records can be queried like any other object, useful for debugging.

 For the ultimate in flexibility, you can write logic within an Apex Trigger or Scheduled Job to directly create, update, or delete the sharing records, for example, in the `RaceData__Share` object. In this case, the criteria for sharing records can be practically anything you can express in code. You first define a sharing reason against the applicable Custom Object, which will be automatically included in your package. This is used as a kind of tag for the sharing records your application code creates versus sharing records created through sharing rules defined in the subscriber org. Also note that if the platform detects references to the `Share` object for a given object listed on the **Sharing Settings** page, it will prevent the subscriber org administrator from changing the default access from private to public.

Your code and security review considerations

The platform will enforce record visibility in cases where the user attempts to navigate to the record directly in the Salesforce UI, including reports they run and access provided via Salesforce APIs when they use third-party applications.

However, keep in mind that your Apex code runs at system level by default; thus, it's important to pay attention to the use of the `with sharing` or `without sharing` keyword (for all key entry points to your code). This is also something the security review scanner will look for. You might as well ask when using the `without sharing` keyword makes sense; such a use case might be when you explicitly want a system-level logic to see all records on behalf of an operation or validation the user is performing.

Platform APIs

Salesforce provides a number of APIs to access and manipulate records in its own objects that belong to applications such as CRM; these APIs are also extended to support Custom Objects created by admins or provided by packages installed in the subscriber org. Salesforce dedicates a huge amount of its own and community-driven documentation resources you can reference when educating partners and customer developers on the use of these APIs. Thus, it is important that your application works well with these APIs.

Platform APIs are enabled for Enterprise Edition orgs and above, though if you have a need to consume them in Professional or Group Edition orgs, Salesforce can provide a Partner API token (following security review completion) to enable their use; this is unique to your application and so does not provide access for code other than yours.

Typically, unless you are developing an off-platform utility or integration to accompany your application, you may not find your application consuming these APIs at all, though there are some you might want to consider, highlighted in the following bullets. Keep in mind, however, that if you do, in addition to the Partner API token, the subscriber org's daily API limit will also be consumed; hence, ensure that your usage is as network optimal as possible.

Enterprise-level customers often have complex integration requirements both on and off platform; typically, Salesforce utilizes the SOAP and REST technologies to make these APIs available to any number of platforms and languages such as Java and Microsoft .NET. In *Chapter 9, Providing Integration and Extensibility*, we will discuss how you can extend the features of the platform data-orientated APIs with your own more application process-orientated APIs.

> Note that not all platform APIs have an Apex variant that can be called directly, though this does not necessarily mean that they cannot be used. Apex supports making outbound HTTP callouts either via a WSDL or by directly creating and parsing the required requests and responses. A good example of this is the Metadata API, which can be used to develop Visualforce wizards to automate common setup tasks via Apex, as shown in an Apex example shown later in this chapter.

The following list details some of the main APIs that may be of use to your Enterprise-level customers wishing to develop solutions around your application:

- **Enterprise API**: This SOAP API is dynamically generated based on the objects present at the time in the subscriber org, meaning that any tool (such as data-mapping tools) or developer consuming it will find the information it exposes more familiar and easier to access. One downside, however, is that this can end up being quite a large API to work with, as Enterprise customer orgs often have hundreds of objects and fields in them.

- **Partner API**: This is also a SOAP API; unlike the Enterprise API, it provides a more generic CRUD-based API to access the record in the subscriber org. Its name can be a bit misleading, as there is no restriction to non-partners using it, and as it is lighter than the Enterprise API, it's often a first choice.

- **REST API**: This provides another CRUD style API, similar to the Partner API, but in this case, it is based on the more popular REST technology standard. It's often preferred when building mobile applications and is also fast becoming popular as the default API for Java and .NET.

- **Metadata API and Tooling API**: These SOAP APIs provide a means to automate many of the tasks performed under the **Setup** menu and those performed by developers when editing code. While these might not be of direct interest to those integrating with your application, as many of these tasks are performed initially and then only rarely, it might be something to consider using in tools you want to provide to keep the implementation times for your application low.

- **Streaming API**: This API utilizes a HTTP long polling protocol known as the Bayeux protocol to allow callers to monitor in near real time and record activity in Salesforce. This API can be used on a page to monitor race data as it arrives and display it in near real time to the user.

- **Replication API**: Sometimes it is not possible or desirable to migrate all data into Salesforce through Custom Objects. In some cases, this migration is too complex or cost prohibitive. This REST and Apex API allows replication solutions to determine for a given period of time which records for a given object that has been created, updated, or deleted.

- **Bulk API**: This REST-based API allows the import and export of large amounts of records in CSV or XML format up to 10 MB in size per batch job.

Considerations when naming objects and fields

The following are some considerations to ensure that your application objects are well placed to work well with the platform APIs:

- **Naming Custom Objects and fields**: When naming your Custom Objects and fields, pay attention to **API Name** (or **Developer Name**, as it is sometimes referenced). This is the name used when referencing the object or field in the APIs and Apex code mentioned in the previous section. Personally, I prefer to remove the underscore characters the Salesforce Setup UIs place in the default API names when you tap out of the **Label** field, as doing so makes the API name shorter and is easier to type with fewer underscore characters. It then ends up reflecting the camel case used by most APIs, for example, `RaceData__c` instead of `Race_Data__c`.

- **Label and API name consistency**: While it is possible to rename the label of a custom field between releases of your application, you cannot rename the API name. Try to avoid doing so, as causing an inconsistency between the field label and API name makes it harder for business users and developers to work together and locate the correct fields.

- **Naming Relationships**: Whenever you define **Master-Detail** or **Lookup Relationship**, the platform uses the plural label value of the object to form a relationship API name. This API name is used when querying related records as part of a subquery, for example, `select Id, Name, (select Id, Name from Races) from Season__c`. When creating relationship fields, pay attention to the default value entered into the **Child Relationship Name** field, removing underscores if desired and checking whether the names make sense.

For example, if you create a lookup field to the `Driver__c` object called **Fastest Lap By** on the `Race__c` object, the default relationship API name will be **Races**. When using this in a subquery context, it will look like `select Id, Name, (select Id, Name from Races) from Race__c`. However, by naming the relationship `FastestLaps`, this results in a more self-describing query: `select Id, Name, (select Id, Name from FastestLaps) from Race__c`.

- **Apex Triggers bulkification and performance**: When testing Apex Triggers, ensure that you accommodate up to 200 records; this is the default chunk size that Salesforce recommends when utilizing its bulk APIs. This tests the standard guidelines around bulkification best practices; although smaller chunk sizes can be configured, it will typically reduce the execution time of the overall process. Also related to execution time is the time spent within Apex Trigger code, when users solely update fields that have been added in the subscriber org. In these cases, executing the Apex Trigger logic is mostly redundant, as none of the fields this logic is interested in will have changed. Therefore, encourage the optimization of the Apex Trigger logic to execute expensive operations (such as execution of SOQL) only if fields that have been packaged have changed.

Localization and translation

It is important to take localization and translation into consideration from the beginning as it can become difficult and costly to apply it later. Fortunately, the platform can do a lot of work for you.

Localization

When using the native user interface, it automatically formats the values of the numeric and date fields according to the **Locale** field on the **user profile**. **Visualforce** pages. Using the `apex:outputField` and `apex:inputField` components will automatically format values, and outputting local sensitive values in any other way will need to be handled manually in your Apex Controller code or in your JavaScript code.

It's not always possible to use the Visualforce `apex:inputField` and `apex:outputField` tags as described earlier in this chapter. For example, if the information you are displaying is not contained within a Custom Object field, but in some calculated view state in your Apex Controller. The format methods on various type classes such as `Date`, `DateTime`, and `Decimal`, can be used to generate a formatted string value that you can bind to on your pages. You can also determine the users' ISO locale code via `UserInfo.getLocale()`.

Translation

Literal text entered when defining components such as Custom Objects, fields, and layouts are automatically available to the Salesforce Translation Workbench tool. However, literal text used in the Apex code and Visualforce pages need special attention from the developer through the use of Custom Labels.

It is important to avoid concatenation of Custom Label values when forming messages to the end user, as it makes it harder for translators to understand the context of the messages and if needed, resequence the context of the message for other languages. For example, take the message `The driver XYZ was disqualified`. The bad practice is:

```
String message =
    Label.TheDriver + driverName + Label.WasDisqualified;
```

The good practice is as follows:

```
String message = String.format(
    Label.DriverDisqualified, new String[] { driverName});
```

The `DriverDisqualified` Custom Label will be defined as follows:

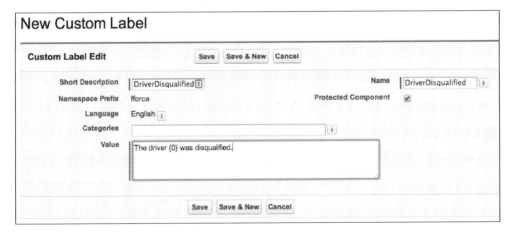

When creating Custom Labels, be sure to pay attention to the **Protected** checkbox. If you uncheck it, end users can reference your labels, which you might want to consider if you wish them to reuse your messages, for example in custom **Email Templates** or **Visualforce** pages. However, the downside is that such labels cannot ever (currently) be deleted from your package as your functionality changes.

Finally, remember that you can utilize `apex:ouputField` within `apex:apex:pageBlockSection` and the field labels will automatically be rendered next to the fields on the page.

Building customizable user interfaces

The most customizable aspect of the user interface your application delivers is the one provided by Salesforce through its highly customizable layout editor that provides the ability to customize the standard user interface pages (including those now delivered via the mobile client Salesforce1) used to list, create, edit, and delete records.

In contrast, a user interface constructed with Visualforce applying customization features takes added effort on behalf of the developer typically utilizing Custom Settings and Fieldsets. Visualforce pages can be used to customize parts of or completely replace the standard user interface. This will be covered in more detail in *Chapter 8, User Interface*.

It is worth noting that subscriber org administrators can modify the page overrides defined and packaged on your Custom Objects to re-enable the Salesforce standard user interface instead of using your packaged Visualforce page. As such, it's worth keeping in mind to give some aesthetic attention to all your Custom Object layouts. Also, note that action overrides and layout components do not get upgraded.

Layouts

The following is a brief summary of the customization features available beyond the standard sections and field ordering. These allow you to add graphs and custom UIs that help combine the layout customization with the flexibility and power of Visualforce:

- **Visualforce**: Layout sections allow you to embed a Visualforce page using the Standard Controllers. While this is only supported on the standard view pages, you are able to do whatever you wish on the Visualforce page itself.

- **Report charts**: Recently, the ability to embed a report chart into a layout has been added to the platform. This is a powerful feature to enhance the information provided to the user using a parameterized report.

- **Actions**: This allows you to describe, either declaratively or programmatically, additional actions beyond the standard platform actions. They are only applicable if you have enabled Chatter for the object.

- **Custom Buttons**: Much like actions, this allows additional buttons on the detail and list view pages to invoke application specific functionality. Creating Custom Buttons and hooking them up to your Apex code is covered in *Chapter 8, User Interface*.

Visualforce

When you are considering building dedicated or even embedded (within layouts) Visualforce pages, always give consideration to end users who want to extend the layout and/or tables on the page with their own custom fields. Fieldsets offer the best means to achieve this; a later chapter will go into this in more detail.

E-mail customization with e-mail templates

Using Apex, you can write code to send e-mails using the Messaging API. This allows you to dynamically generate all attributes of the e-mails you wish to send, the from and to address, subject title, and body. However, keep in mind that end users will more than likely want to add their own logo and messaging to these e-mails, even if such e-mails are simply notifications aimed at their internal users.

Instead of hardcoding the structure of e-mails in your code, consider using email templates (under the **Setup** menu). This feature allows administrators in the subscriber org to create their own e-mails using replacement parameters to inject dynamic values from records your objects define. Using a Custom Setting, for example, you can ask them to configure `DeveloperName` of the e-mail template to reference in your code. You can package email templates as starting points for further customization, though keep in mind that they are not upgradable.

> If data being included in the e-mail is not stored as a field on a Custom Object record or formula field, consider providing some Visualforce custom components in your package that can be used in Visualforce email templates. These components can be used to invoke the Apex code from the email template to query information and/or perform calculations or a reformat of information.

Workflow and Flow

Salesforce provides two declarative tools to implement business processes that either occur as a result of end user operations such as creating, updating, or starting an approval process for a record; this tool is known as **Workflow**. When you need to implement a UI flow that provides a wizard or interview style user experience, this tool is known as **Flow** or sometimes **Visual Flow**.

As an application developer, both can be created and packaged as part of your application. Such components are upgradable (provided that they are marked as **Protected**). Typically, however, package developers tend to leave utilization of these features to consultants and subscriber org admins in preference to Apex and/or Visualforce, where more complex logic and user experiences can be created.

> You may want to consider exposing your application business processes that are not accessible through manipulation of your application objects as Flow plugins.

Social features and mobile

Chatter is a key social feature of the platform; it can enable users of your application to collaborate and communicate contextually around the records in your application as well as optionally invite their customers to do so, using the Chatter Communities feature. It is a powerful aspect of the platform but covering its details is outside the scope of this book.

You can enable Chatter under the **Chatter Settings** page under **Setup**, after which you can enable **Feed Tracking** (also under **Setup**) for your Custom Objects. This setting can be packaged, though it is not upgradable and can be disabled by the subscriber org administrator. Be careful when packaging references to Chatter such as this, as well as including references to the various Chatter-related objects, since this will place a packaging install dependency on your package, requiring all your customers to also have this feature enabled.

By creating actions on your Custom Objects, you can provide a quick way for users to perform common activities on records, for example, updating a contestant's status to DNF. These actions are also visible through the Salesforce1 Mobile application, so they enhance the productivity of the mobile user further compared to standard record editing.

Perform the following steps in the packaging org to try out the steps:

1. Enable **Feed Tracking** for the `Race`, `Driver`, and `Contest` Custom Objects as described above; the fields being tracked are not important for the following steps, but you may want to select them all to get a better feel for the type of notifications Chatter generates. Also enable **Publisher Actions** from the **Chatter Settings** page.

2. Navigate to the `Contestant` object definition and locate the **Buttons, Links and Actions** section. Create a new action and complete the screen as follows:

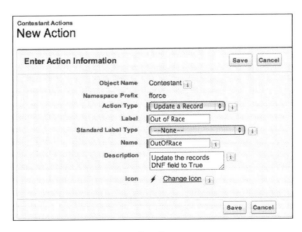

3. When prompted to design the layout of the action, accept the default layout shown and click on **Save**. On the **Contestant Action** page shown, click on **New** to add a new **Predefined Field Value** option to assign TRUE to the DNF field as part of action to update the record:

4. Finally, edit the **Contestant** layout and drag the **Out of Race** action onto the layout (you may need to click on the **override the global publisher layout** link in the layout editor before you can do this). After performing these steps, you will see the **Out of Race** action being displayed in the browser UI as shown in the following screenshot:

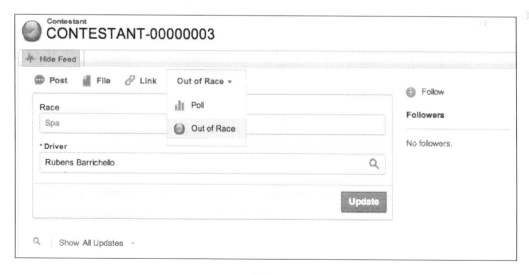

If you are viewing the record via the Salesforce1 Mobile application, it looks like this:

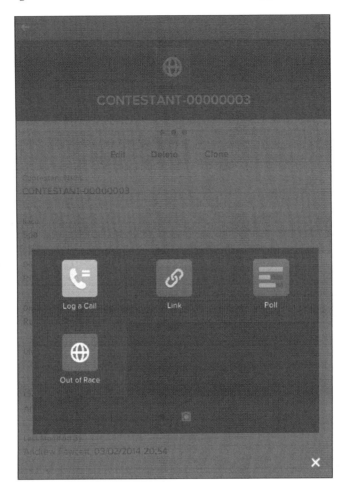

Take time to review your package contents after completing the steps in this chapter and then perform another upload and test an upgrade of the package in your testing org. When installing the upgrade, you should see a confirmation page like the one shown in the following screenshot, showing new or changed components being installed:

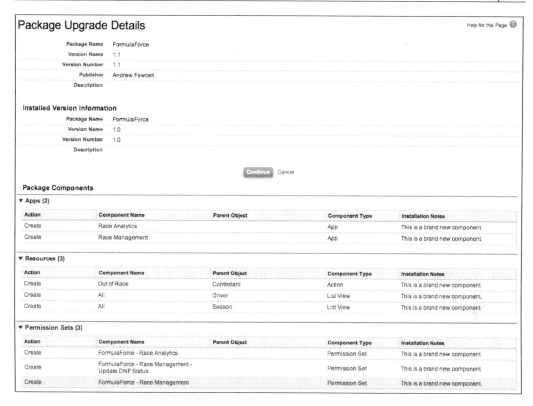

Only a part of the screenshot is shown, though you can see that it shows the custom application, action, and Permission Set components added in this chapter. Further down, the upgraded confirmation page shows the updated Custom Object and new custom fields are shown in the following screenshot:

Action	Component Name	Parent Object	Component Type	Installation Notes
▼ Objects (2)				
Update	Contestant		Custom Object	This is an upgraded component. It will be updated to the new version.
Update	Driver		Custom Object	This is an upgraded component. It will be updated to the new version.
▼ Fields (8)				
Create	Active	Driver	Custom Field	This is a brand new component.
Create	DNF	Contestant	Custom Field	This is a brand new component.
Create	Nationality	Driver	Custom Field	This is a brand new component.
Update	Driver	Contestant	Custom Field	This is an upgraded component. It will be updated to the new version.
Create	Total DNFs	Race	Custom Field	This is a brand new component.
Create	Fastest Lap By	Race	Custom Field	This is a brand new component.
Create	Driver and Race	Contestant	Custom Field	This is a brand new component.
Create	Year	Season	Custom Field	This is a brand new component.

Notice that once you have upgraded the package in your testing org, the layouts for **Season**, **Driver**, and **Race** do not feature the new fields added in this release of the package. This is due to the fact that layouts are not upgraded.

Summary

In this chapter, you have seen a number of platform features that directly help you build key structural and functional aspects of your application without writing a line of code, and in turn, further enabling your customers to extend and customize their application. The chapter also focused on optimizing the tasks performed by consultants and administrators to install and configure the application. Finally, you were made aware of limits imposed within the subscriber org, the ways to avoid them, and now have an awareness of them when packaging.

Continue to review and evolve your application by first looking for opportunities to embrace these and other platform features, and you will ensure that you and your customers' strong alignment with the current and future platform features continue to grow. In the next chapter, we will dive deeper into options and features surrounding the storage of data on the platform.

Make sure to reference the *Salesforce Limits Quick Reference Guide* PDF describing the latest limits of the features discussed in this chapter and others at `http://login.salesforce.com/help/pdfs/en/salesforce_app_limits_cheatsheet.pdf`.

3
Application Storage

It is important to consider your customers' storage needs and use cases around their data creation and consumption patterns early in the application design phase. This ensures that your object schema is the most optimum one with respect to large data volumes, data migration processes (inbound and outbound), and storage cost. In this chapter, we will extend the Custom Objects in the **FormulaForce** application as we explore how the platform stores and manages data.

You will obtain a good understanding of the types of storage provided, and how the costs associated with each are calculated. It is also important to understand the options that are available when it comes to reusing or attempting to mirror the Standard Objects such as **Account**, **Opportunity**, or **Product**, which extend the discussion further into license cost considerations. You will also become aware of the options for standard and custom indexes over your application data, which will lead to the topic of handling large data volumes, covered in an entire chapter later in this book. Finally, we will have some insight into new platform features for *consuming external data storage* from within the platform.

In this chapter, we will cover the following topics:

- Mapping out end user storage requirements
- Understanding the different storage types
- Record identification, uniqueness, and auto numbering
- Record relationships
- Reusing existing Standard Objects
- Applying external IDs and unique fields
- Importing and exporting application data
- Options for replicating and archiving data
- External data sources

Mapping out end user storage requirements

During the initial requirements and design phase of your application, the best practice is to create user categorizations known as personas. Personas consider the users' typical skills, needs, and objectives. From this information, you should also start to extrapolate their data requirements, such as the data they are responsible for creating (either directly or indirectly, by running processes), and what data they need to consume (reporting). Once you have done this, try to provide an estimate of the number of records that they will create and/or consume per month.

> Share these personas and their data requirements with your executive sponsors, your market researchers, early adopters, and finally the whole development team, so that they can keep them in mind and test against them as the application is developed.

For example, in our FormulaForce application, it is likely that **managers** will create and consume data, whereas **race strategists** will mostly consume a lot of data. Finally, there will likely be a background process in the application, generating a lot of data, such as the process that records **Race Data** from the cars and drivers during the qualification stages and the race itself, such as sector (a designated portion of the track) times.

> You may want to capture your conclusions regarding personas and data requirements in a spreadsheet along with some formulas that help predict data storage requirements (discussed later in this chapter). This will help in the future as you discuss your application with Salesforce during the AppExchange Listing process, and will be a useful tool during the Sales cycle as prospective customers wish to know how to budget their storage costs with your application installed.

Understanding the different storage types

The storage used by your application records contribute to the most important part of the overall data storage allocation on the platform. There is also another type of storage used by the files uploaded or created on the platform. From the **Storage Usage** page under the **Setup** menu, you can see a summary of the records used, including those that reside in the Salesforce Standard Objects.

Storage Usage

Help for this Page

Your organization's storage usage is listed below.

Storage Type	Limit	Used	Percent Used
Data Storage	250.0 MB	290 KB	0%
File Storage	250.0 MB	0 B	0%

Current Data Storage Usage

Record Type	Record Count	Storage	Percent
Opportunities	31	62 KB	21%
Cases	26	52 KB	18%
Leads	22	44 KB	15%
Contacts	20	40 KB	14%
Campaigns	4	32 KB	11%
Accounts	12	24 KB	8%
Solutions	10	20 KB	7%
Lap Records	3	6 KB	2%
System Streaming Channels	2	4 KB	1%
Contestants	2	4 KB	1%
Drivers	2	4 KB	1%
Races	1	2 KB	1%
Seasons	1	2 KB	1%
Tasks	0	0 B	0%

The preceding page also shows which users are using the most amount of storage. In addition to the individual's **User** details page, you can also locate the **Used Data Space** and **Used File Space** fields; next to these are the links to view the users' data and file storage usage.

The limit shown for each is based on a calculation between the minimum allocated data storage depending on the type of organization or the number of users multiplied by a certain amount of MB, which also depends on the organization type; whichever is greater becomes the limit. For full details of this, click on the **Help for this Page** link shown on the page.

Note that a new object, `Lap Records`, is shown in the preceding screenshot; we will create this object later in this chapter; it has some special storage considerations.

Data storage

Unlike other database platforms, Salesforce typically uses a fixed 2 KB per record size as part of its storage usage calculations, regardless of the actual number of fields or the size of the data within them on each record. There are some exceptions to this rule, such as **Campaigns** that take up 8 KB, and stored **Email Messages** use up the size of the contained e-mail, though all Custom Object records take up 2 KB. Note that this record size also applies even if the Custom Object uses large text area fields.

Columns versus rows

Given the calculation in the preceding section, you may want to consider whether your data model has multiple occurrences of data that has a known maximum value. In these cases, consider the option of creating multiple columns (or multiple sets of columns) instead of a new object that will use up additional storage. Enterprise Edition orgs currently support up to 500 fields per object. For example, in Formula 1 racing, it is well established that there are only three rounds of qualification before the race in order to determine the starting positions, where each driver competes for the fastest lap.

This could be modeled as a **Qualification Lap** child object to the **Contestant** object; however, in this case, it will only ever have a maximum of three records per contestant in it. A more optimal data storage design is a set of new fields in the **Contestant** object.

Perform the following steps in the packaging org to try out this process:

1. Create three fields of type `Number(6,3)`, for example, **Qualification 1 Lap Time** (`Qualification1LapTime__c`), on the **Contestant** object. Ensure that the **Required** checkbox is unchecked when creating these fields, since not all drivers make it through to the final qualification rounds. Note that here we have used numerals instead of words, for example `QualificaitonOneLapTime__c`, as this can help in situations where dynamic Apex is iterating over the fields.

2. Create a roll-up summary field on the **Race** object, `Poll Position Lap Time`, utilize the **MIN** option when selecting **Roll-Up Type**, and select the `Qualification 1 Lap Time` field in **Field to Aggregate**, as shown in the following screenshot:

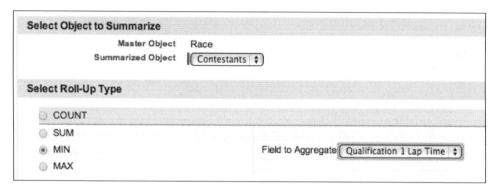

3. Finally, update the permission sets to grant read and write access to the new fields that you have just added in the **Race Management** permission set and read access within the **Race Analytics** permission set.

Keep in mind that you can also use **Formula fields** to add or apply further logic to data stored in columns, emulating what would have been filtered or aggregating queries over equivalent rows. There is also a benefit to reducing the number of SOQL and DML operations that your code needs to perform when taking this approach.

Visualizing your object model

It is an essential idea to build an **Entity Relationship Diagram** (**ERD**) of your object model; not only is this a good resource for you and your team, but it can also help your customers understand where the data that they are creating resides, and help them build reports and integration solutions. Salesforce provides an interactive tool known as **Schema Builder** (accessed via the button from the **Objects** page under **Setup**) that can help with this; it can also be used to create new objects and fields. At this stage in the book, the FormulaForce application data model should look something like this:

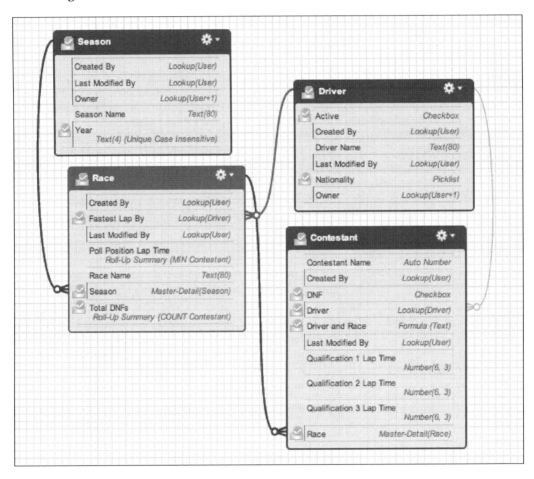

If you are creating **logging** solutions in your application, keep in mind the storage usage for this type of data. For example, how does the user perform bulk deletion of the records? Should this be scheduled? Also, how do you communicate this information to them? A log object can be configured with Workflow rules by the subscriber to perhaps e-mail users as critical log entries are inserted.

If your users are using **Chatter**, you may want to consider providing the facility (perhaps as an option through dynamic Apex, to avoid a package dependency) of using a **Chatter post** to notify the user. Chatter posts, comments, and track changes are not counted by Salesforce under storage usage. However, any files and photos you upload are counted against file storage.

Custom settings storage

Custom settings are slightly different from Custom Objects with respect to data storage limits, in that they do not exist in the same storage area. Custom settings are ideal for data that is read often but written to infrequently. Salesforce caches data in these objects in something it calls the **Application Cache** and provides a means to query it quickly without query governor limits being applied. However, unlike Custom Objects, they do not support **Apex Triggers** or **validation rules**.

There are limits on the storage they can consume, per organization, per namespace. This means that if you create a custom setting and add it to your managed package, it gets its own storage limit. The storage limit for custom settings starts with 1 MB for a full licensed user and can go up to a maximum of 10 MB.

You can see the current storage utilization from the **Custom Settings** page under **Setup**, as follows:

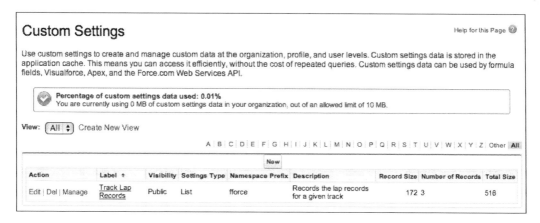

On this page, perform the following steps in the packaging org to create a custom setting and populate it:

1. Create a **Track Lap Records** custom setting by clicking on **New**, and enter `TrackLapRecords` as the API name.

2. Select **List** as **Setting Type** and **Public** as **Visibility**.

3. Create the following fields as described in the following table.

4. Finally, add the custom setting to the package.

Object	Field Name and Type
TrackLapRecords__c	DriverName__c Text(60)
	Time__c Number(5,3)
	Year__c Text(4)

Enter the following sample data, click on **Manage** to begin entering data, and observe the **Number of Records** and **Total Size** columns on the **Custom Settings** page:

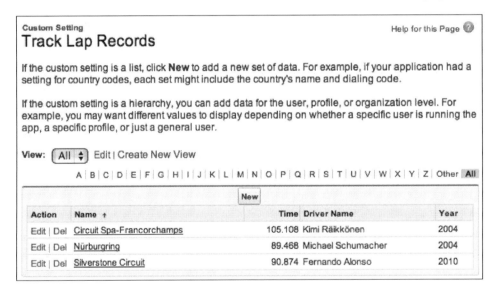

You can also define a **List View** to make it easier for your users to review the custom setting records they create. You cannot initially edit the default **All** view, though you can create one with the same name; click on **Create New View**. This List View will also be packaged.

Note that while the **Storage Usage** page lists custom settings as shown in the following screenshot, they are not included in the total shown. Instead, you need to use the **Custom Settings** page to understand the storage limit and current usage.

| Lap Records | 3 | 6 KB | 2% |

File storage

Salesforce has a growing number of ways to store file-based data, ranging from the historic **Document** tab, to the more sophisticated **Content** tab, to using **Chatter Files**, not to mention **Attachments**, which can be applied to your Custom Object records if enabled. Each has its own pros and cons for end users and file size limits that are well defined in the Salesforce documentation.

From the perspective of application development, as with data storage, be aware of how much your application is generating on behalf of the user and give them a means to control and delete that information. In some cases, consider if the end user would be happy to have the option to recreate the file on demand (perhaps as a PDF) rather than always having the application to store it.

Record identification, uniqueness, and auto numbering

Every record in Salesforce has an **Id** field, and with a few exceptions, also a **Name** field. The **Id** field is unique, but is not human readable, meaning it cannot be entered or, for most of us on this planet, easily remembered!

The default value for the **Name** field is to provide a means for the user to enter their own textual description for the record, such as the race name or the driver name. The **Name** field is not enforced as being unique. Being the primary means by which the user identifies records; this can be a problem and is something that the end user needs to avoid. This aspect of the platform can be particularly problematic with accounts and contacts; hence, AppExchange has a number of so-called "Deduplication" applications you can try.

 The Database.merge and merge DML statements support merging of accounts, leads, and contact records.

Unique and external ID fields

When adding fields, you can indicate that the values stored within them are **unique** and/or **external identifiers**. For unique fields, the platform will automatically enforce this rule regardless of how records are created or updated, rejecting records with no unique values. By utilizing fields designated as external ID fields, you can simplify the data-loading process for users; this will be discussed later in this chapter in more detail. Both of these field modifiers result in a custom index being created, which can help optimize query performance.

 You can help users avoid creating duplicate records with the same name by ensuring that other identifying fields such as these are also added to the **lookup layout** as described in the previous chapter.

Let's add a **Unique** and **External Id** field to record the driver's Twitter handle. Perform the following steps in the packaging org to try this out:

1. Create a new **Text** field, **Twitter Handle** (TwitterHandle__c), with a length of **15** on the **Driver** object, and check the **Unique** and **External Id** checkboxes.

2. Utilize the **Driver** records entered in the previous chapters to update the fields and confirm that the system prevents duplicate Twitter handles. Lewis Hamilton's Twitter handle is LewisHamilton and Ruben's is rubarrichello.

3. Update the permission sets that have read and write permissions for the new field to **Race Management**, and the read-only permission to **Race Analytics**.

Auto Number fields

The platform supports an auto sequence field type, which can be applied to the **Name** field during and after object creation (as long as the object has not been previously included as part of a prior package release upload). It can also be applied to a brand new field. The platform handles incrementing the sequence and ensures there are no duplicates.

Apply **Auto Number** within the FormulaForce application to give a unique auto incrementing identifier to the **Race Data** records as they are inserted. Perform the following steps in the packaging org to try this out:

1. Create a new **Race Data** (RaceData__c) object; for **Record Name**, enter Race Data Id, and select **Auto Number** from the **Data Type** field.

2. In the **Display Format** field, enter RDID-{000000000} and 1 in the **Starting Number**. Finally, check the **Allow Reports** field.

3. Add a **Lookup** field called Race (Race__c) to relate records in this object to the existing Race object. Select the **Don't allow deletion of the lookup record that's part of a lookup relationship** option to prevent the deletion of race records if race data exists. We will add further fields to this object in a later chapter.

4. Create a tab for the **Race Data** object that we just created and add the tab to the **Race Management** and **Race Analytics** applications. By doing this, the tab and object will automatically be added to the package ready for the next upload.

5. Create a test record to observe the **Race Data Name** field value.

6. Update the permission sets with the new object and fields, giving a read and write permission to **Race Management** and a read-only permission to **Race Analytics**.

While it is possible to add new custom fields to objects that have already been packaged and released to your customers, you cannot currently add new **Auto Number** fields to an object that has already been packaged, for example, the **Driver** object.

Apex tests creating test records that utilize **Auto Number** fields can be configured by an org setting to not increment the sequence number outside of the test, which would create gaps in the sequence from the end user's perspective. Access this setting in the subscriber org via the **Options...** button on the **Apex Test Execution** page under **Setup**:

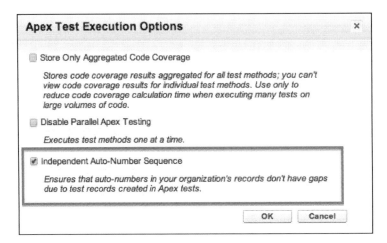

Display Format determines the formatting but not the maximum sequence number. For example, if a format of SEQ{0000} is used, and the next sequence number created is 10,000, the platform will display it as SEQ10000, ignoring the format digits. The maximum of an Auto Number field is stated in the Salesforce documentation as being a maximum length of 30 characters, of which 10 are reserved for the prefix characters. It also states that the maximum starting number must be less than 1,000,000,000.

The platform does not guarantee that there will be no gaps in an auto number sequence field. Errors in creating records can create gaps as the number assigned during the insert process is not reused. Thus, set expectations accordingly with your users when using this feature.

One workaround to creating an unbroken sequence would be to create a Custom Object with the **Name** field that utilizes the **Auto Number** field type, for example, Job References. Then, create a relationship between this object and the object records you require the sequence applied to, for example Jobs. Then, write an **Apex Scheduled** job that inserts records on a daily basis into the Job References object for each Jobs record that is currently without a Job Reference relationship. Then, run reports over the Job References object. To ensure that no Job records are deleted, thus creating gaps, you can also enable the lookup referential integrity feature described in the following sections.

Subscribers customizing the Auto Number Display Format

Be aware that **Display Format** cannot be customized once it is packaged and installed in the subscriber org. However, it is possible to create a custom **Formula field** in the subscriber org to remove the prefix from the **Name** field value and reapply whatever prefix is needed. For example, the following formula will isolate the numeric portion of the **Name** field value and apply a new prefix specified in the formula (this could also be driven by a custom setting or conditional logic in the formula):

```
'MYID-' + MID(Name, 4, LEN(Name) + 4)
```

When this formula field is applied for a record who's Auto Number is RD-000000001, the formula would display as follows:

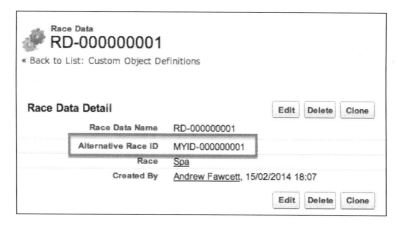

Record relationships

A relationship is formed by a **Lookup** field being created from one object to another, often referred to as a parent and child relationship. There are two types of relationships in Salesforce: **Master-Detail** and **Lookup**.

In some aspects, they share similarities in how they are referenced when using SOQL and Apex and how they are input through the user interface (such as **lookup filters** described in the previous chapter). However, there are differences regarding **limits** and **referential integrity** features, and they are as follows:

- Utilizing the Master-Detail form of relationship provides a powerful way to model containment, where one parent object record acts as a container for other child records; in our example, a race contains **Contestants**.

    ◦ The platform will automatically cascade deletion of child records when the parent is deleted, and it will also enforce the need for a parent reference when the child records are created.

- By default, the platform prevents users from moving the child records to another parent by editing the relationship field. However, you can disable this validation and permit this by selecting the **Child records can be reparented to other parent records after they are created** option.

- With the use of **Rollup Summary** fields, it also becomes possible to build calculated fields based on values of the child record fields.

- Salesforce, however, does recommend that this kind of parent-and-child relationship does not exceed 10,000 child records; otherwise, the platform will not support the cascade delete of child records.

- You can define up to three levels of Master-Detail relationships.

- Utilizing the **Lookup** type of relationship allows you to model connections between related records that are optional and may also have other relationships not necessarily in an ownership or containing aspect with their parents. Keep in mind the following points when using Lookup fields to define relationships:

  - Deletion of parent records will not result in a cascade delete of related child records; this can be enabled via **Salesforce Support**, though this setting will not be packaged.

  - Unlike Master-Detail, you can elect for the platform to enforce referential integrity during the creation of the field by utilizing the **Don't allow deletion of the lookup record that's part of a lookup relationship** option.

  - Currently, the **Rollup Summary** fields are not supported when using a Lookup relationship.

Lookup fields of either kind are automatically indexed by the platform, making queries in some cases faster. We will focus more on indexes in a later chapter. The maximum number of relationship fields per object is 40.

 While it is possible to add new custom fields to objects that have already been packaged and released to your customers, you cannot add a new Master-Detail relationship to an object that has already been packaged.

Reusing the existing Standard Objects

When designing your object model, a good knowledge of the existing **Standard Objects** and their features is the key to knowing when and when not to reference them. Keep in mind the following points when considering the use of Standard Objects:

- **From a data storage perspective**, ignoring Standard Objects creates a potential data duplication and integration effort for your end users if they are already using similar Standard Objects as pre-existing Salesforce customers. Remember that adding additional custom fields to the Standard Objects via your package will not increase the data storage consumption for those objects.

- **From a license cost perspective**, conversely, referencing some Standard Objects might cause additional license costs for your users, since not all are available to the users without additional licenses from Salesforce. Make sure that you understand the differences between **Salesforce (CRM)** and **Salesforce Platform** licenses with respect to the Standard Objects available. Currently, the Salesforce Platform license provides **Accounts** and **Contacts**; however, to use **Opportunity** or **Product** objects, a Salesforce (CRM) license is needed by the user. Refer to the Salesforce documentation for the latest details on these.

Use your user personas to define what Standard Objects your users use and reference them via lookups, Apex code, and Visualforce accordingly. You may wish to use **extension packages** and/or **dynamic Apex** and SOQL to make these kind of references optional. Since **Developer Edition** orgs have all these licenses and objects available (although in a limited quantity), make sure you review your **Package dependencies** before clicking on the **Upload** button each time to check for unintentional references.

Importing and exporting data

Salesforce provides a number of its own tools for **importing** and **exporting** data, as well as a number of third-party options based on the Salesforce APIs; these are listed on AppExchange. When importing records with other record relationships, it is not possible to predict and include the IDs of related records, such as the **Season** record ID when importing **Race** records; this section will present a solution to this.

Salesforce provides **Data Import Wizard**, which is available under the **Setup** menu:

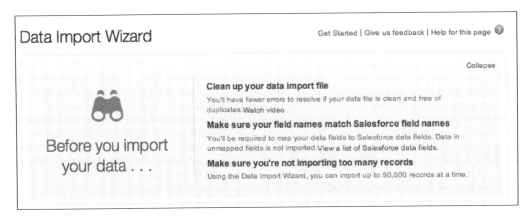

It is straightforward to import a CSV file with a list of race **Season** since this is a top-level object and has no other object dependencies. However, to import **Race** information (which is a related child object to **Season**), the **Season** and **Fasted Lap By** record IDs are required, which will typically not be present in a **Race** import CSV file by default. Note that IDs are unique across the platform and cannot be shared between orgs.

External ID fields help address this problem by allowing Salesforce to use the existing values of such fields as a secondary means to associate records being imported that need to reference parent or related records. All that is required is that the related record **Name** or, ideally, a unique external ID be included in the import data file.

The Races.csv file is included in the sample code for this chapter in the /data folder. This CSV file includes three columns: Year, Name, and Fastest Lap By (of the driver who performed the fastest lap of that race, indicated by their Twitter handle). You may remember that a **Driver** record can also be identified by this since the field has been defined as an **External ID** field:

	A	B	C
1	Year	Name	Fasted Lap By
2	2014	Melbourne	LewisHamilton
3	2014	Shanghai	LewisHamilton
4	2014	Monte Carlo	LewisHamilton
5	2014	Budapest	LewisHamilton

Both the 2014 **Season** record and the Lewis Hamilton **Driver** record should already be present in your packaging org. If not, refer to the previous chapter to create these. Now, run **Data Import Wizard** and complete the settings as shown in the following screenshot:

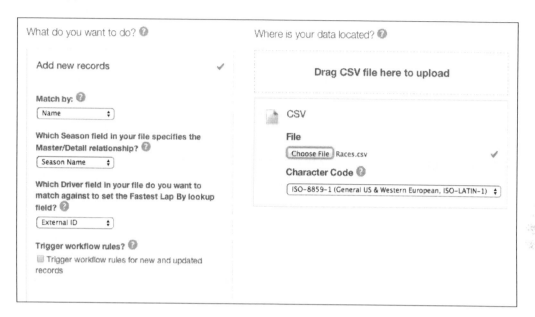

Next, complete the field mappings as shown in the following screenshot:

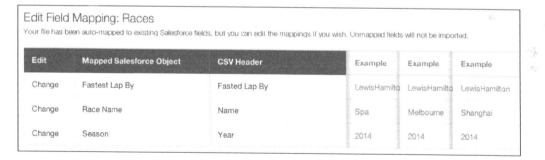

Click on **Start Import** and then on **OK** to review the results once the data import has completed. You should find that four new **Race** records have been created under 2014 **Season**, with the **Fasted Lap By** field correctly associated with the Lewis Hamilton **Driver** record.

Note that these tools will also stress your **Apex Trigger** code for volumes, as they typically have the bulk mode enabled and insert records in chunks of 200 records. Thus, it is recommended that you test your triggers to at least this level of record volumes. Later chapters will present coding patterns to help ensure that code supports the bulk mode.

Options for replicating and archiving data

Enterprise customers often have legacy and/or external systems that are still being used or that they wish to phase out in the future. As such, they may have requirements to replicate aspects of the data stored in the Salesforce platform to another. Likewise, in order to move unwanted data off the platform and manage their data storage costs, there is a need to archive data.

The following lists some platform and API facilities that can help you and/or your customers build solutions to replicate or archive data. There are, of course, a number of **AppExchange** solutions listed that provide applications that use these APIs already:

- **Replication API**: This API exists in both the web service SOAP and Apex form. It allows you to develop a scheduled process to query the platform for any new, updated, or deleted records between a given time period for a specific object. The getUpdated and getDeleted API methods return only the IDs of the records, requiring you to use the conventional Salesforce APIs to query the remaining data for the replication. The frequency in which this API is called is important to avoid gaps. Refer to the Salesforce documentation for more details.

- **Outbound Messaging**: This feature offers a more real-time alternative to the replication API. An outbound message event can be configured using the standard workflow feature of the platform. This event, once configured against a given object, provides a **Web Service Definition Language (WSDL)** file that describes a web service endpoint to be called when records are created and updated. It is the responsibility of a web service developer to create the end point based on this definition. Note that there is no provision for deletion with this option.

- **Bulk API**: This API provides a means to move up to 5000 chunks of Salesforce data (up to 10 MB or 10,000 records per chunk) per rolling 24 hour period. Salesforce and third-party data loader tools, including the Salesforce Data Loader tool, offer this as an option. It can also be used to delete records without them going into the recycle bin. This API is ideal for building solutions to archive data.

External data sources

One of the downsides with moving data off the platform in an archive use case or with not being able to replicate data onto the platform is that the end users have to move between applications and logins to view data; this causes an overhead as the process and data is not connected.

A relatively new feature of the platform is the ability to surface external data within the Salesforce user interface via the so-called **External Objects** and **External Data Sources** configurations under **Setup**. They offer a similar functionality to Custom Objects, such as **List views**, **Layouts**, **Custom Buttons**, **Reports**, and **Dashboards**. At the time of writing, Salesforce supports Microsoft Sharepoint's external data sources in this way (through a beta program), though it is likely that this will be extended in the up coming releases. This technology also offers some interesting integration possibilities for the future.

Summary

This chapter has further explored the declarative aspects of developing an application on the platform that applies to how an application is stored and how relational data integrity is enforced through the use of the lookup field deletion constraints and applying unique fields. The Master-Detail relationships allow you to model containment concepts in our data model. We also considered the data storage implications of extending your schema across columns instead of rows and the benefits on the cost of storage for your end users.

Upload the latest version of the **FormulaForce** package and install it into your test org. The summary page during the installation of new and upgraded components should look something like the following screenshot. Note that the permission sets are upgraded during the install.

▼ Tabs (1)

Action	Component Name	Parent Object	Component Type	Installation Notes
Create	Race Data		Tab	This is a brand new component.

▼ Resources (2)

Action	Component Name	Parent Object	Component Type	Installation Notes
Create	All	RaceData__c	List View	This is a brand new component.
Create	Race Data Layout	RaceData__c	Page Layout	This is a brand new component.

▼ Objects (2)

Action	Component Name	Parent Object	Component Type	Installation Notes
Create	Race Data		Custom Object	This is a brand new component.
Create	Track Lap Records		Custom Setting	This is a brand new component.

▼ Fields (9)

Action	Component Name	Parent Object	Component Type	Installation Notes
Create	Time	TrackLapRecords__c	Custom Field	This is a brand new component.
Create	Driver Name	TrackLapRecords__c	Custom Field	This is a brand new component.
Create	Twitter Handle	Driver	Custom Field	This is a brand new component.
Create	Qualification 3 Lap Time	Contestant	Custom Field	This is a brand new component.
Create	Qualification 1 Lap Time	Contestant	Custom Field	This is a brand new component.
Create	Poll Position Lap Time	Race	Custom Field	This is a brand new component.
Create	Race	RaceData__c	Custom Field	This is a brand new component.
Create	Year	TrackLapRecords__c	Custom Field	This is a brand new component.
Create	Qualification 2 Lap Time	Contestant	Custom Field	This is a brand new component.

In this chapter, we have now covered some major aspects of the platform with respect to packaging, platform alignment, and how your application data is stored as well as the key aspects of your application's architecture.

In the next few chapters of this book, we will start to look at **Enterprise coding patterns** and effectively engineer your application code to work in harmony with the platform features, and grow with your needs and the platform.

4
Apex Execution and Separation of Concerns

When starting to write Apex, it is tempting to start with an Apex Trigger or Apex Controller class and start placing the required logic in these classes to implement the desired functionality. This chapter will explore a different starting point, one that gives the developer focus on writing application business logic (the core logic of your application) in a way that is independent of the calling context. It will also explain the benefits that it brings in terms of reuse, code maintainability, and flexibility, especially when applying code to different areas of the platform.

We will explore the ways in which Apex code can be invoked, the requirements and benefits of these contexts, their commonalities, their differences, and best practices that are shared. We will distill these into a layered way of writing code that teaches and embeds **Separation of Concerns (SOC)** in the code base from the very beginning. We will also introduce a naming convention to help with code navigation and enforce SOC further.

At the end of the chapter, we will have written some initial code, setting out the framework to support Separation of Concerns and the foundation for the next three chapters to explore some well-known **Enterprise Application Architecture** patterns in more detail. Finally, we will package this code and install it in the test org.

This chapter will cover the following topics:

- Apex execution contexts
- Apex governors and namespaces
- Where is Apex used?
- Separation of Concerns
- Patterns of Enterprise Application Architecture
- Unit testing versus system testing
- The packaging code

Execution contexts

An execution context on the platform has a beginning and an end; it starts with a user or system action or event, such as a button click or part of a scheduled background job, and is typically short lived; seconds or minutes instead of hours before it ends. It is especially important in multitenant architecture because each context receives its own set of limits around queries, database operations, logs, and duration of the execution.

In the case of background jobs (**Batch Apex**), instead of having one execution context for the whole job, the platform splits the information being processed and hands it back through several execution contexts in a serial fashion. For example, if a job was asked by the user to process 1000 records and the batch size (or scope size in Batch Apex terms) was 200 (which is the default), this would result in five distinct execution contexts one after another. This is done so that the platform can throttle up or down the execution of jobs or if needed, pause them between scopes.

You might think that an execution context starts and ends with your Apex code, but you would be wrong. Using some Apex code is introduced later in this chapter; we will use the debug logs to learn how the platform invokes the Apex code.

Exploring execution contexts

In the next two examples, imagine for now an Apex Trigger has been created for the **Contestant** object and an Apex class has been written to implement some logic to update the contestants' championship points dependent on their position when the race ends.

In the first example, the **Contestant** record is updated directly from the UI and the **Apex Debug** log shown in the next screenshot is captured.

Notice the **EXECUTION_STARTED** and **EXECUTION_FINISHED** lines; these show the actual start and end of the request on the Salesforce server. The **CODE_UNIT_STARTED** lines show where the platform invokes Apex code. Also, note that the line number shows **EXTERNAL**, indicating the platform's internal code called the Apex code. The rest of the execution of the code is collapsed in the screenshot for brevity at this point.

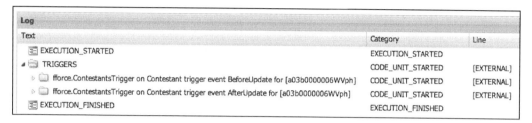

In this second example, imagine that some Apex code was executed to calculate the contestants' championship points once the race ends. In this case, the code was executed from an **Execute Anonymous** prompt (though in the application, this would be a button); again, the Apex Debug log was captured and is shown in the next screenshot.

Again, you can see the **EXECUTION_STARTED** and **EXECUTION_FINISHED** entries, along with the three **CODE_UNIT_STARTED** entries, one for the `RaceService.awardChampionshipPoints` Apex method called from the **Execute Anonymous** prompt and two others for the Apex Trigger code.

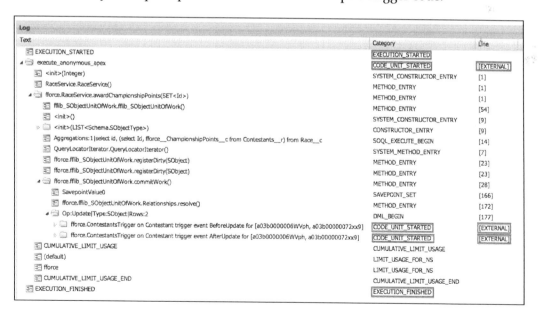

What is different from the first example is, which you can see by looking at the **Line** column, that the execution transitions show lines of the Apex code being executed and EXTERNAL. When DML statements are executed in Apex to update the **Contestants** records, the Apex code execution pauses while the platform code takes over to update the records. During this process, the platform eventually then invokes Apex Triggers and once again, the execution flows back into Apex code.

Essentially, the execution context is used to wrap a request to the Salesforce server; it can be a mix of execution of the Apex code, Validation Rules, workflow rules, trigger code, and other logic executions. The platform handles the overall orchestration of this for you. The Salesforce Developer Console tool offers some excellent additional insight into the time spent in each of these areas.

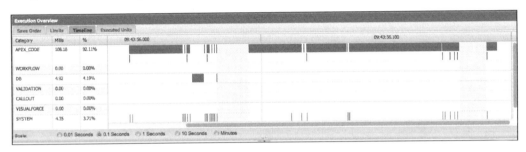

If the subscriber org has added Apex Triggers to your objects, these are executed in the same execution context. If any of these Apex code units throw unhandled exceptions, the entire execution context is stopped and all database updates performed are rolled back, which is discussed in more detail later in this chapter.

Execution context and state

The server memory storage used by the Apex variables created in an execution context can be considered the state of the execution context; in Apex, this is known as the **heap**. On the whole, the server memory resources used to maintain an execution context's state are returned at the end; thus, in a system with short lived execution contexts, resources can be better managed. By using the CPU and heap governors, the platform enforces the maximum duration of an execution context and Apex heap size to ensure the smooth running of the service; these are described in more detail later in this chapter.

State management is the programming practice of managing the information the user or job needs between separate execution contexts (requests to the server) invoked as the user or job goes about performing the work, such as a wizard-based UI or job aggregating information. Users, of course, do not really understand execution contexts and state; they see tasks via the user interface or jobs they start based on field inputs and criteria they provide. It is not always necessary to consider state management, as some user tasks can be completed in one execution context; this is often preferable from an architecture perspective as there are overheads in the managing state. Although the platform provides some features to help with state management, using them requires careful consideration and planning, especially from a data volumes perspective.

In other programming platforms such as Java or Microsoft .NET, static variables are used to maintain state across execution contexts, often caching information to reduce the processing of subsequent execution contexts or to store common application configuration. The implementation of the `static` keyword in Apex is different; its scope applies only to the current execution context and no further. Thus, an Apex static variable value will not be retained between execution contexts, though they are preserved between multiple Apex code units (as illustrated in the previous section). Thus, in recursive Apex Trigger scenarios, allow the sharing of the static variable to control recursion.

 Custom Settings may offer a potential parallel in Apex where other programming languages use static variables to store the application configuration. Such settings can be configured to be org, user, or profile scope and are low cost to read from Apex.

Execution context and security

As discussed in the last chapter, the platform provides security features to allow subscribers or administrators to manage CRUD operations on your objects as well as individual field-level security (FLS) ideally through the assignment of some carefully considered Permission Sets that you have included in your package, in addition to providing the ability to define sharing rules to control record visibility and editing.

Within an Apex execution context, it is important to understand whose responsibility it is (the platform's or developer's) to provide enforcement of these security features. With respect to sharing rules, there is a default security context, which is either set by the platform or can be specified using specific keywords used within Apex code. The two types of security are described in further detail in the following bullets:

- **Sharing security**: Through the use of the `with sharing` keyword when applied to an Apex class declaration, the Apex runtime provides support to filter out records returned by SOQL queries automatically that do not meet the sharing rules for the current user context. If it is not specified, then this is inherited from the outermost Apex class that controls the execution. Conversely, the `without sharing` keyword can be used to explicitly enable the return of all records meeting the query regardless of sharing rules. This is useful when implementing referential integrity, for example, where the code needs to see all the available records regardless of the current users sharing rules.

- **CRUD and FLS security**: As discussed in the previous chapter, it is the Apex developers' responsibility to use appropriate programming approaches to enforce this type of security. On a Visualforce page, CRUD and FLS are only enforced through the use of the appropriate Visualforce components such as `apex:inputField` and `apex:outputField`. The Apex code within an execution context runs within the system mode with respect to CRUD and FLS accessibility, which means unless your code checks for permitted access, the platform will always permit access. Note that this is regardless of the use of the `with sharing` keyword, which only affects the records that are visible to your code.

In summary, both are controlled and implemented separately as follows:

- Row-level security applies only to the `with sharing` usage
- CRUD security and FLS needs separate coding considerations

In the later chapters of this book, we will see some places to position this logic to make it easier to manage and less intrusive for the rest of the code.

Execution context transaction management

Handling database transactions in Apex is simpler than other platforms. By default, the scope of the transaction wraps the entire execution context. This means that if the execution context completes successfully, any record data is committed. If an unhandled exception or error occurs, the execution context is aborted and all record data is rolled back.

Unhandled Apex exceptions, governor exceptions, or Validation Rules can cause an execution context to abort. In some cases, however, it can be desirable to perform only a partial rollback. For these cases, the platform provides **Savepoints** that can be used to place markers in the execution context to record what data is written at the point the Savepoint was created. Later, a Savepoint can be used in the execution as the rollback position to resume further processing in response to error handling or a condition that causes the alternative code path resulting in different updates to the database.

It is important to realize that catching exceptions using the Apex `try` and `catch` keywords, for example, in Visualforce controller methods, results in the platform committing any data written up until the exception occurs. This can lead to partially updated data across the objects being updated in the execution context giving rise to data integrity issues in your application. Savepoints can be used to avoid this by using a rollback in the `catch` code block. This does, however, present quite a boilerplate overhead for the developer each time. Later in this book, we will review this practice in more detail and introduce a pattern known as **Unit Of Work** to help automate this.

Apex governors and namespaces

Platform governors prevent any one execution context from consuming excessive resources on the service, which could be detrimental to its users. Overall, an execution context cannot exceed 10 minutes, though within an execution context in practice, other limits would likely be reached before this.

For example, Apex code units executing within an execution context can only collectively execute for a maximum 10 or 60 seconds depending on the context. Over the years, Salesforce has worked hard to consolidate what was once a confusing array of governors, which also varied based on a number of Apex code contexts. Thankfully, these days governors are much easier to follow and vary only based on the context being interactive or batch (asynchronous).

The namespaces and governor scope

An important consideration for a packaged solution is the scope of a governor. In other words, does it apply only to the packaged code or for all code executing in the execution context? Remember that an execution context can contain code from other developers within the subscriber org or other packaged solutions installed.

Your package namespace acts as a container for some governors, which protects your code from limits being consumed by other packaged code (triggers for example) running in the execution context. The platform supports up to 10 namespace scopes within one execution context. For code that has not been deployed as part of a managed package, such as code developed directly in the subscriber org, there is a default namespace.

You can see evidence of namespaces in play when you observe the debug logs within your packaging org. Just before each Apex code unit completes, notice how the LIMIT_USAGE_FOR_NS section of the debug log is repeated for the default and fforce namespaces (your namespace will be different) as follows, allowing you to review the incremental usage of governors throughout the execution context:

```
13:47:43.712 (412396000)|CUMULATIVE_LIMIT_USAGE
13:47:43.712|LIMIT_USAGE_FOR_NS|(default)|
  Number of SOQL queries: 0 out of 100
  Number of query rows: 0 out of 50000
  Number of SOSL queries: 0 out of 20
  Number of DML statements: 0 out of 150
  Number of DML rows: 0 out of 10000
  Number of code statements: 0 out of 200000
  Maximum CPU time: 0 out of 10000
  Maximum heap size: 0 out of 6000000
  Number of callouts: 0 out of 10
  Number of Email Invocations: 0 out of 10
  Number of fields describes: 0 out of 100
  Number of record type describes: 0 out of 100
  Number of child relationships describes: 0 out of 100
  Number of picklist describes: 0 out of 100
  Number of future calls: 0 out of 10

13:47:43.712|LIMIT_USAGE_FOR_NS|fforce|
  Number of SOQL queries: 1 out of 100
  Number of query rows: 1 out of 50000
  Number of SOSL queries: 0 out of 20
  Number of DML statements: 2 out of 150
  Number of DML rows: 3 out of 10000
  Number of code statements: 85 out of 200000
```

```
Maximum CPU time: 0 out of 10000

Maximum heap size: 0 out of 6000000

Number of callouts: 0 out of 10

Number of Email Invocations: 0 out of 10

Number of fields describes: 0 out of 100

Number of record type describes: 0 out of 100

Number of child relationships describes: 0 out of 100

Number of picklist describes: 0 out of 100

Number of future calls: 0 out of 10
```

```
13:47:43.712|CUMULATIVE_LIMIT_USAGE_END
```
```
13:47:43.412|CODE_UNIT_FINISHED|execute_anonymous_apex
```

Note that all governors are shown in the summary regardless of their scope; for example, the CPU time governor is an execution scope governor. This allows you to follow the consumption of the Apex CPU time across Apex code units from all namespaces. The **Developer Console** option provides some excellent tools to profile the consumption of governors.

Deterministic and non-deterministic governors

When considering governors from a testing and support perspective, you should be aware of which governors are deterministic and which are not. For example, when profiling your application, this is being able to obtain the exact same results (such as the preceding results) from the debug logs from repeated running of the exact same test. The following outlines examples of both types of governors:

- Examples of deterministic governors are the SOQL and DML governors. If you repeat the same test scenario (within your development or packaging orgs), you will always get the same utilization of queries and updates to the database; thus, you can determine reliably if any changes in these need to be investigated.

- An example of a non-deterministic governor is the CPU time governor. The amount of time used between executions will vary based on the load at any given time on the Salesforce servers. Thus, it is hard to determine accurately whether changes in your application are truly affecting this or not. That being said, it can be a useful indicator depending on the variance you're seeing between builds of your software. However, keep in mind that the base line information you capture will become increasingly less accurate as time goes by, for example, between platform releases.

In the CPU governor, the platform limits the length of time the execution context is allowed to spend executing the Apex code to 10 seconds for interactive context and 60 seconds for asynchronous context (for example, batch Apex), though in practice the platform appears to exercise some tolerance. In contrast, the number of SOQL queries or DML statements is always constant when applied to a consistent test scenario.

As the CPU governor is non-deterministic, it should only be used as a guideline when testing. My recommendation is not to use the `Limits.getCPULimit()` method as a branching mechanism between interactive and batch processing in your application. If you require this type of branching, focus on using aspects of your application such as selection criteria, number of rows selected, or some other configurable setting in the subscriber org perhaps via a Custom Setting.

You may want to consider testing certain governors within an Apex test context to monitor for changes in how many queries or DML are being consumed. Such tests can give you an early warning sign that inefficiency has crept into your code. Use the `Limits` class methods to capture the before and after state of the SOQL and/or DML governors. Then, apply either a strict comparison of the expected usage (for example, 10 queries expected after the execution of the test) or a plus or minus tolerance to allow for code evolution.

Key governors for Apex package developers

The following table is a summary of key governors, their scope, and whether they are deterministic. Note that Salesforce is constantly monitoring the use of its service and adapting its governors. Always check for the latest information on governors in the *Apex Developer's Guide*.

Governor	Scope	Deterministic
Execution context timeout	Execution context	No
Apex CPU governor	Execution context	No
SOQL queries	Namespace	Yes
DML statements	Namespace	Yes
Query rows	Namespace	Yes

Where is Apex used?

The following table lists the types of execution contexts the Apex code can run from and considerations with respect to security and state management. While a description of how to implement each of these is outside the scope of this book, some aspects such as batch Apex are discussed in more detail in a later chapter when considering data volumes.

Execution context	Security	State management
Anonymous Apex	Sharing is enforced by default, unless disabled by applying the `without sharing` keyword to the enclosing class. CRUD and FLS are enforced by default, but only against the code entered directly into the **Execute Anonymous** window. The code will fail to compile if the user does not have access to the objects or fields referenced. Note that the checking is only performed by the platform at compilation time; if the code calls a pre-existing Apex class, there is no enforcement within this class and any other class it calls.	See Note 2.
Apex Controller action method	Sharing is not enforced by default; the developer needs to apply the `withsharing` keyword to the enclosing class. CRUD and FLS are not enforced by default; the developer needs to enforce this in code.	Any member variable declared on the Apex Controller that is not static or marked with the transient keyword will be included in **View State**. Visualforce automatically maintains this between interactions on the page. Use it carefully, as large View State sizes can cause performance degradation for the page. **Developer Console** has an excellent View State browser tool.

Execution context	Security	State management
Apex Controller remote action	Sharing is not enforced by default; the developer needs to apply the `withsharing` keyword to the enclosing class. It is required for Salesforce security review. CRUD and FLS are not enforced by default; the developer needs to check this in code.	Remote action Apex methods are already static, as stated previously; any static data is not retained in Apex. Thus, there is no state retained between remote action calls made by the client JavaScript. Typically, in these cases, the state of the task the user is performing is maintained on the page itself via the client-side state. As a result of not having to manage the state for the developer, remote action methods are much faster than action methods.
Apex Trigger	Sharing is not enforced by default; the developer needs to apply the `withsharing` keyword in the outermost Apex class (if present, for example, Apex Controller). Triggers invoked through the Salesforce UIs or APIs run without sharing implicitly; if you need to apply with sharing, move your trigger code into an Apex class and call that from the trigger code. CRUD and FLS are not enforced by default; the developer needs to enforce this in the code.	Static variables are shared between Apex Trigger invocations within an execution context. This allows some caching of commonly used information and/or recursive trigger protection to be implemented if needed.

Execution context	Security	State management
Batch Apex	Sharing is not enforced by default; the developer needs to apply the `withsharing` keyword to the enclosing class. CRUD and FLS are not enforced by default; the developer needs to enforce this in the code.	Batch Apex splits work into distinct execution contexts, driven by splitting up the data into scopes (typically, 200). If the `Database.Stateful` interface is implemented, class member variable values of the implementing Apex class are retained between each invocation. The `transient` keyword also applies here. The `final` keyword can be used to retain the initial member variable values throughout the job execution.
Apex scheduler	See Note 1.	See Note 2.
Inbound messaging	See Note 1.	See Note 2.
Flow plugin	See Note 1.	See Note 2.
Apex REST API	See Note 1.	See Note 2.
Apex web service	See Note 1.	See Note 2.

Note 1: Unless otherwise stated in the preceding table, the default position is as follows regarding security:

- Sharing is not enforced by default; the developer needs to apply the `withsharing` keyword to the enclosing class

- CRUD and FLS are not enforced by default; the developer needs to check this in the code

Note 2: For state management, unless stated otherwise in the previous table, the default position is as follows:

- No static or member variable values are retained between invocations of the Apex class methods between execution contexts

Separation of Concerns

As you can see there are a number of places Apex code is invoked by various platform features. Such places represent areas for valuable code to potentially hide. It is hidden because it is typically not easy or appropriate to reuse such logic as each of the areas mentioned in the previous table has its own subtle concerns with respect to security, state management, transactions, and other aspects such as error handling (for example, catching and communicating errors) as well as varying needs for bulkification.

Throughout the rest of this chapter, we will review these requirements and distill them into a Separation of Concerns that allows a demarcation of responsibilities between the Apex code used to integrate with these platform features versus the code implementing your application business logic, such that the code can be shared between platform features today and in future more readily. Wikipedia describes the benefits of Separation of Concerns as the following:

> *"The value of Separation of Concerns is simplifying development and maintenance of computer programs. When concerns are well separated, individual sections can be developed and updated independently. Of especial value is the ability to later improve or modify one section of code without having to know the details of other sections, and without having to make corresponding changes to those sections."*

Apex code evolution

Apex Triggers can lead to a more traditional pattern of `if/then/else` style coding resulting in a very procedural logic that is hard to maintain and follow. This is partly due to them not being classes and as such they don't naturally encourage breaking up the code into methods and separate classes. As we saw in the previous table, Apex Triggers are now not the only execution context for Apex; others do support Apex classes and **object-orientated programming** (OOP) style, often leveraging system-defined Apex interfaces to allow the developer to integrate with the platform such as batch Apex.

Apex has come a long way since its early introduction as a means to write more complex Validation Rules in Apex Triggers. These days, the general consensus in the community is to write as little code as possible directly in Apex Trigger, instead of delegating the logic to separate Apex classes. For a packaged application, there is no real compelling reason to have more than one Apex Trigger per object. Indeed, the Salesforce security review has been known to flag this even if the code is conditioned to run independently.

A key motivation to move the Apex Trigger code into an Apex class is to gain access to the more powerful language semantics of the Apex language such as OOP, allowing the developer to structure the code more closely to the functions of the application and gain better code reuse and visibility.

Separating concerns in Apex

Each execution context has its own requirements for your code, such as implementing system interfaces, annotations, or controller bindings. Within this code are further coding requirements relating to how you engineer your application code, which lead to a set of common architecture layers of concern, such as loading records, applying validations, and executing business logic.

Understanding these layers allows us to discover a different way to write the application code than simply writing all our code in a single Apex class, which becomes tightly coupled to the execution context and thus less flexible in the future.

To manage these layers of concern in the code, create separate classes—those that are bound to the specific execution context (such as Batch Apex, Scheduler, Apex REST, and Inbound Messaging) and those that contain the application business logic that implements the actual task for the user.

The following UML diagram shows Apex classes that implement the requirements (or concerns) of the execution context and Apex classes to execute the application business logic. The dotted line indicates a Separation of Concerns between the controller classes and classes implementing the application business logic.

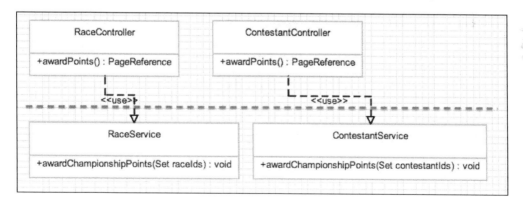

Execution context logic versus application logic concerns

In this section, we will review the needs/concerns of the execution context and how each can lead to a common requirement of the application business logic. This helps define the guidelines around writing the application business logic, thus making it logical and more reusable throughout the platform and application:

- **Error handling**: When it comes to communicating errors, traditionally, a developer has two options: let the error be caught by the execution context or catch the exception to display it in some form. In the Visualforce Apex controller context, it's typical to catch exceptions and route these through the `ApexPage.addMessage` method to display messages to the user via the `apex:pageMessages` tag. In contrast to Batch Apex, letting the platform know that the job has failed involves allowing the platform to catch and handle the exception instead of your code. In this case, Apex REST classes, for example, will automatically output exceptions in the REST response.

  - **Application business code implication**: The point here is that there are different concerns with regard to error handling within each execution context. Thus, it is important for application business logic to not dictate how errors should be handled by calling the code.

- **Transaction management**: As we have seen earlier in this chapter, the platform manages a single default transaction around the execution context. This is important to consider with the error handling concern, particularly if errors are caught, as the platform will commit any records written to the database prior to the exception occurring, which may not be desirable and may be hard to track down.

  - **Application business code implication**: Understanding the scope of the transaction is important, especially when it comes to writing application business logic that throws exceptions. Callers, especially those catching exceptions, should not have to worry about creating `Database.Savepoint` to rollback the state of the database if an exception is thrown.

- **Number of records**: Some contexts deal with a single database record, such as a Visualforce Standard Controller, and others deal with multiple records, such as Visualforce Standard Set Controllers or Batch Apex. Regardless as to the type of execution context, the platform itself imposes governors around the database operations that are linked with the number of records being processed. Every execution context expects code to be bulkified (minimal queries and DML statements).

  ○ **Application business code implication**: Though some execution contexts appear to only deal with a single record at a time in reality because database-related governors apply to all execution context types, it is good practice to assume that the application code should consider bulkification regardless. This also helps make the application code more reusable in future from different contexts.

- **State management**: Execution contexts on Force.com are generally stateless; although as described earlier in this chapter, there are some platform facilities to store state across execution contexts.

  ○ **Application business code implications**: As the state management solutions are not always available and are also implemented in different ways, the application code should not attempt to deal directly with this concern and should make itself stateless in nature. If needed, provide custom Apex types that can be used to exchange the state with the calling execution context code, for example, a controller class.

- **Security**: It could be said that the execution context should be the one concerned with enforcing this, as it is the closest to the end user. This is certainly the case with a controller execution context where Salesforce recommends the `with sharing` keyword is placed. Though when it comes to CRUD and FLS security, the practicality of placing enforcement at the execution context entry point will become harder from a maintenance perspective, as the code checking the users' permissions will have to be continually maintained (and potentially repeated) along with the needs of the underlying application business code.

  ○ **Application business code implication**: The implication here is that it is the concern of both the execution context and the application business logic to enforce the users permissions. Though in the case of sharing, mainly the initial Apex caller should be respected. As we dive deeper into the engineering application business logic in later chapters, we will revisit security several times.

A traditional approach for logging errors for later review by administrators or support teams is to use a **log table**. While in Force. com this can be implemented to some degree, keep in mind that some execution contexts work more effectively with the platform features if you don't catch exceptions and let the platform handle it. For example, the **Apex Jobs** page will correctly report failed batches along with a summary of the last exception. If you implement a logging solution and catch these exceptions, visibility of failed batch jobs will be hidden from administrators. Make sure that you determine which approach suites your users best. If you decide to implement your own logging, keep in mind that this requires some special handling of Apex database transactions and provision of application functionality to allow users to clean up old logs.

Improving incremental code reuse

There is Separation of Concerns between code invoked directly through an execution context and the application business logic code within an application. This knowledge is important to ensure whether you can effectively reuse application logic easily, incrementally, and with minimal effort. It is the developer's responsibility to maintain this Separation of Concerns by following patterns and guidelines set out in the chapters of this book and those you devise yourself as part of your own coding guidelines.

Reuse needs may not always be initially obvious. However, by following Separation of Concerns and the design patterns in this book, when they do arise as your application evolves and/or new platform features are added, the process is more organic without refactoring, or at worst, copy and pasting the code!

To illustrate a reuse scenario, imagine that in the first iteration of the FormulaForce application, awarding points to a race contestant was accomplished by the user through an **Award Points** button on the **Contestant** detail page for each contestant. Also, the newsletter functionality was accessed by manually clicking a **Send News Letter** button on the **Season** detail page each month.

The class diagram for the first iteration is shown in the next diagram. Note that you can already see the beginning of a separation of concern between the Apex controller logic and application business logic, which is contained in the classes ending in `Service`. The Service layer is discussed in more detail later in this chapter.

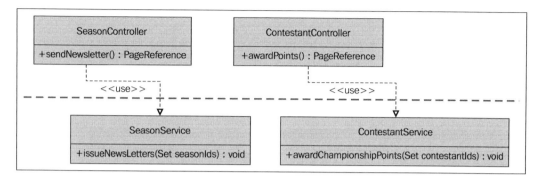

Now, imagine that in the second iteration of the application, user feedback requested that awarding of points should also be available at the race level and applied in one operation for all contestants through a button on the **Race** detail page. In the following class diagram, you can see that the `ContestService` class is now reused by the `RaceService` class in order to implement the `RaceController.awardPoints` service method:

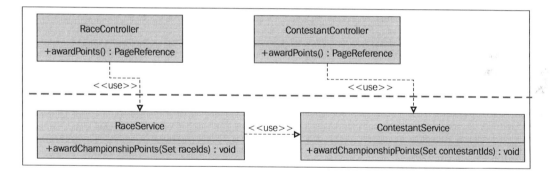

An additional enhancement was also requested to permit the newsletter functionality to use the platform scheduler to automatically issue the newsletter. The following diagram shows that the `SeasonService` class is now reused by both the `SeasonNewsLetterSchedule` class as well as the `SeasonController` class:

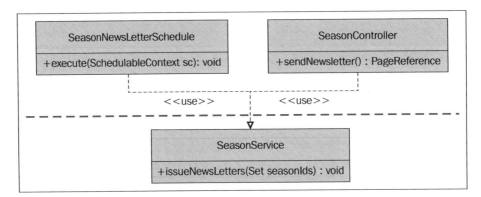

The preceding examples have shown that code from the first iteration can be reused either from the new application business logic or from a new execution context in the case of the scheduler. In the next chapter, we will take a further look at the Service layer, including its design guidelines that make this kind of reuse possible.

Patterns of Enterprise Application Architecture

So far, we have only discussed Separation of Concerns between the Apex code invoked from an execution context (Apex Controller, Scheduler, Batch Apex, and so on) and reusable application business logic code placed in the `Service` classes. However, there are further levels of granularity and patterns that help focus and encapsulate application logic further, known as Enterprise Application Architecture patterns.

The general definitions of the patterns used in the next three chapters of this book are not inherently new, but are a new implementation for this platform. They have been and continue to be incredibly popular on other platforms. The original author of these patterns is Martin Fowler, who describes the other patterns in his book, *Patterns of Enterprise Application Architecture* (http://www.martinfowler.com/books/eaa.html)

This book takes some of the patterns in Martin Fowler's book and applies them to the platform while also taking the opportunity to bake in a few best practices on the Force.com platform. The next section is a short summary of those we will be taking a closer look at.

The Service layer

The following is Martin Fowler's definition of the Service layer
(`http://martinfowler.com/eaaCatalog/serviceLayer.html`):

> *"Defines an application's boundary with a layer of services that establishes a set of available operations and coordinates the application's response in each operation."*

You had a little preview of this pattern in action within this chapter. You can see that for the business application logic, it forms an initial entry point, encapsulating operations and tasks the end users perform.

Its methods and behavior is designed such that it is agnostic of the caller, making it adaptable to multiple execution contexts easily, as shown in the earlier examples. It also has a role to play in your applications API strategy.

The Domain Model layer

The following is Martin Fowler's definition of the Domain layer (`http://martinfowler.com/eaaCatalog/domainModel.html`):

> *"An object model of the domain that incorporates both behavior and data. At its worst, business logic can be very complex. Rules and logic describe many different cases and slants of behavior, and it's this complexity that objects were designed to work with."*

If you think of the Service layer as the band conductor, the Apex classes that make up the Domain layer are the instruments it conducts, each with its own role and responsibility in making the music!

The Domain layer in a Force.com context helps group and encapsulate logic specific to each physical Custom Object in the application. Also, while utilizing object-oriented concepts like interfaces and inheritance to apply common behavioral aspects between your Custom Objects in your application, such as security, it is responsible for applying validations and processing historically done in the Apex Triggers code directly. Note that the Service layer can leverage these classes to form high-level business application logic that spans multiple objects and thus can access and reuse domain object-specific logic.

The Data Mapper (Selector) layer

The following is Martin Fowler's definition of the Data Mapper layer (http://martinfowler.com/eaaCatalog/dataMapper.html):

> *"A layer of Mappers (473) that moves data between objects and a database while keeping them independent of each other and the mapper itself."*

Making effective use of database queries to fetch data is as important on Force.com as any other platform. For complex object models, having SOQL do some of the heavy lifting can lead to some fairly sophisticated queries. Encapsulating how data from the database is mapped into memory is the role of the Data Mapper layer.

In Martin Fowler's world, this usually involves mapping database result set records returned into Java classes (known as **Plain Old Java Objects (POJO)** or **Data Transformation Objects (DTO)**). However, Apex provides us with these data structures for each of our custom objects in the form of SObject. Thus, the role of this pattern is slightly different, as the SOQL query itself explicitly selects SObject representing the data. Hence, this pattern has been renamed to reflect its key responsibility more accurately.

Introducing the FinancialForce.com Apex Commons library

There exists an Apex class library used to support these patterns, which is also used in this book. The Apex Commons library is from an open source project started by FinancialForce.com and launched to the community at the Dreamforce 2012 event.

Since then, the patterns have been adopted by other developers on the platform and have been extended with additional features such as Fieldsets and Security. We will be using this library in the next three chapters as we explore the enterprise patterns they support in more detail. The GitHub repository can be found at https://github.com/financialforcedev/fflib-apex-common.

Unit testing versus system testing

When it comes to testing the Apex code, we know the drill: write good tests to cover your code, assert its behavior, and obtain at least 75 percent coverage. Force.com will not allow you to upload packaged code unless you obtain this amount or higher. You also have to cover your Apex Trigger code, even if it's only a single line, as you will soon see is the case with the implementation of the Apex Triggers in this book.

When it comes to unit testing, what Force.com currently lacks, however, is a mocking framework to permit more focused and isolated testing of the layers mentioned in the previous sections without having to set up all the records needed to execute the code you want to test. This starts to make your Apex tests feel more like system-level tests having to execute the full functional stack each time.

While conventions such as **test-driven development (TDD)** are possible, they certainly help you think about developing true unit tests on the platform. Doing so can also get quite time consuming to develop and then wait for these tests to run due to growing data setup complexity. Such tests end up feeling more like system- or integration-level tests because they end up testing the whole stack of code in your application.

The good news is that the layering described in this book does give you opportunities to isolate smaller tests to specific aspects, such as validation or insert logic. As we progress through each layer in the upcoming chapters, we will revisit this topic of writing Apex tests, which are akin to unit tests.

Although outside the scope of this book, it is worth noting that FinancialForce.com has also recently shared its ApexMocks class library and supporting tool. This is an early development and is starting to show great promise at providing a framework for those used to mocking approaches in languages such as Java via Mockito. You can read more about this and the author at the GitHub repository at `https://github.com/financialforcedev/fflib-apex-mocks`.

The packaging code

The source code provided with this chapter contains skeleton Apex classes shown in the UML diagrams used earlier in this chapter. In the upcoming chapters, we will flesh out the methods and logic within them. For now, deploy them into your packaging org and add them into your package. Note that once you add Apex classes, any Apex classes they subsequently go on to reference will be automatically pulled into the package. The following is a list of the Apex classes added in this chapter and the application architecture layer they apply to:

Apex class	Layer
SeasonController.cls	Visualforce Controller
SeasonControllerTest.cls	Apex test
ContestantController.cls	Visualforce Controller
ContestantControllerTest.cls	Apex test
RaceController.cls	Visualforce Controller
RaceControllerTest.cls	Apex test
SeasonNewsletterScheduler.cls	Apex Scheduler
SeasonNewsletterSchedulerTest.cls	Apex test
RaceService.cls	Race Service
RaceServiceTest.cls	Apex test
SeasonService.cls	Season Service
SeasonServiceTest.cls	Apex test
ContestantService.cls	Contestant Service
ContestantServiceTest.cls	Apex test

Note that there is one class, SeasonNewsLetterSchedule, that requires the use of the global access modifier. This ensures that this class cannot be deleted or renamed in future releases. This might feel restrictive, but is the key to support the Apex Scheduler feature in this case. As it is important when users upgrade to new versions of your package, the schedules they have defined continue to reference the code in your package.

Upload a new version of the package and install it into your test org. You should see a confirmation install summary page that looks something like the following:

Action	Component Name	Parent Object	Component Type	Installation Notes
Create	SeasonNewsletterScheduler		Apex Class	This is a brand new component.
Create	SeasonController		Apex Class	This is a brand new component.
Create	SeasonService		Apex Class	This is a brand new component.
Create	RaceService		Apex Class	This is a brand new component.
Create	RaceServiceTest		Apex Class	This is a brand new component.
Create	SeasonNewsletterSchedulerTest		Apex Class	This is a brand new component.
Create	RaceController		Apex Class	This is a brand new component.
Create	ContestantServiceTest		Apex Class	This is a brand new component.
Create	SeasonControllerTest		Apex Class	This is a brand new component.
Create	ContestantControllerTest		Apex Class	This is a brand new component.
Create	ContestantController		Apex Class	This is a brand new component.
Create	RaceControllerTest		Apex Class	This is a brand new component.
Create	SeasonServiceTest		Apex Class	This is a brand new component.
Create	ContestantService		Apex Class	This is a brand new component.

Summary

In this chapter, we have taken an in-depth look at how the platform executes the Apex code and the different contexts from which it does so. We have also taken time to understand how key concepts like state and security are managed, in addition to highlighting some Apex governors and their respective scopes.

This has allowed us to observe some common needs from which we have distilled into a Separation of Concerns, which we can start to apply as guidelines into layers in our business application code, making the Apex logic more reusable and accessible from different contexts as your application functionality and indeed the platform itself evolves.

As we progress further into practicing Separation of Concerns, the Domain, Service, and Selector layers' patterns will become a further layer of separation within our application business logic. We will continue to define the naming and coding guidelines as we progress through the next three chapters so that it becomes easier to maintain a good Separation of Concerns for the existing developers and those just starting to work on the code base.

If you have an existing code base and are wondering where to start with refactoring its code up into the layers described in this chapter, my advice is to concentrate initially on forming your Service layer contract and refactoring as much true business logic code into it as possible. Make your execution context classes, such as controllers and batch Apex classes (but not triggers initially), as thin as possible, leaving them to focus solely on their responsibilities such as error handling. This will get some of your true business application logic at least contained below the Service layer, even if it might not be factored precisely how you would want it had you have written it from scratch. After this, you can focus on expanding this out to refactoring the Trigger logic into Domain, then the Query logic into separate Selector classes, perhaps incrementally, as you revise the areas of the application for enhancements.

Application Service Layer

5

If your application was considered a living organism, the Service layer would be its beating heart. Regardless as to how the environment and the things that interact with it change over time, it must remain strong and able to adapt. In this chapter, we begin our journey with the three coding patterns: Service, Domain, and Selector, which were introduced in *Chapter 4, Apex Execution and Separation of Concerns*.

In this chapter, we will review the pattern as set out by Martin Fowler and then review how this has been applied on the Force.com platform in Apex, describing design guidelines born from the Separation of Concerns we defined in the previous chapter.

One concern of this layer is interacting with the database; a later chapter will cover querying in more detail. This chapter will focus on updating the database and introducing a new pattern, Unit Of Work, which helps make your code more streamlined and bulkified.

At the end of this chapter, we will extend the FormulaForce application to provide a means to calculate driver championship points and issue a newsletter. The code developed in the Service layer will be invoked from Custom buttons and the Apex Scheduler. Later chapters will also cover further uses of the Service layer.

The following aspects of the Service layer will be covered in this chapter:

- Introducing the Service layer pattern
- Implementation design guidelines
- Handling DML with the Unit Of Work
- Services calling services
- Contract Driven Development
- Testing the services
- Calling the services

Introducing the Service layer pattern

The following is Martin Fowler's definition of the Service layer
(`http://martinfowler.com/eaaCatalog/serviceLayer.html`):

> *"Defines an application's boundary with a layer of services that establishes a set of available operations and coordinates the application's response in each operation."*

The use of the word "boundary" in Martin's definition is interesting, as this literally represents the point of separation or boundary between the concerns of the application's business logic in the Service layer and execution context or caller, be that a Visualforce Controller class or a Batch Apex class, as illustrated in the UML diagrams shown in the previous chapter.

The following illustration shows just some of the types of callers that an Apex Service layer is designed to support. By following the design guidelines given in the next diagram, you can ensure that your Service layer code can be called from any one of these features and others in the future:

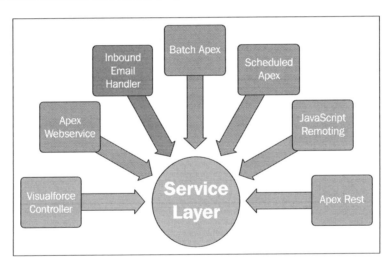

This book will illustrate the use of the Service layer in a number of these areas.

The reference to coordinates in Martin's definition is also an important point with respect to the encapsulation of the application's true business logic. You must be diligent about this encapsulation since the Service layer cannot coordinate the behavior of the application without it. The patterns in this book help to promote better thinking about encapsulation. However, there is no way to express dependencies between Apex code in the way other languages such as Java might use the `package` and `protected` keywords, for example. As such, it is down to us to make sure that there is a solid awareness and desire to honor them.

Code reviews are an integral part of any development process. One easy indicator that your application business logic may be leaking outside of your service layer is the increasing amount of code in the calling classes, such as Visualforce Controllers or Batch Apex classes. Remember that these classes have their own concerns as well, such as handling and reporting errors and presenting information that the Service layer or your Custom Objects need. Though generally, if the code looks to be doing more than this, it could be a sign that there is some code that should have been factored into a service method. The hard part is often failing a code review based on this observation, particularly if the author claims there is no current reuse case. While that may be true, ignoring it in the beginning and letting it remain increases technical debt, limits reuse (will the next developer have time to refactor?), and increases the risk of inconsistent behavior across your application.

Finally, keep in mind that the information exchanged with the Service layer is not necessarily targeted to a specific use case or caller requirement. It is the responsibility of the calling code, such as a Visualforce Controller or even code written by a subscriber org developer, to translate between the chosen client user interface and the Service layer interface.

In a later chapter, we will also explore exposing your Service layer as an API for external consumption. For these reasons, the Service layer has to be agnostic or unbiased towards any particular caller.

Implementation of design guidelines

Having studied the Separation of Concerns in the previous chapter and reflected on the previous illustration, the following design guidelines help ensure that the Service layer is agnostic of the caller, easy to locate, and encourages some Force.com best practices, such as bulkification. Note that bulkification is not just a concept for Apex Triggers; all the logic in your application must make efficient use of governed resources.

Naming conventions

A colleague of mine used to reference the following when talking about naming:

> *"There are only two hard things in Computer Science: cache invalidation and naming things."*

> *–Phil Karlton*

In my career so far, I have come to realize that there is some truth in this statement. Naming conventions have never been so important on Force.com as it is currently without a means to group or structure code files, using a directory structure for example. Instead, all classes are effectively in one root folder called /classes.

Thus, it comes down to the use of naming conventions to help clarify purpose (for developers, both new and old, working on the code base) and to which layer in your architecture a class belongs. Naming does not, however, stop at the class name level; the enums, methods, and even parameter names all matter.

> It is a good idea to work with those designing and documenting your application in order to establish and agree on an **application vocabulary of terms**. This is not only a useful reference for your end users to get to know your application, but also helps in maintaining consistency throughout your user interface and can also be used in the implementation of it, right down to the method and class names used. This comes in handy, especially if you are planning on exposing your Service layer as a public API. (I'm a big fan of clear self-documenting APIs.)

The following points break down some specific guidelines for the Service layer, though some are also applicable throughout your application code:

- **Avoid acronyms**: In general, try to avoid using acronyms (as far as possible); while these might be meaningful to those experienced in working on the application, newcomers will find it harder to navigate the code as they learn the application functionality and code base. This applies more so if you're using your Service layer as an API. Though it can be tempting from a typing perspective, a good editor with auto completion should resolve this concern pretty well. Widely used and understood acronyms like ID are reasonable.

- **Class names**: Ending your class name with the Service suffix allows developers to filter easily to find these critical classes in your application code base. The actual name of the service can be pretty much anything you like, typically a major module or a significant object in your application. Make sure, however, that it is something from your application's vocabulary. If you've structured your application design well, your service class names should roughly fall into the groupings of your application's modules; that is, the naming of your Service layer should be a by-product of your application's architecture, and not a thing you think up when creating the class.

○ Some bad examples are `UtilService`, `RaceHelper`, `BatchApexService`, and `CalcRacePointsService`. These examples either use acronyms that are platform feature bias or potentially to contextualized. Classes with the name `Helper` in them are often an indication that there is a lack of true understanding of where code should be located; watch out for such classes.

○ Some good examples are `CommonService`, `RaceService`, and `SeasonService`. These examples clearly outline some major aspects of the application and are general enough to permit future encapsulation of related operations as the application grows.

- **Method names**: The `public` or `global` method names are essentially the business operations exposed by the service. These should also ideally relate or use terms expressed in your application's end user vocabulary, giving the same thought to these as you would give to a label or button for the end user, for example. Avoid naming them in a way that ties them to their caller; remember that the Service layer doesn't know or care about the caller type.

  ○ Some bad examples are `RaceService.recalcPointsOnSave`, `SeasonService.handleScheduler`, and `SeasonService.issueWarnings`. These examples are biased either towards the initial caller use case or towards the calling context; nor does `handleScheduler` really express enough about what the method is actually going to perform.

  ○ Some good examples are `RaceService.awardChampionshipPoints`, `SeasonService.issueNewsLetter`, and `DriverService.issueWarnings`. These examples are named according to what they do, correctly located, and unbiased to the caller.

- **Parameter names and types**: As with method and class names, keep them focused on the data they represent, and ideally use consistent terms. Keep in mind that the type of your parameter can also form a part of the meaning of the parameter, and may help in some cases with the implementation of the service method. For example, if the parameter is intended to receive a list of IDs, consider using `Set` instead of `List`, as typically, duplicate IDs in the list are unwanted. For the `Map` parameters, I always try to use the `somethingABySomethingB` convention in my naming so it's at least clear what the map is keyed by. In general, I actually try to apply these conventions to all variables, regardless of them being method parameters.

- ○ Some bad examples are `List<String> driverList` and `Map<String, DriverPerformance> mapOfPerformance`; these examples are either not using the correct data type and/or are using unclear data types as to the list or map contents; there is also some naming redundancy.

- ○ Some good examples are `Set<Id> driverIds` and `Map<String,DrivePerformance> drivePerformanceByName`; these examples use the correct types and help in documenting how to use the map correctly; the reader now knows that the `String` key is a name. Another naming approach would be `somethingsToName`, for example. Also, the map parameter name no longer refers to the fact that it is a map because the type of parameter communicates this well enough.

- **Inner class names**: While there is no formal structure to Apex classes in the form of a typical directory facility (or package structure, in Java terms), Apex does support the concept of inner classes to one level. These can sometimes be used to define classes that represent parameter data that is only relevant to the service methods. Because inner classes are always qualified by the name of the parent class, you do not need to repeat it.

  - ○ Some bad examples are `SeasonService.SeasonSummary` and `DriverService.DriverRaceData`; these examples repeat the parent class name.

  - ○ Some good examples are `SeasonService.Summary` and `DriverService.RaceDetails`; these examples are shorter as they are qualified by the outer class.

These guidelines should not only help to ensure whether your Service layer remains more neutral to its callers and thus more consumable now and in the future, but also follow some best practices around the platform. Finally, as we will discuss in *Chapter 9, Providing Integration and Extensibility*, following these guidelines leaves things in good shape to expose as an actual API if desired.

If you're having trouble agreeing on the naming, you can try a couple of things. Firstly, try presenting the name and/or method signatures to someone not as close to the application or functionality to see what they interpret from it. This approach could be considered as parallel to a popular user experience acceptance testing approach, **fly-by reviews**. Obviously, they may not tell you precisely what the actual intent is, but how close or not they get can be quite useful when deciding on the naming.

Secondly, try writing out pseudo code for how calling code might look; this can be useful to spot redundancy in your naming. For example, `SeasonService.issueSeasonNewsLetter(Set<Id> seasonIdList)` could be reduced to `SeasonService. issueNewsLetter(Set<Id> seasonIds)`, since the scope of the method within the `SeasonService` method need not include `Season` again, and the parameter name can also be shortened since its type infers a list.

Bulkification

It's well known that the best practice of Apex is to implement bulkification within Apex Triggers, mainly because they can receive and process many records of the same type. This is also true for the use of Standard Set Controller or Batch Apex, for example.

As we identified in the previous chapter, handling bulk sets of records is a common requirement. In fact, it's one that exists throughout your code paths, since DML or SOQL in a loop at any level in your code will risk hitting governor limits.

For this reason, when designing methods on the Service layer, it is appropriate that you consider list parameters by default. This encourages development of bulkified code within the method and avoids the caller having to call the service method in a loop.

The following is an example of non-bulkified code:

```
RaceService.awardChampionShipPoints(Id raceId)
```

The following is another example of non-bulkified code:

```
RaceService.awardChampionShipPoints(Set<Id> raceIds)
```

A non-bulkified method with several parameters might look like this, for example:

```
RaceService.retireFromRace(Id raceId, String reason)
```

A bulkified version of this method can utilize an Apex inner class as described earlier and shown in the following example (in the next sub-section).

 Sometimes, implementing bulkified versions of service methods are more costly and complex than what the callers will realistically require, so this should not be seen as a fixed guideline, but should at least always be considered.

Defining and passing data

While defining data to be exchanged between the Service layer and its callers, keep in mind that the responsibility of the Service layer is to be caller-agnostic. Unless you're explicitly developing functionalities for such data formats, avoid returning information through JSON or XML strings; allow the caller (for example, a JavaScript remoting controller) to deal with these kinds of data-marshalling requirements.

As per the guidelines, using inner classes is a good way to express and scope data structures used by the service methods; the following code also illustrates a bulkified version of the multi-parameter non-bulkified method shown in the previous section:

 Thinking about using inner classes this way can also be a good way to address the symptom of primitive obsession (http://c2.com/cgi/wiki?PrimitiveObsession).

```
public class ContestantService
{
  public class RaceRetirement
  {
    public Id contestantId;
    public String reason;
  }

  public static void retireFromRace(
    List<RaceRetirement> retirements)
  {
      // Process race retirements...
  }
}
```

Try to avoid too much service coupling by reusing inner classes between services. If this is starting to happen, it may be an indication that you need a new shared or common service perhaps.

Always keep in mind that the service method really only needs the minimum information to do its job, and express this through the method signature and related types so that callers can clearly see that only that information is required or returned. This avoids doubt and confusion in the calling code, which can result in it passing too little or redundant information.

This example utilizes read and write member variables in the `RaceRetirement` class, indicating both are required. The inner class of the `RaceRetirement` class is only used as an input parameter to this method. Give some consideration before using an inner class such as both input and output types, since it is not always clear which member variables in such classes should be populated for the input use case or which will be populated in the output case.

However, if you find such a need for the same Apex type to be used as both an output and input parameter, and some information is not required on the input, you can consider indicating this via the **Apex property syntax** by making the property read-only. This prevents the caller from populating the value of a member field unnecessarily; for example, consider the following service methods in the `RaceService` method:

```
public static
    Map<Id, List<ProvisionalResult>>
        calculateProvisionalResults(Set<Id> raceIds)
{
    // Implementation
}


public static void
    applyRaceResults(
        Map<Id, List<ProvisionalResult>>
            provisionalResultsByRaceId){    // Implementation
}

public class ProvisionalResult
{
    public Integer racePosition {get; set;}
    public Id contestantId {get; set;}
    public String contestantName {get; private set;}
}
```

While calling the `calculateProvisionalResults` method, the `contestantName` field is returned as a convenience, but is marked as read-only since it is not needed when applied in the context of the `applyRaceResults` method.

Considerations when using SObjects in the Service layer interface

In the following example, the service method appears to add the **Race** records as the input, requiring the caller to query the object and also to decide which fields have to be queried. This is a loose contract definition between the service method and the caller:

```
RaceService.awardChampionShipPoints(List<Race__c> races)
```

A better contract to the caller is to just ask for what is needed, in this case, the IDs:

```
RaceService.awardChampionShipPoints(Set<Id> raceIds)
```

Even though IDs that relate to records from different object types could be passed (one might consider performing some parameter validation to reject such lists), this is a more expressive contract, focusing on what the service really needs. The caller now knows that only the ID is going to be used.

In the first example when using the `Race__c` SObject type as a parameter type, it is not clear which fields callers need to populate, which can make the code fragile, as it is not something that can be expressed in the interface definition. Also, the fields required within the service code could change and require caller logic to be refactored. This could also be an example of failing in the encapsulation concern of the business logic within the Service layer.

It can be said that this design approach incurs additional overhead, especially if the caller has already queried the **Race** record for presentation purposes and the service must then re-query the information. However, in such cases, maintaining the encapsulation and reuse concerns can be more compelling reasons. Careful monitoring of this consideration makes the service interface clearer, better encapsulated, and ultimately more robust.

Transaction management

A simple expectation of the caller when calling the Service layer methods is that if there is a failure via an exception, any work done within the Service layer up until that point is rolled back. This is important as it allows the caller to handle the exception without fear of any partial data being written to the database. If there is no exception, then the data modified by the service method can still be rolled back, but only if the entire execution context itself fails, otherwise the data is committed.

This can be implemented using a `try/catch` block in combination with `Database.Savepoint` and the `rollback` method, as follows:

```
public static void awardChampionshipPoints(Set<Id> raceIds)
{
  // Mark the state of the database
  System.Savepoint serviceSavePoint = Database.setSavePoint();
  try
  {
    // Do some work
  }
  catch (Exception e)
  {
    // Rollback any data written before the exception
    Database.rollback(serviceSavePoint);
    // Pass the exception on for the caller to handle
    throw e;
  }
}
```

Later in this chapter, we will look at the Unit Of Work pattern, which helps manage the Service layer transaction management in a more elegant way than having to repeat the preceding boilerplate code in each service method.

Compound services

As your Service layer evolves, your callers may find themselves needing to call multiple service methods at a time, which should be avoided.

To explain this, consider that a new application requirement has arisen for a single custom button to update the **Drivers** standings (the position in the overall season) in the championship with the feature to issue a new season newsletter.

The code behind the Apex Controller action method might look like the following code:

```
try
{
    Set<Id> seasons = new Set<Id> { seasonId };

    SeasonService.updateStandings(seasons);

    SeasonService.issueNewsLetters(seasons);
}
catch (Exception e)
{
    ApexPages.addMessage(e);
}
```

The problem with the preceding code is that it erodes the encapsulation and thus reuses the application Service layer by putting functionality in the controller, and also breaks the transactional encapsulation.

For example, if an error occurs while issuing the newsletter, the standings are still updated (since the controller handles exceptions), and thus, if the user presses the button again, the driver standings in the championship will get updated twice!

The best way to address this type of scenario when it occurs is to create a new compound service, which combines the functionality into one new service method call. This example also uses an inner class to pass the season ID and provide the issue newsletter option:

```
try
{
    SeasonService.UpdateStandings updateStandings =
        new SeasonService.UpdateStandings();
    updateStandings.seasonId = seasonId;
    updateStandings.issueNewsletter = true;

    SeasonService.updateStandings(
        new List<SeasonService.UpdateStandings>
            { updateStandings });
}
catch (Exception e)
{
    ApexPages.addMessage(e);
}
```

It may be desirable to retain the original service methods used in the first example in cases where this combined behavior is not always required.

Later in this chapter, we will see how the implementation of the preceding new service method will reuse the original methods and thus introduce the ability for existing service methods to be linked to each other.

A quick guideline checklist

Here is a useful table that summarizes the earlier guidelines:

When thinking about...	The guidelines are...
Naming conventions	• Suffix class names with service • Stick to application vocabulary • Avoid acronyms • Class, method, and parameter names matter • Avoid redundancy in names • Utilize inner classes to scope by service
Bulkification	• On service methods, utilize list parameters over single parameters to encourage optimized service code for bulk callers • Single instance parameters can be used where it's overly expensive to engineer bulkified implementations and there is little functional benefit
Defining and passing data	• Keep data neutral to the caller • Leverage inner classes to scope data • Pass only what is needed
Transaction management	• Callers can assume that work is rolled back if exceptions are raised by the service methods, so they can safely handle exceptions themselves • Wrap service method code in `SavePoint`
Compound services	• Maintain the Service layer's functional encapsulation by monitoring for multiple service method calls in one execution context • Create new service methods to wrap existing ones or merge existing methods as needed

Handling DML with the Unit Of Work pattern

The database maintains relationships between records using record IDs. Record IDs are only available after the record is inserted. This means that the related records, such as child object records, need to be inserted in a specific dependency order. Parent records should be inserted before child records, and the parent record IDs are used to populate the relationship (lookup) fields on the child record objects before they can be inserted.

The common pattern for this is to use `List` or `Map` to manage records inserted at a parent level, in order to provide a means to look up parent IDs, as child records are built prior to being inserted. The other reasoning for this is bulkification; minimizing the number of DML statements being used across a complex code path is vital to avoid hitting governor limits on the number of DML statements required as such lists are favored over executing individual DML statements per record.

The focus on these two aspects of inserting data into objects can often detract from the actual business logic required, making code hard to maintain and difficult to read. The following section introduces another of Martin Fowler's patterns, the Unit Of Work, which helps address this, as well as provides an alternative to the boilerplate transaction management using `SavePoint`, as illustrated earlier in this chapter.

The following is Martin Fowler's definition of Unit Of Work (`http://martinfowler.com/eaaCatalog/unitOfWork.html`):

> *"Maintains a list of objects affected by a business transaction and coordinates the writing out of changes and the resolution of concurrency problems."*

In an extract from the given webpage, he also goes on to make these further points:

> *"You can change the database with each change to your object model, but this can lead to lots of very small database calls, which ends up being very slow.*
>
> *A Unit of Work keeps track of everything you do during a business transaction that can affect the database. When you're done, it figures out everything that needs to be done to alter the database as a result of your work."*

Although these statements don't appear to relate to Force.com, there are parallels with respect to the cost of making multiple DML statements, both in terms of governors and general performance. There is also a statement about transaction management at a business (or service) level, which applies to the responsibility of the Service layer.

In order to best illustrate these benefits, let's review the implementation of a service to load some historic data into the `Season`, `Race`, `Driver`, and `Contest` objects. Each of these objects has several relationships, as illustrated in the following screenshot:

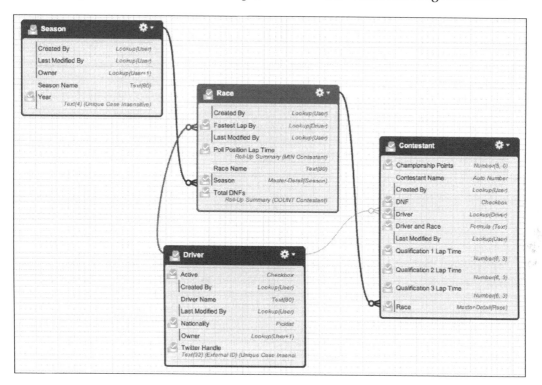

Consider the following sample JSON format to import data into the application:

```
{
    "drivers": [
        {
            "name": "Lewis Hamilton",
            "nationality": "British",
            "driverId": "44",
            "twitterHandle": "lewistwitter"
        }
    ],
    "seasons": [
        {
            "year": "2013",
            "races": [
                {
```

```
                        "round": 1,
                        "name": "Spain",
                        "contestants": [
                            {
                                "driverId": "44",
                                "championshipPoints": 44,
                                "dnf": false,
                                "qualification1LapTime": 123,
                                "qualification2LapTime": 124,
                                "qualification3LapTime": 125
                            }
                        ]
                    }
                ]
            }
        ]
    }
```

Without a Unit Of Work

This first example shows a traditional approach using Map and List to import the data, obeying bulkificaiton and inserting a dependency order. The important logic highlighted in the following code copies data from the imported data structures into the objects; everything else is purely managing transaction scope and inserting dependencies:

```
public static void importSeasons(String jsonData)
{
  System.Savepoint serviceSavePoint = Database.setSavePoint();
  try
  {
    // Parse JSON data
    SeasonsData seasonsData =
        (SeasonsData) JSON.deserializeStrict(jsonData,
          SeasonService.SeasonsData.class);

    // Insert Drivers
    Map<String, Driver__c> driversById =
      new Map<String, Driver__c>();
    for(DriverData driverData : seasonsData.drivers)
      driversById.put(driverData.driverId,
        new Driver__c(
          Name = driverData.name,
```

```
      DriverId__c = driverData.driverId,
      Nationality__c = driverData.nationality,
      TwitterHandle__c = driverData.twitterHandle));
insert driversById.values();

// Insert Seasons
Map<String, Season__c> seasonsByYear =
  new Map<String, Season__c>();
for(SeasonData seasonData : seasonsData.seasons)
  seasonsByYear.put(seasonData.year,
    new Season__c(
      Name = seasonData.year,
      Year__c = seasonData.year));
insert seasonsByYear.values();

// Insert Races
Map<String, Race__c> racesByYearAndRound =
  new Map<String, Race__c>();
for(SeasonData seasonData : seasonsData.seasons)
  for(RaceData raceData : seasonData.races)
    racesByYearAndRound.put(
      seasonData.Year + raceData.round,
      new Race__c(
        Season__c = seasonsByYear.get(seasonData.year).Id,
        Name = raceData.name));
insert racesByYearAndRound.values();

// Insert Contestants
List<Contestant__c> contestants =
  new List<Contestant__c>();
for(SeasonData seasonData : seasonsData.seasons)
  for(RaceData raceData : seasonData.races)
    for(ContestantData contestantData
          : raceData.contestants)
      contestants.add(
        new Contestant__c(
          Race__c = racesByYearAndRound.get(
            seasonData.Year + raceData.round).Id,
          Driver__c = driversById.get(
            contestantData.driverId).Id,
          ChampionshipPoints__c =
            contestantData.championshipPoints,
          DNF__c = contestantData.dnf,
```

```
                    Qualification1LapTime__c =
                       contestantData.qualification1LapTime,
                       Qualification2LapTime__c =
                          contestantData.qualification2LapTime,
                       Qualification3LapTime__c =
                          contestantData.qualification3LapTime
                 ));
        insert contestants;
      }
      catch (Exception e)
      {
        // Rollback any data written before the exception
        Database.rollback(serviceSavePoint);
        // Pass the exception on
        throw e;
      }
    }
```

 This data import requirement could have been implemented by using the **Salesforce Data Loaders** and external field references, as described in the earlier chapter. One reason you may decide to take this approach is to offer an easier option from your own UIs that can be made available to general users without administrator access.

With Unit Of Work

Before we take a closer look at how the **FinancialForce Apex Enterprise Pattern** library has implemented this pattern, let's first take a look at the following revised example of the code shown earlier, this time using a new Apex class called `Application`. This class exposes a static property and method to create an instance of a Unit Of Work.

This class is used to capture the database work as records are created, thus the remaining logic is more focused and avoids `Map` and `List` and repeated iterations over the imported data shown in the previous example. It also internally bulkifies the work (DML) for the caller. Finally, the `commitWork` method call performs the actual DML work in the correct dependency order while applying transaction management. Consider the following code:

```
// Construct a Unit Of Work to capture the following working
fflib_SObjectUnitOfWork uow =
Application.UnitOfWork.newInstance();
```

```
// Create Driver__c records
Map<String, Driver__c> driversById =
  new Map<String, Driver__c>();
for(DriverData driverData : seasonsData.drivers)
{
  Driver__c driver = new Driver__c(
    Name = driverData.name,
    DriverId__c = driverData.driverId,
    Nationality__c = driverData.nationality,
    TwitterHandle__c = driverData.twitterHandle);
  uow.registerNew(driver);
  driversById.put(driver.DriverId__c, driver);
}

for(SeasonData seasonData : seasonsData.seasons)
{
  // Create Season__c record
  Season__c season = new Season__c(
    Name = seasonData.year,
    Year__c = seasonData.year);
  uow.registerNew(season);
  for(RaceData raceData : seasonData.races)
  {
    // Create Race__c record
    Race__c race = new Race__c(Name = raceData.name);
    uow.registerNew(race, Race__c.Season__c, season);
    for(ContestantData contestantData : raceData.contestants)
    {
      // Create Contestant__c record
      Contestant__c contestant = new Contestant__c(
        ChampionshipPoints__c =
          contestantData.championshipPoints,
        DNF__c = contestantData.dnf,
        Qualification1LapTime__c =
          contestantData.qualification1LapTime,
        Qualification2LapTime__c =
          contestantData.qualification2LapTime,
        Qualification3LapTime__c =
          contestantData.qualification3LapTime);
      uow.registerNew(contestant,
        Contestant__c.Race__c, race);
      uow.registerRelationship(contestant,
```

```
                Contestant__c.Driver__c,
                driversById.get(contestantData.driverId));
        }
    }
}
// Insert records registered with uow above
uow.commitWork();
```

The following is the implementation of the Application class and the UnitOfWork static property. It leverages a simple factory class that dynamically creates instances of the fflib_SObjectUnitOfWork class provided with the **FinancialForce Apex Enterprise Patterns library** (also included in this chapter's source code):

```
public class Application
{
    // Configure and create the UnitOfWorkFactory for
    //   this Application
    public static final UnitOfWorkFactory UnitOfWork =
        new UnitOfWorkFactory(
            new List<SObjectType> {
                Driver__c.SObjectType,
                Season__c.SObjectType,
                Race__c.SObjectType,
                Contestant__c.SObjectType });
    /**
     * Class implements a Unit of Work factory
     **/
    public class UnitOfWorkFactory
    {
        private List<SObjectType> objectTypes;

        private UnitOfWorkFactory(List<SObjectType> objectTypes)
        {
            this.objectTypes = objectTypes;
        }

        public fflib_SObjectUnitOfWork newInstance()
        {
            return new fflib_SObjectUnitOfWork(objectTypes);
        }
    }
}
```

The factory method `newInstance` creates a `fflib_SObjectUnitOfWork` instance. The purpose of this library class is to provide the methods used in the preceding code to register records for insert, update, or delete, and implement the `commitWork` method.

I recommend that you create a single application Apex class like the one shown previously, where you can maintain the full list of objects used in the application and their dependency order; as your application's objects grow, it will be easier to maintain.

The `fflib_SObjectUnitOfWork` base class has the following methods in it. The preceding example uses the `registerNew` and `registerRelationship` methods to insert records and ensure that the appropriate relationship fields are populated. Review the documentation of these methods in the code for more details. The following screenshot shows a summary of the methods in the `fflib_SObjectUnitOfWork` class:

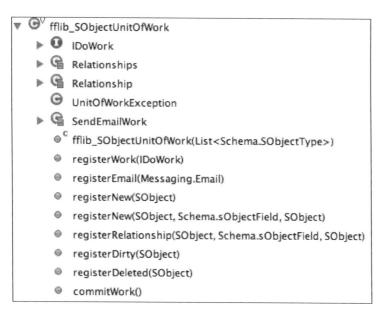

Call the `registerDirty` method with a `SObject` record you want to update and the `registerDeleted` method to delete a given `SObject` record. You can also call a combination of the `registerNew`, `registerDirty`, and `registerDeleted` methods.

The Unit Of Work scope

To make the most effective use of the Unit Of Work's ability to coordinate database updates and transaction management, maintain a single instance of the Unit Of Work within the scope of the service method, as illustrated in the previous section.

If you need to call other classes that also perform database work, be sure to pass the same Unit Of Work instance to them, rather than allowing them to create their own instance. We will explore this a little later in this chapter.

It may be tempting to maintain a static instance of Unit Of Work so that you can refer to it easily without having to pass it around. The downside of this approach is that the scope becomes broader than the service layer execution scope as Apex can be invoked within an execution context multiple times. Code registering records with a static execution scope Unit Of Work is depending on an outer Apex code unit committing the work. It also gives a false impression that the Unit Of Work is useable after a commit has been performed.

Unit Of Work special considerations

Depending on your requirements and use cases, the standard methods of Unit Of Work may not be appropriate. The following is a list of some use cases that are not handled by default and may require a custom work callback to be registered:

- **Self and recursive referencing**: Records within the same object that have lookups to each other are not currently supported, for example, account hierarchies.

- **More granular DML operations**: The `Database` class methods allow the ability to permit some records to be processed when others fail. The DML statements executed in the Unit Of Work are defaulted to all or nothing.

- **Sending e-mails**: Sending e-mails is considered a part of the current transaction; if you want to register this kind of work with the Unit Of Work, you can do so via the `registerEmail` method. Multiple registrations will be automatically bulkified.

The following is a template for registering a customer work callback handler with Unit Of Work. This will be called during the `commitWork` method within the transaction scope it creates. This means that if work fails in this work callback, it will also call other work registered in the standard way with Unit Of Work to rollback.

```
public class CustomAccountWork
  implements fflib_SObjectUnitOfWork.IDoWork
{
    private List<Account> accounts;

    public CustomAccountWork (List<Account> accounts)
    {
      this.accounts = accounts;
    }

    public void doWork()
    {
        // Do some custom account work e.g. hierarchies
    }
}
```

Then, register the custom work as per the following example:

```
uow.registerNew...
uow.registerDirty...
uow.registerDeleted...
uow.registerWork(new CustomAccountWork(accounts));
uow.commitWork();
```

Services calling services

In the previous chapter, I described a reuse use case around a FormulaForce application feature that awards championship points to contestants. We imagined the first release of the application providing a Custom Button only on the **Contestant** detail page and then the second release also providing the same button but on the **Race** detail page.

In this part of the chapter, we are going to implement the respective service methods, emulating this development cycle and, in turn, demonstrating an approach to call between Service layer methods, passing the Unit Of Work correctly.

First, let's look at the initial requirement for a button on the **Contestant** detail page; the method in the `ContestantService` class looks like this:

```
public static void awardChampionshipPoints(
    Set<Id> contestantIds)
{
  fflib_SObjectUnitOfWork uow =
    Application.UnitOfWork.newInstance();
  for(Contestant__c contestant :
       new ContestantsSelector().selectById(contestantIds))
  {
    // Determine points to award for the given position
    ChampionshipPoints__c pointsForPosition =
      ChampionshipPoints__c.getInstance(
        String.valueOf(contestant.RacePosition__c));
    if(pointsForPosition!=null)
    {
      // Apply points and register for udpate with uow
      contestant.ChampionshipPoints__c =
        pointsForPosition.PointsAwarded__c;
      uow.registerDirty(contestant);
    }
  }
  uow.commitWork();
}
```

This method utilizes the concept of a **Selector** to query the database; this will be described in its own chapter later in this book. The method also uses a custom setting to look up the championship points awarded for each position the contestants finished in the race. This custom setting is provided with the source code for this chapter. Enter the values as shown in the next screenshot, where the **Name** field represents the position in which the drivers finished the race:

```
Custom Setting
Championship Points

If the custom setting is a list, click New to add a new set of
had a setting for country codes, each set might include the

If the custom setting is a hierarchy, you can add data for the
For example, you may want different values to display depe
running the app, a specific profile, or just a general user.

View:  [ All ♦ ]  Edit | Create New View
```

			New
Action	**Name**		**Points Awarded**
Edit | Del	1		25
Edit | Del	2		18
Edit | Del	3		15
Edit | Del	4		12
Edit | Del	5		10
Edit | Del	6		8
Edit | Del	7		6
Edit | Del	8		4
Edit | Del	9		2
Edit | Del	10		1

The service is called from the `ContestantController` action method, which is bound
to the button on the **Contestant** detail page (via a Visualforce page), as follows:

```
public PageReference awardPoints()
{
   try
   {
     ContestantService.awardChampionshipPoints(
       new Set<Id> { standardController.getId() });
   }
   catch (Exception e)
   {
     ApexPages.addMessages(e);
   }
   return null;
}
```

In the next release, the same behavior is required from the `RaceController` method to apply the logic to all contestants in the **Race** page. The controller method looks like this:

```
public PageReference awardPoints()
{
  try
  {
    RaceService.awardChampionshipPoints(
      new Set<Id> { standardController.getId() });
  }
  catch (Exception e)
  {
    ApexPages.addMessages(e);
  }
  return null;
}
```

In order to provide backward compatibility, the original custom button on the **Contestant** detail page and thus the service method used by the controller are to be retained. Because the original method was written with bulkificaiton in mind to begin with, reusing the `ContestantService` logic from the new `RaceService` method is made possible.

This is what the `RaceService.awardChampionshipPoints` method looks like. Again, a `Selector` class is used to query the **Race** records and the **Contestant** child records in a single query such that the child records are also available:

```
public static void awardChampionshipPoints(Set<Id> raceIds)
{
  fflib_SObjectUnitOfWork uow =
    Application.UnitOfWork.newInstance();

  // Query Races and contestants, bulkify contestants
  List<Contestant__c> contestants = new List<Contestant__c>();
  for(Race__c race :
    new RaceSelector().selectByIdWithContestants(raceIds))
      contestants.addAll(race.Contestants__r);

  // Delegate to contestant service
  ContestantService.awardChampionshipPoints(uow, contestants);
  // Commit work
  uow.commitWork();
}
```

By using method overloading, a new version of the existing `ContestantService.awardChampionshipPoints` method has been added, which takes as its first parameter the Unit Of Work (created in `RaceService`) and then the **Contestant** list.

 The problem with this additional method is that it inadvertently exposes an implementation detail of the service to potential non-service calling code. It would be ideal if Apex supported the concept of the **protected keyword** found in other languages, which would hide this method from code outside of the Service layer. The solution is to simply ensure that developers understand that such method overrides are only for use by other Service layer callers.

The following resultant code shows that the `ContestantService` methods now support both the new `RaceService` caller and the original `ContestantController` caller. Also, there is only one instance of Unit Of Work in either code path, and the `commitWork` method is called once all the work is done.

```
public static void awardChampionshipPoints(
  Set<Id> contestantIds)
{
  fflib_SObjectUnitOfWork uow =
    Application.UnitOfWork.newInstance();

  // Apply championship points to selected contestants
  awardChampionshipPoints(uow,
    new ContestantSelector().selectById(contestantIds));

  uow.commitWork();
}
public static void awardChampionshipPoints(
  fflib_SObjectUnitOfWork uow, List<Contestant__c> contestants)
{
  // Apply championship points to given contestants
  for(Contestant__c contestant : contestants)
  {
    // Determine points to award for the given position
    ChampionshipPoints__c pointsForPosition =
      ChampionshipPoints__c.getInstance(
        String.valueOf(contestant.RacePosition__c));
    if(pointsForPosition!=null)
    {
      // Apply points and register for udpate with uow
      contestant.ChampionshipPoints__c =
        pointsForPosition.PointsAwarded__c;
      uow.registerDirty(contestant);
    }
  }
}
```

Contract Driven Development

If you have a large piece of functionality to develop, with a complex Service layer and Visualforce client logic, it can be an advantage to decouple these two streams of development activity so that developers can continue in parallel, meeting up sometime in the future to combine efforts.

An approach to this is sometimes referred to as **Contract Driven Development**. This is where there is an agreement on a contract (or service definition) between the two development streams before they start their respective developments. Naturally, the contract can be adjusted over time, but having a solid starting point will lead to a smoother parallel development activity.

This type of development can be applied by implementing a small factory pattern within the Service layer class. The main methods on the service class are defined as normal, but their internal implementation can be routed to respective inner classes to provide an initial **dummy implementation** of the service, which is active for the client developers, for example, and another **production implementation**, which can be worked on independently by the service developers.

 Because the static service methods actually exposed to callers don't expose this factory implementation, it can easily be removed later in the development cycle easily.

Take for example a requirement in the FormulaForce application to provide a Visualforce page to preview the final finishing positions of the drivers once the race is complete (known as the provisional positions). Development needs to start on the user interface for this feature as soon as possible, but the Service layer code has not been written yet. The client and Service layer developers sit down and agree what is needed, and define the skeleton methods in the Service layer together.

The first thing they do within the service class is create an inner Apex interface that describes the service methods, which is the contract. The methods on this interface follow the same design guidelines as described earlier in this chapter.

 The only difference is that a _x suffix is applied to the end of the method names, which avoids an Apex compiler issue where Apex defined the methods later to implement the interface clash with those defined in the service class.

The following shows the definition of the `IRaceService` Apex interface:

```
public class RaceService
{
  private interface IRaceService
  {
    Map<Id, List<ProvisionalResult>>
      calculateProvisionResults_x(Set<Id> raceIds);

    void applyRaceResults_x(Map<Id,
      List<ProvisionalResult>> provisionalResultsByRaceId);

    void awardChampionshipPoints_x(Set<Id> raceIds);
  }
}
```

Next, an implementation of this interface for the dummy client implementation of this service is added as an inner class, along with another inner class for the service developers to continue to develop independently as the client developer goes about their work. Consider the following code:

```
public class DummyImplementation implements IRaceService
{
  public Map<Id, List<ProvisionalResult>>
    calculateProvisionResults_x(Set<Id> raceIds)
  {
    // Dummy behavior to allow the client to be developed
    //   independent of the main service implementation
    Id raceId = new List<Id>(raceIds)[0];
    ProvisionalResult hamilton = new ProvisionalResult();
    hamilton.racePosition = 1;
    hamilton.contestantName = 'Lewis Hamilton';
    hamilton.contestantId = 'a03b0000006WVph';
    ProvisionalResult rubens = new ProvisionalResult();
    rubens.racePosition = 2;
    rubens.contestantName = 'Rubens Barrichello';
    rubens.contestantId = 'a03b00000072xx9';
    return new Map<Id, List<ProvisionalResult>> {
        new List<Id>(raceIds)[0] =>
          new List<ProvisionalResult> { hamilton, rubens } };
  }

  public void applyRaceResults_x(Map<Id,
    List<ProvisionalResult>> provisionalResultsByRaceId) { }
```

```
    public void awardChampionshipPoints_x(Set<Id> raceIds) { }
}


public class ProductionImplementation implements IRaceService
{
  public Map<Id, List<ProvisionalResult>>
    calculateProvisionResults_x(Set<Id> raceIds)
  {
    return null;
  }

  public void applyRaceResults_x(Map<Id,
    List<ProvisionalResult>> provisionalResultsByRaceId) { }

  public void awardChampionshipPoints_x(Set<Id> raceIds) { }
}
```

Finally, the standard service methods are added, but are implemented via a method used to resolve the correct implementation of the service methods to use. The following service methods leverage the appropriate implementation of the preceding interface:

```
public class RaceService
{
  public static Map<Id, List<ProvisionalResult>>
    calculateProvisionResults(Set<Id> raceIds)
  {
    return service().calculateProvisionResults_x(raceIds);
  }

  public static void applyRaceResults(
   Map<Id,List<ProvisionalResult>> provisionalResultsByRaceId)
  {
    service().applyRaceResults_x(provisionalResultsByRaceId);
  }
  public static void awardChampionshipPoints(Set<Id> raceIds)
  {
    service().awardChampionshipPoints_x(raceIds);
  }

  private static IRaceService service()
    {
      if(ApexPages.currentPage()!=null)
        if(ApexPages.currentPage()
```

```
        .getParameters().containsKey('dummy'))
          return (IRaceService)
            new DummyImplementation();
      return (IRaceService) new ProductionImplementation();
  }
 }
```

The `service` method can use any approach you want in order to determine which implementation of the service interface to use. How you determine which implementation to use at runtime is up to you. In the preceding example, the **Visualforce client developer** can add `?dummy` to their page URL, and this will ensure that the dummy behavior of the service will be used when their controller code calls the service methods.

As mentioned, this simple factory implementation can easily be removed later in the development cycle once the client development and service development are completed. This is done by migrating the code from the `ProductionImplementation` methods into the Service class methods or by having the `service` method return this class only.

 You may have noticed that the interface was defined as `private` in the previous example. This is purely because the requirement to implement the factory pattern around the service implementation was purely internal. By making the interface `public` and adjusting the logic in the `service` method to something more general, you can follow the same principles discussed here to utilize a more general factory pattern (perhaps to provide extensibility outside of your application) or a test-mocking facility in your tests. Note that if your interface implementations are made outside of the service class, through top-level classes, the interface method names need not utilize the _x suffix.

Testing the Service layer

It is tempting to allow the testing of the Service layer to be done via tests around the calling code, such as Visualforce controller tests. However, depending solely on this type of testing leaves the Service layer logic open to other use cases that may not strictly be covered by the controller logic. For example, a custom controller using `StandardController` will only pass in a single record and not multiple ones.

Make sure to develop specific Apex tests against the Service layer as the functionality is developed. Although outside the scope of this book, Service layer development is an ideal candidate for practicing **Test Driven Development**.

Mocking the Service layer

Sometimes, the data setup requirements of the Service layer are such that it makes writing Apex tests for controllers or other callers, such as Batch Apex, quite complex and thus expensive, not only in server time for the test to run (due to data setup for each test method) but also in developer time, while preparing a full set of test data.

While you still need to test the full stack of your code, there is an approach called **mocking**, which can be used in conjunction with the previously mentioned factory pattern, which will allow the test context for the given service caller to implement its own test implementation of the service that mimics (with hardcoded test responses) different behaviors that the controller is expecting from the service method. This allows the controller tests to be more varied and focused when devising tests. Again, this mocking approach has to be used in combination with full stack tests that truly execute all the code required.

Calling the Service layer

The preceding examples have shown the use of the service class methods from Visualforce Controller methods. Let's take a closer look at what is happening here, the assumptions being made, and also at an Apex Scheduler example. Other examples of service methods in action will feature throughout later chapters.

The following code represents code from a controller class utilizing `StandardController` that provides support for the Visualforce page associated with a Custom Button on the `Race` object. Notice how it wraps the record ID in `Set`, honoring the bulkified method signature:

```
public PageReference awardPoints()
{
  try
  {
    RaceService.awardChampionshipPoints(
      new Set<Id> { standardController.getId() });
  }
  catch (Exception e)
  {
    ApexPages.addMessages(e);
  }
  return null;
}
```

> The constructor of these controllers is not shown, but it essentially stores `StandardController` or `StandardSetController` in a member variable for later reference by the controller methods.

Here is a similar version that can be used when `StandardSetController` is being used, in the case where a Custom Button is required on the objects' list view:

```
public PageReference awardPointsToRaces()
{
  try
  {
    RaceService.awardChampionshipPoints(
      new Map<Id, SObject>(
        standardSetController.getRecords()).keySet() );
  }
  catch (Exception e)
  {
    ApexPages.addMessages(e);
  }
  return null;
}
```

> The `Map` constructor in Apex will take a list of SObjects and automatically build a map based on the IDs of the SObjects passed in. Combining this with the `keySet` method allows for a quick way to convert the list of records contained in `StandardSetController` into a list of IDs required by the service method.

In both cases, any exceptions are routed to the `apex:pageMessages` component on the page (which should be one of the first things you should consider adding to a page) by calling the `ApexPages.addMessages` method that is passing in the exception.

Note that there is no need for the controller code to roll back changes made within the service that may have been made to object records up to the exception being thrown, since the controller is safe in the assumption that the service method has already ensured this is the case. This arrangement between the two is essentially a Separation of Concerns at work!

Finally, let's look at an example from the `SeasonNewsletterScheduler` class. As with the controller example, it handles the exceptions itself, in this case, e-mails the user with any failures:

```
global void execute(SchedulableContext sc)
{
  try
  {
    SeasonService.issueNewsLetterCurrentSeason();
  }
  catch (Exception e)
  {
    Messaging.SingleEmailMessage mail = new
      Messaging.SingleEmailMessage();
    mail.setTargetObjectId(UserInfo.getUserId());
    mail.setSenderDisplayName(UserInfo.getUserName());
    mail.setSubject('Failed to send Season Newsletter');
    mail.setHtmlBody(e.getMessage());
    mail.setSaveAsActivity(false);
    Messaging.sendEmail(
      new Messaging.SingleEmailMessage[] { mail });
  }
}
```

Updating the FormulaForce package

Finally, deploy the code included in this chapter and ensure any new Apex classes (especially test classes) are added to the package and perform a release upload. You may want to take some time to further review the code provided with this chapter, as not all of the code has been featured in this chapter. Some new fields have been added to the **Contestant** and **Season** objects also, which will automatically be added to the package.

The package confirmation page should look something like this:

Action	Component Name	Parent Object	Component Type	Installation Notes
Objects (3)				
Update	Contestant		Custom Object	This is an upgraded component. It will be updated to the new version.
Update	Driver		Custom Object	This is an upgraded component. It will be updated to the new version.
Create	Championship Points		Custom Setting	This is a brand new component.
Fields (6)				
Create	Points Awarded	ChampionshipPoints__c	Custom Field	This is a brand new component.
Create	Driver Id	Driver	Custom Field	This is a brand new component.
Create	Grid Position	Contestant	Custom Field	This is a brand new component.
Create	Race Time	Contestant	Custom Field	This is a brand new component.
Create	Current	Season	Custom Field	This is a brand new component.
Create	Race Position	Contestant	Custom Field	This is a brand new component.
Code (26)				
Create	fflib_StringBuilderTest		Apex Class	This is a brand new component.
Create	TestData		Apex Class	This is a brand new component.
Update	SeasonNewsletterScheduler		Apex Class	This is an upgraded component. It will be updated to the new version.
Update	SeasonController		Apex Class	This is an upgraded component. It will

This screenshot shows only part of the installation summary that relates to new objects and fields added to the package; your screen will display additional Apex classes also.

Summary

In this chapter, we have taken the first step in developing a robust coding convention to manage and structure the coding complexities of an enterprise application. This first layer encapsulates your application's business process logic in an agnostic way, in a way that allows it to be consumed easily across multiple Apex entry points, both those required today by your application and those that will arise in the future as the platform evolves.

We have also seen how the Unit Of Work pattern can be used to help bulkify DML statements, manage record relationships and implement a database transaction, and allow your Service layer logic to focus more on the key responsibility of implementing business logic. In the upcoming chapters, we will see how it quickly becomes the backbone of your application. Careful adherence to the guidelines around your Service layer will ensure it remains strong and easy to extend.

In the next chapter, we will look at the Domain layer, a pattern that blends the data from a Custom Object alongside applicable logic related to a Custom Object's behavior that relates to that data. This includes logic traditionally placed in Apex Triggers but it is also optional to further distribute and layer code executed in the Service layer.

6
Application Domain Layer

The objects used by your application represent its domain. Unlike other database platforms where the record data is, by default, hidden from end users, the Force. com platform displays your record data through the standard Salesforce UI, reports, dashboards, and Salesforce1 mobile application. Surfacing the labels and relationships, you give your objects and fields directly to the end user. From the moment you create your first object, you start to define your application's domain, just as Salesforce Standard Objects represent the CRM application domain.

Martin Fowler's *Patterns of Enterprise Application Architecture* also recognizes this concept as a means of code encapsulation to combine the data expressed by each object with behaviors written in code that affect or interact with that data. This could be Apex Trigger code, providing defaulting and validation, or code awarding championship points to contestant records or checking rules compliance.

This chapter will extend the functionality of the FormulaForce application using the Domain layer pattern, as well as highlight specific concerns, guidelines, and best practices, and how it integrates with both Apex Triggers and the application's Service layer code.

The following aspects will be covered in this chapter:

- Introducing the Domain layer pattern
- Implementing design guidelines
- The Domain class template
- Implementing the Domain Trigger logic
- Implementing the custom Domain logic
- Object-orientated programming
- Testing the Domain layer
- Calling the Domain layer

Introducing the Domain layer pattern

The following is Martin Fowler's definition of the Domain layer (`http://martinfowler.com/eaaCatalog/domainModel.html`):

> *"An object model of the domain that incorporates both behavior and data".*

Like the Service layer, this pattern adds a further layer of Separation of Concerns and factoring of the application code, which helps manage and scale a code base as it grows.

> *"At its worst business logic can be very complex. Rules and logic describe many different cases and slants of behavior, and it's this complexity that objects were designed to work with. A Domain Model creates a web of interconnected objects, where each object represents some meaningful individual, whether as large as a corporation or as small as a single line on an order form."*

Martin's reference to objects in the preceding quote is mainly aimed at objects created from instantiating classes that are coded in an object-orientated programming language such as Java or .NET. In these platforms, such classes act as a logical representation of the underlying database-table relationships. This approach is typically referred to as **Object Relational Mapping (ORM)**.

In contrast, a Force.com developer reading the term object will tend to first think about Standard or Custom Objects rather than something resulting from a class instantiation. This is because Salesforce has done a great job in binding the data with behavior through their declarative definition of an object, which as we know is much more than just fields. It has formulas, filters, referential integrity, and many other features that we have discussed in earlier chapters available without writing any code.

Taking into consideration these declarative features are essentially a means to enable certain behaviors, a Force.com Custom or Standard Object does already meet some of the encapsulation concerns of the Domain layer pattern.

Encapsulating an object's behavior in code

Apex Triggers present a way to write code to implement additional behavior for Custom Objects (or Standard Objects for that matter). They provide a place to implement more complex behavior associated with database events such as **create**, **update**, and **delete**.

However, as an Apex Trigger cannot have **public** methods, it does not provide a means to write code that logically belongs with the object but is not necessarily linked with a database event. An example of this would be logic to calculate **Contestants** championship points or checking compliance against the many **Formula1 rules and regulations**, which we will look at later in this chapter. Furthermore, they do not present the opportunity to leverage **object-orientated programming (OOP)** approaches, also discussed later in this chapter.

As a result, developers often end up putting this logic elsewhere, sometimes in a controller or helper class of some kind. Thus, the code implementing the behavior for a given object becomes fragmented and there is a breakdown of *Separation of Concerns*.

Lifting your Apex Trigger code out of the body of the trigger and into an **Apex Class**, perhaps named by some convention based on the object name, is a good start to mitigating this fragmentation, for example `RaceTriggerManager` or `RaceTriggerHandler`. Using such approaches, it then becomes possible to create other methods and break up the code further. These approaches are only the start in seeking a more complete interpretation of the domain model concept described in this chapter.

Using the `Manager` or `Handler` approach tends to attract logic relating to the Apex Trigger event model and nothing else, leaving other object-related logic to find less obvious locations in the code base.

Interpreting the Domain layer in Force.com

In this chapter, we look at the Force.com interpretation of the Domain layer pattern, one which ensures behavior invoked both through Apex Trigger events and through direct Apex method calls (from the Service layer and other Domain classes) are considered.

A single Domain class can be created to encapsulate all of the behavior and will begin to leverage OOP principles, such as interfaces, to further enrich the code for reuse and Separation of Concerns, which we will explore later in this chapter.

The following diagram illustrates two consumers of the Domain layer classes—the code from the **Service layer** and also direct interactions with objects resulting in **Apex Trigger** events, which will also be routed to the same Domain layer class:

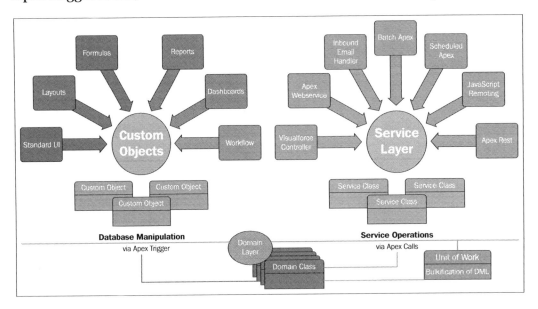

Domain classes in Apex compared to other platforms

As we have seen in earlier chapters, a Standard or Custom Object is exposed within the Apex runtime as a **concrete type** that can be instantiated to populate record fields for insertions in the database or to determine which types are used to return records queried from it.

When considering the Domain pattern, the first inclination is perhaps to extend the applicable SObject such as `Account` or `Race__c` through **Apex inheritance** with the `extends` keyword. Unfortunately, the **Apex compiler** does not support this approach. Even if it were to support this, given best practices of bulkification, writing code that deals with a single record instance at a time will quickly lead to governor issues.

Instead, the Domain class implementation covered here uses the **composition** approach to combine record data and behavior. This is sometimes known as the **wrapper class** approach; it is so named because it wraps the data that it relates to as a class member variable.

The Apex implementation of the wrapper class is no different, except that we choose to wrap a list of records to enforce **bulkified implementations** of the logic within. The following pseudocode illustrates the instantiation of an **Apex Domain class**:

```
Race__c raceRecords =
  [select Id, Name from Races__c where Id in :raceIds];

Races races = new Races(raceRecords);
```

Another implementation difference compared to other platforms, such as Java and .NET, is the creation of accessor methods to obtain related parent and child records. Though it is possible to write such methods, these are not recommended, for example `Contestants.getRaces` or `Races.getContestants`.

This implementation avoids coding these types of accessors, as the `SObject` objects in Apex already provide a means to traverse relationships (if queried) as needed. The bulk nature of Apex Domain classes also makes these types of methods less useful and more appropriate for the caller to use the `Selector` classes to query the required records as and when needed, rather than as a result of invoking an accessor method.

To summarize, the Apex Domain classes described in this chapter focus on wrapping lists of records and methods that encapsulate the object's behavior and avoid providing accessor methods for query-related records.

Implementation design guidelines

As with the previous chapter, this section provides some general design and best practice guidelines around designing a **Domain layer class** for a given object. Note that some of these conventions are shared by the **Service layer**, as it also calls the Domain layer because conventions such as bulkification apply to the logic written here as well.

Naming conventions

The key principle of the Domain layer pattern is to lay out the code in such a way that it maps to the business domain of the application. In a Force.com application, this is typically supported by the Custom Objects. As such, its important to clearly indicate which Domain layer class relates to which Standard or Custom Object:

- **Avoid acronyms**: As per the previous chapter, try to avoid these unless it makes your class names unworkably long.

- **Class names**: Use the plural name of your Custom Object for the name of your Domain class. This sets the tone for the scope of the record that the class deals with as clearly being bulkified, as described in the following subsection.
  - Some bad examples are `Race.cls` and `RaceDomain.cls`
  - Some good examples are `Races.cls` and `Teams.cls`

- **Method names**: Methods that relate to the logic associated with database operations or events should follow the `onEventName` convention. Other method names should be descriptive and avoid repeating the name of the class as part of the name.
  - Some bad examples are `Races.checkInserts` and `Races.startRace`
  - Some good examples are `Races.onBeforeInsert` and `Races.start`

- **Parameter Names and Types**: Much of what was described in the previous chapter applies here. Though passing in a list of records to the Domain class methods is not required, this is available as a class member variable to all the domain class methods, as you will see later in this chapter.
  - Some bad examples are:

```
Races.onBeforeInsert(
   List<Race__c> racesBeingInserted)
Races.start(
   List<Id> raceIds)
```

  - Some good examples are:

```
Races.onBeforeInsert()
Races.start()
```

- **Inner classes and interfaces**: Much of what was described in the previous chapter also applies here. As the data being managed is expressed in terms of the actual Custom Object themselves and that information is available as a class member variable, there is typically less of a need for inner classes representing data to be passed in and out of a Domain class.

The following diagram shows how the Domain classes that are used in this chapter map to their respective **Custom Objects**. Each Domain class receives the records that it's methods act on in its constructor. The methods shown in the Domain classes are described in more detail as we progress through this chapter.

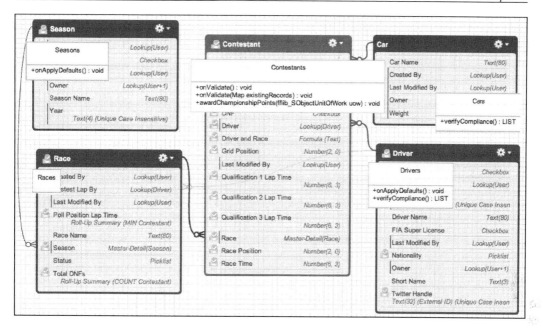

Bulkification

As with the Service layer, code written in the Domain layer is encouraged to think about records in a bulk context. This is important when Domain class methods are being called from an Apex Trigger context and the Service layer code, both of which carry the same bulkification requirement.

Instead of enforcing bulkification through passing parameters and ensuring that parameter types are bulkified, as with the Service layer, the information in the Domain class logic acts on and is driven by its member variables, which are themselves bulkified. In this case, the `Records` class property returns a `List<SObject>` object:

```
public void onValidate()
{
  for(Contestant__c race : (List<Contestant__c>) Records)
  {
  }
}
```

Defining and passing data

Most methods on Domain classes already have the information they need through the `Records` property (the state the Domain class was constructed with). As such, there is little need to pass data information on the methods themselves. However, for some custom behavior methods (those not reflecting the Apex Trigger logic), you might want to pass other domain objects and/or a **Unit Of Work** as additional parameters. Examples later in this chapter help illustrate this.

Transaction management

For Domain class methods that perform database operations, there are two design guidelines: utilize a transaction context (Unit Of Work) passed as a parameter to the method or create one for the scope of the Domain class method execution.

Domain class template

The Domain class implementation in this chapter utilizes the **FinancialForce.com Apex Enterprise Patterns** library, which is open source and is included in the sample code of this chapter. In this library, the Apex base class, `fflib_SObjectDomain`, is provided to help implement the Domain layer pattern.

A basic template for a Domain class utilizing this base class is shown in the following code snippet:

```
public class Races extends fflib_SObjectDomain
{
  public Races(List<Race__c> races)
  {
    super(races);
  }

  public class Constructor
    implements fflib_SObjectDomain.IConstructable
  {
    public fflib_SObjectDomain construct(
      List<SObject> sObjectList)
    {
      return new Races(sObjectList);
    }
  }
}
```

The first thing to note is that the **constructor** for this class takes a list of Race__c records, as per the guidelines described previously. The code implemented in a domain class is written with bulkification in mind. The base class constructor initializes the Records base class property.

 The inner class, Constructor, is present to permit the dynamic creation of the Domain class in an Apex Trigger context. This is actually working around the lack of full reflection (the ability to reference the class constructor dynamically) in the Apex language. The name of this inner class must always be Constructor.

By extending the fflib_SObjectDomain class, the Domain class inherits properties and methods it can override to implement its own methods, such as the Records property, which provides access to the actual record data. There are virtual methods provided to make the **Apex Trigger** behavior implementation easier as well as some specialized events such as onValidate and onApplyDefaults. The following class overview illustrates some of the key methods in the base class that the Domain classes can override:

```
fflib_SObjectDomain(List<SObject>)
onApplyDefaults()
onValidate()
onValidate(Map<Id, SObject>)
onBeforeInsert()
onBeforeUpdate(Map<Id, SObject>)
onBeforeDelete()
onAfterInsert()
onAfterUpdate(Map<Id, SObject>)
onAfterDelete()
handleBeforeInsert()
handleBeforeUpdate(Map<Id, SObject>)
handleBeforeDelete()
handleAfterInsert()
handleAfterUpdate(Map<Id, SObject>)
handleAfterDelete()
triggerHandler(Type)
```

Implementing Domain Trigger logic

The most common initial use case for a Domain class is to encapsulate the Apex Trigger logic. In order to enable this, a small Apex Trigger is required to invoke the `triggerHandler` method. This will route the various Trigger events to the appropriate methods in the Domain class (as shown in the preceding screenshot), avoiding the need for the usual `if/else` logic around `Trigger.isXXXX` variables.

The name of this trigger can be anything, though it makes sense to match it with that of the corresponding Domain class. Once this is in place, you can ignore it and focus on implementing the Domain class methods as follows:

```
trigger Seasons on Season__c (
  after delete, after insert, after update,
  before delete, before insert, before update) {
  fflib_SObjectDomain.triggerHandler(Seasons.class);
}
```

At the time of writing this book, the base class did not support `undelete` events from Apex Triggers. If this is required, you can consider extending the base class routing of this event and perhaps contributing your improvement to the community.

Routing trigger events to Domain class methods

The following diagram illustrates the flow of execution from the Apex Trigger to the Domain class, `triggerHandler`, to the individual methods:

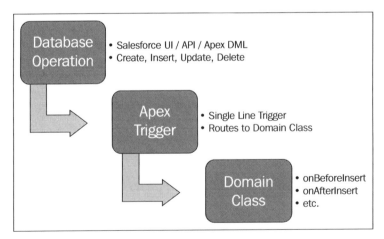

To help you understand how traditional Apex Trigger events are mapped to the various virtual methods in the base class, this table describes the code path taken from when the base class's `fflib_SObjectDOmai.triggerHandler` method is invoked through the specific event-based methods that can be overridden by a Domain class:

Trigger context	Base class Records property value	Base class handle method called (refer to the following note)	Base class event method(s) called (refer to the following note)
`Trigger.isBefore`			

`Trigger.isInsert`	`Trigger.new`	`handleBeforeInsert()`	`onApplyDefaults()`
			
			`onBeforeInsert()`

`Trigger.isUpdate`	`Trigger.new`	`handleBeforeUpdate(`
		`Map<Id,SObject>`
		`existingRecords)`
			`onBeforeUpdate(`
			`Map<Id,SObject>`
			`existingRecords)`

`Trigger.isDelete`	`Trigger.oldMap`	`handleBeforeDelete()`	`onBeforeDelete()`
`Trigger.isAfter`			

`Trigger.isInsert`	`Trigger.new`	`handleAfterInsert()`	`onValidate()`
			
			`onAfterInsert()`

`Trigger.isUpdate`	`Trigger.new`	`handleAfterUpdate(`
		`Map<Id,SObject>`
		`existingRecords)`
			`onValidate(`
			`Map<Id,SObject>`
			`existingRecords)`
			
			`onAfterUpdate(`
			`Map<Id,SObject>`
			`existingRecords)`

`Trigger.isDelete`	`Trigger.oldMap`	`handleAfterDelete()`	`onAfterDelete()`

Note: Handle methods cannot be overridden. The `existingRecords` parameter represents the value of `Trigger.oldMap`.

The base class uses the template method pattern (`http://en.wikipedia.org/wiki/Template_method_pattern`). This ensures that when overriding the onXXX methods from the base class, you do not need to worry about calling the base class version of the method, as is the typical developer requirement when overriding methods in OOP.

Enforcing object security

Salesforce requires packaged applications to implement the **CRUD (Create, Read, Update, and Delete)** security checks via the methods on the `SObjectDescribe` Apex runtime type.

The preceding handle methods in the `fflib_SObjectDomain` base class used in this chapter automatically perform the Create, Update, and Delete checks on behalf of the Domain class (the Selector base class introduced in the next chapter provides assistance for Read checking). The handler method checks the required security before calling the preceding event methods and will throw a `DomainException` exception if the user does not have the required access (forcing the entire Trigger context to stop). The following table lists the `SObjectDescribe` methods called by each handler method listed in the previous table:

Base class handle method	SObjectDescribe method used
handleAfterInsert	SObjectDescribe.isCreateable()
handleAfterUpdate	SObjectDescribe.isUpdateable()
handleAfterDelete	SObjectDescribe.isDeletable()

 Domain classes can access the `SObjectDescribe` instance for `SObject` wrapped through the `SObjectDescribe` base property.

Apex Trigger event handling

The upcoming sections illustrate some Apex Trigger examples with respect to the **FormulaForce** application. They utilize the `Drivers` and `Contestants` Domain classes included in the sample code for this chapter along with the following new fields:

- In the `Driver__c` object, a new field called `ShortName__c` as a **Text** type, with a maximum size of 3 characters, has been created.

- In the `Race__c` object, there is a new field called `Status__c` as a **Picklist** type, with the **Scheduled**, **In Progress**, **Red Flagged**, and **Finished** values. The default value is scheduled by ticking the **Use first value as default value** checkbox.

Defaulting field values on insert

Although the `onInsertBefore` method can be overridden to implement logic to set default values on record insert, the following code, added to the `Contestants` Domain class, has chosen to override the `onApplyDefaults` method instead. This was used as it is more explicit and permits a **Separation of Concerns** between the defaulting code and the record insert code, although both are fired during the insert phase:

```
public override void onApplyDefaults()
{
  for(Driver__c driver : (List<Driver__c>) Records)
  {
    if(driver.ShortName__c == null)
    {
      // Upper case first three letters of drivers last name
      String lastName = driver.Name.substringAfterLast(' ');
      driver.ShortName__c = lastName.left(3).toUpperCase();
    }
  }
}
```

The preceding code attempts to populate the **Drivers** short name, which is typically made up of the first three characters of their second name in upper case, so **Lewis Hamilton** will become **HAM**.

Validation on insert

The following validation logic applies during record creation. It has been added to the `Contestants` Domain class and ensures that contestants are only added when the race is in the **Scheduled** state.

It also demonstrates the use of a **Selector** pattern class to bulk load records from the `Race__c` Custom Object, and this pattern will be covered in detail in the next chapter:

```
public override void onValidate()
{
  // Bulk load the associated races
  Set<Id> raceIds = new Set<Id>();
  for(Contestant__c contestant :
      (List<Contestant__c>) Records)
    raceIds.add(contestant.Race__c);
```

```
Map<Id, Race__c> associatedRaces =
  new Map<Id, Race__c>(
    new RacesSelector().selectById(raceIds));
// Only new contestants to be added to Scheduled races
for(Contestant__c contestant :
  (List<Contestant__c>) Records)
{
  Race__c race = associatedRaces.get(contestant.Race__c);
  if(race.Status__c != 'Scheduled')
    contestant.addError(
      'Contestants can only be added to scheduled races');
}
}
```

By overriding the onValidate method, the logic always invokes the after phase of the Apex Trigger. As no further edits can be made to the record fields, this is the safest place to perform the logic. Always keep in mind that your Apex Trigger might not be the only one assigned to the object. For example, once your package is installed in a subscriber org, a subscriber-created custom trigger on your object might fire before yours (the order of trigger invocation is non-deterministic) and will attempt to modify fields. Thus, for managed package triggers, it is highly recommended that validation be performed in the after phase to ensure complete confidence and security, as the data will not be modified further after validation.

Validation on update

An alternative method, override, is provided to implement the validation logic applicable to record updates. It is an overload of the onValidate method shown in the preceding example, used to pass in the current records on the database for comparison if needed:

```
public override void onValidate(
  Map<Id,SObject> existingRecords)
{
  // Bulk load the associated races
  Map<Id, Race__c> associatedRaces = queryAssociatedRaces();

  // Can only change drivers in scheduled races
  for(Contestant__c contestant :
    (List<Contestant__c>) Records)
  {
    Race__c contestantRace =
```

```
      associatedRaces.get(contestant.Race__c);
    Contestant__c oldContestant   =
      (Contestant__c) existingRecords.get(contestant.Id);
    if(contestantRace.Status__c != 'Scheduled' &&
       contestant.Driver__c !=  oldContestant.Driver__c)
      contestant.Driver__c.addError(
        'You can only change drivers for scheduled races');
  }
}
```

The preceding code leverages a new custom Domain class method to share the code responsible for loading associated **Race** records for **Contestants** across the onValidate method shown in the previous example. This method also uses the Records property to determine **Contestants** in scope:

```
private Map<Id, Race__c> queryAssociatedRaces()
{
  // Bulk load the associated races
  Set<Id> raceIds = new Set<Id>();
  for(Contestant__c contestant :
    (List<Contestant__c>) Records)
    raceIds.add(contestant.Race__c);
  return new Map<Id, Race__c>(
    new RacesSelector().selectById(raceIds));
}
```

The preceding method is marked as private, as there is currently no need to expose this functionality to other classes. Initially, restricting methods this way is often considered best practice and permits easier internal refactoring or improvements in the future. If a need arises that needs access to this functionality, the method can be made public.

Implementing custom Domain logic

A Domain class should not restrict itself to containing logic purely related to Apex Triggers. In the following example, the code introduced in the previous chapter to calculate championship points has been refactored into the Contestants Domain class. This is a more appropriate place for it, as it directly applies to the **Contestant** record data and can be readily shared between other Domain and Service layer code (which we will look at later in this chapter):

```
public void awardChampionshipPoints(
  fflib_SObjectUnitOfWork uow)
```

```
{
  // Apply championship points to given contestants
  for(Contestant__c contestant :
    (List<Contestant__c>) Records)
  {
    // Determine points to award for the given position
    ChampionshipPoints__c pointsForPosition =
      ChampionshipPoints__c.getInstance(
        String.valueOf(contestant.RacePosition__c));
    if(pointsForPosition!=null)
    {
      // Apply points and register for udpate with uow
      contestant.ChampionshipPoints__c =
        pointsForPosition.PointsAwarded__c;
      uow.registerDirty(contestant);
    }
  }
}
```

Note that the **Unit Of Work** is passed as a parameter here so that the method can register work (record updates) with the calling Service layer method responsible for committing the work. Once again, as with the previous Domain class methods, the Records property is used to access the **Contestant** records to process.

Object-oriented programming

One of the big advantages of using Apex classes is the ability to leverage the power of **OOP**. OOP allows you to observe commonalities in data or behavior across your objects to share code or apply common processing across different objects.

An example of such a commonality in the Formula1 world are rules; every aspect of the sport has a set of rules and regulations to comply with, such as **drivers** owning a **FIA Super License**, the weight of the car they drive should be at least above a defined minimum, and ensuring that a **team** has not exceeded the maximum distance in testing their cars. Such compliances are checked regularly, both before and after a race.

Creating a compliance application framework

In our FormulaForce application, we want to create a compliance framework that will check these regulations across the different objects while also providing a consistent user interface experience for the end user to verify compliance. The initial requirement is to place a **Verify Compliance** button on the **Detail Pages** on all applicable objects.

The **Visualforce Controller** and **Service code** that perform the verification process should be generic and reusable across these objects, while the actual compliance-checking logic associated with each object will be specific. By using an **Apex Interface**, we can define this common requirement for the applicable Domain classes to implement.

In this section, we will implement this requirement using an Apex Interface and a generic service that can be passed record IDs for different Domain objects across the application. Creating such a service avoids code duplication by having to repeat the logic of handling the results within the code of each Domain class and provides a centralized service for the controller to consume regardless of the object type in scope.

By using an Apex Interface and a generic service, we separate the functional concerns of implementing compliance functionality as follows:

- The Service layer code is concerned solely with executing the compliance-checking process through the interface

- The Controller code is concerned with calling the service class method to execute the compliance check and then presenting the results to the user consistently

- The Domain layer classes that implement the interface focus solely on validating the record data against the applicable rules according to the type of the object

Having these Separation of Concerns makes it easy to significantly modify or extend the ways in which the checking is invoked and presented to the user without having to revisit each of the Domain layer classes, or conversely, modify the compliance logic of one object without impacting the overall implementation across the application.

An Apex Interface example

Interfaces help express common attributes or behaviors across different domain classes. In this section, we will use an Apex Interface to help expose the compliance-checking logic encapsulated in each of the applicable Domain classes.

In order to exercise and implement the compliance framework, the FormulaForce application has gained a few extra fields and objects. These objects, additional classes, and Visualforce pages are all included in the code samples of this chapter.

To summarize, the following steps have been taken to implement the compliance framework requirement. You can follow along with these or simply refer to the sample code of this chapter:

1. Create a new **Car** object and tab.

2. Create a new **Weight** field of type **Number** and length **6** on the **Car** object.

3. Create a new **FIA Super License** field to the **Driver** object.

4. Create a new `Cars` Domain class and `CarsSelector` Selector class.

5. Create a new `ComplianceService` class and `ICompliant` interface.

6. Create new `Cars` and `Drivers` Domain classes and implement the `ICompliant` interface.

7. Update the `Application` class to implement a Domain class factory.

8. Create a new `ComplianceService.verify` method that utilizes the Domain factory.

9. Create a new `ComplianceController` class and Visualforce pages per object.

The following sections describe in further detail the Apex coding from step 5 onwards.

Step 5 – defining a generic service

The aim is to develop a common service to handle all compliance verifications across the application. So, a new `ComplianceService` class has been created with a `verify` method on it, which is capable of receiving IDs from various objects. If there are any verification errors, they will be thrown as part of an exception. If the method returns without throwing an exception, the given records are compliant. The following code snippet shows the creation of a new `ComplianceService` class with a `verify` method:

```
public class ComplianceService
{
  /**
   * Provides general support to verify compliance in the
   * application
   * @throws ComplianceException for any failures
   **/
  public static void verify(Set<Id> recordIds)
  {
    // Query the given records and delegate to the
    //   corresponding Domain class to check compliance
    //   and report failures via ComplianceException
  }
```

Before we look further into how this service method can be implemented, take a look at the new `ICompliant` interface and the `verifyCompliance` method that will be implemented by the `Drivers` and `Cars` Domain classes:

```
public class ComplianceService
{
  /**
   * Interface used to execute compliance checking logic
   * in each domain class
   **/
  public interface ICompliant
  {
    List<VerifyResult> verifyCompliance();
  }

  /**
   * Results of a compliance verification for a given record
   **/
  public class VerifyResult
  {
    public Id recordId;
    public String complianceCode;
    public Boolean passed;
    public String failureReason;
  }
}
```

Step 6 – implementing the Domain class interface

The `Drivers` Domain class implements the interface as follows (only a portion of the class is shown). It checks whether the **FIA Super License** field is checked and reports an appropriate compliance code and failure message if not:

```
public class Drivers extends fflib_SObjectDomain
  implements ComplianceService.ICompliant
{
  public List<ComplianceService.VerifyResult>
    verifyCompliance()
  {
    List<ComplianceService.VerifyResult> compliances =
      new List<ComplianceService.VerifyResult>();
    for(Driver__c driver : (List<Driver__c>) Records)
    {
      ComplianceService.VerifyResult license =
```

```
      new ComplianceService.VerifyResult();
    license.ComplianceCode = '4.1';
    license.RecordId = driver.Id;
    license.passed = driver.FIASuperLicense__c;
    license.failureReason =
      license.passed ? null :
        'Driver must have a FIA Super License.';
    compliances.add(license);
  }
  return compliances;
  }
}
```

The `Cars` domain class (of which only a portion of the class is shown) implements the `verifyCompliance` method as follows, checking whether the car is over the specified weight:

```
public class Cars extends fflib_SObjectDomain
  implements ComplianceService.ICompliant
{
  public List<ComplianceService.VerifyResult>
    verifyCompliance()
  {
    List<ComplianceService.VerifyResult> compliances =
      new List<ComplianceService.VerifyResult>();
    for(Car__c car : (List<Car__c>) Records)
    {
      // Check weight compliance
      ComplianceService.VerifyResult license =
        new ComplianceService.VerifyResult();
      license.ComplianceCode = '4.1';
      license.RecordId = car.Id;
      license.passed =
        car.Weight__c !=null &&
        car.Weight__c >= 691;
      license.failureReason = license.passed ? null :
        'Car must not be less than 691kg.';
      compliances.add(license);
    }
    return compliances;
  }
}
```

Step 7 – the domain class factory pattern

The next step is to dynamically construct the associated Domain class based on the record IDs passed into the `ComplianceService.verify` method. This part of the implementation makes use of a **Factory pattern** implementation for Domain classes.

> A Wikipedia reference to the Factory pattern can be found at
> `http://en.wikipedia.org/wiki/Factory_method_pattern`.

The implementation uses the Apex runtime `Id.getSObjectType` method to establish `SObjectType`, and then via the `Maps` (shown in the following code), it determines the applicable Domain and Selector classes to use (to query the records).

The Apex runtime `Type.newInstance` method is then used to construct an instance of the Domain and Selector classes. The factory functionality is invoked by calling the `Application.Domain.newInstance` method (from the `DomainFactory` class), as follows:

```
public class Application
{
  public static final DomainFactory Domain =
    new DomainFactory(
      // Map SObjectType to Domain Class Constructors
      new Map<SObjectType, Type> {
        Race__c.SObjectType => Races.Constructor.class,
        Car__c.SObjectType => Cars.Constructor.class,
        Driver__c.SObjectType => Drivers.Constructor.class },
      // Map SObjectType to Selector Class
      new Map<SObjectType, Type> {
        Race__c.SObjectType => RacesSelector.class,
        Car__c.SObjectType => CarsSelector.class,
        Driver__c.SObjectType => DriversSelector.class });
}
```

> This Domain factory is implemented within a new class called `Application`, accessed via the `Domain` static member variable. A detailed walk through of the internals of how the `DomainFactory` class works is outside the scope of this chapter, however feel free to review the class code for further details. The following section demonstrates how the `newInstance` method is used to implement the service.

Step 8 – implementing a generic service

The `Application.Domain.newInstance` method used in the following code is used to access the Domain instance factory defined in the last step.

This method returns `fflib_SObjectDomain`, as this is a common base class to all Domain classes. Then, using the `instanceof` operator, it determines whether it implements the `ICompliant` interface, and if so, it calls the `verifyCompliance` method. The following code shows the implementation of a generic service:

```
public class ComplianceService
{
  public static void verify(Set<Id> recordIds)
  {
    // Dynamically create Domain instance for these records
    fflib_SObjectDomain domain =
      Application.Domain.newInstance(recordIds);
    if(domain instanceof ICompliant)
    {
      // Ask the domain class to verify its compliance
      ICompliant compliantDomain = (ICompliant) domain;
      List<VerifyResult> verifyResults =
        compliantDomain.verifyCompliance();
      if(verifyResults!=null)
      {
        // Check for failed compliances
        List<VerifyResult> failedCompliances =
          new List<VerifyResult>();
        for(VerifyResult verifyResult : verifyResults)
          if(!verifyResult.passed)
            failedCompliances.add(verifyResult);
        if(failedCompliances.size()>0)
          throw new ComplianceException(
            'Compliance failures found.', failedCompliances);
        return;
      }
      throw new ComplianceException(
        'Unable to verify compliance.', null);
    }
  }
}
```

Note that if the `verify` method is passed IDs for an object that does not have a corresponding Domain class, an exception is thrown from the factory. However, if a domain class is found but does not implement the interface, the preceding code simply returns without an error, though what the developer will do in this case is up to them.

Step 9 – using the generic service from a generic controller

Finally, a generic Visualforce Controller, `ComplianceController`, has been created with a `verify` action method that calls the service. Note that at no time have we yet referred to a specific Custom Object or Domain class, ensuring that this controller and the service are generic and able to handle objects of different types. The following code shows how the generic `ComplianceService.verify` method is being called from the `ComplianceController.verify` method:

```
public PageReference verify()
{
  try
  {
    // Pass the record to the compliance service
    ComplianceService.verify(
      new Set<Id> { standardController.getId() });
    // Passed!
    ApexPages.addMessage(
      new ApexPages.Message(
        ApexPages.Severity.Info, 'Compliance passed'));
  }
  catch (Exception e)
  {
    // Report message as normal via apex:pageMessages
    ApexPages.addMessages(e);
    // Display additional compliance failure messages?
    if(e instanceof ComplianceService.ComplianceException)
    {
      ComplianceService.ComplianceException ce
        (ComplianceService.ComplianceException) e;
      for(ComplianceService.VerifyResult verifyResult :
          ce.failures)
        ApexPages.addMessage(
```

```
           new ApexPages.Message(
             ApexPages.Severity.Error,
               String.format('{0} ({1})',
                 new List<String> {
                   verifyResult.failureReason,
                   verifyResult.complianceCode })));
     }
   }
   return null;
 }
```

Visualforce pages are then created to bind this generic controller to Custom Buttons on the **Driver** and **Car** detail pages. This is the only reference made to the specific objects that implement the `ComplianceService.ICompliant` interface and is only needed in order to create the Custom Buttons. The following Visualforce page defines a button that uses the generic `ComplianceController.verify` method defined earlier:

```
<apex:page standardController="Driver__c"
   extensions="ComplianceController" action="{!verify}">
  <apex:pageMessages/>
  <apex:form>
    <apex:commandButton value="Cancel" action="{!cancel}"/>
  </apex:form>
</apex:page>

<apex:page standardController="Car__c"
   extensions="ComplianceController" action="{!verify}">
  <apex:pageMessages/>
    <apex:form>
      <apex:commandButton value="Cancel" action="{!cancel}"/>
    </apex:form>
</apex:page>
```

Visualforce components offer a means to encapsulate Visualforce markups into reusable components.

Summarizing compliance framework implementation

Using an Apex Interface and the Factory pattern, a framework has been put in place within the application to ensure that the compliance logic is implemented consistently, and this is a simple matter of implementing the Domain class interface and creating the Visualforce page to enable the feature for other applicable objects in the future.

 As this has been implemented as a service, it can easily be reused from a Batch Apex or Scheduled context as well.

The following screenshot illustrates the **Verify Compliance** button on the **Driver** object. Ensure that the **FIA Super License** field is unchecked before pressing the button.

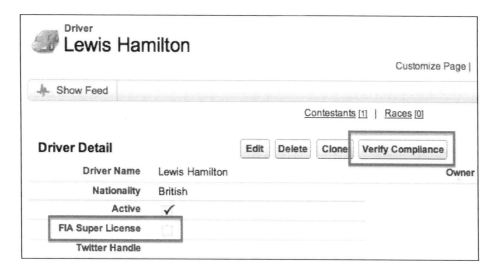

The following errors should be displayed:

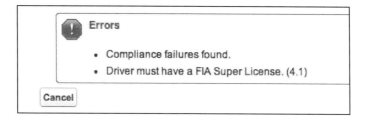

The following screenshot shows the **Verify Compliance** button on the **Car** object:

The following errors are shown by the generic controller defined/created previously:

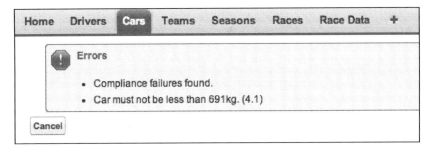

Testing the Domain layer

Testing your Domain code can be accomplished in the standard Force.com manner. Typically, test classes are named by suffixing `Test` at the end of the Domain class name, for example, `RacesTest`. Test methods have the option to test the Domain class code functionality either directly or indirectly.

Indirect testing is accomplished using only the DML and SOQL logic against the applicable Custom Objects and asserting the data and field errors arising from these operations. Here, there is no reference to your Domain class at all in the test code.

However, this only tests the Apex Trigger Domain class methods. For test methods that represent custom domain behaviors, you must create an instance of the Domain class. This section will illustrate examples of both indirect and direct testing approaches.

Unit testing

Although developing tests around the Service layer and related callers (controllers, batch, and so on) will also invoke the Domain layer logic, it is important to test as many scenarios specifically against the Domain layer as possible, passing in different configurations of record data to test both success and failure code paths and making sure that your Domain layer logic is as robust as possible. Wikipedia describes the definition of a **unit test** as follows (`http://en.wikipedia.org/wiki/Unit_ testing`):

> *In computer programming, unit testing is a method by which individual units of source code, sets of one or more computer program modules together with associated control data, usage procedures, and operating procedures are tested to determine if they are fit for use. Intuitively, one can view a unit as the smallest testable part of an application. In procedural programming, a unit could be an entire module, but it is more commonly an individual function or procedure. In object-oriented programming, a unit is often an entire interface, such as a class, but could be an individual method. Unit tests are short code fragments created by programmers or occasionally by white box testers during the development process.*

Testing of the Domain layer falls into this definition. Though without a true mocking framework (such as Mockito in Java), true white-box testing is harder, as there is no way, without implementing your own mocking framework in your code, to invoke specific methods without executing the product code to ensure that the data is in the correct state.

Test methods using DML and SOQL

To test the Apex Trigger methods of the Domain class, the traditional use of DML and SOQL can be applied alongside the use of the Apex runtime `DMLException` methods to assert not only the error message but also other details. The following Apex test method illustrates how to do this:

```
@IsTest
private static void testAddContestantNoneScheduled()
{
  // Test data
  Season__c season =
    new Season__c(Name = '2014', Year__c = '2014');
  insert season;
  Driver__c driver =
    new Driver__c(
      Name = 'Lewis Hamilton', DriverId__c = '42');
  insert driver;
```

```
Race__c race =
 new Race__c(Name = 'Spa',
              Status__c = 'In Progress',
              Season__c = season.Id);
insert race;

Test.startTest();
try
{
  // Insert Contestant to In Progress race
  Contestant__c contestant =
    new Contestant__c(
      Driver__c = driver.Id,
      Race__c = race.Id);
  insert contestant;
  System.assert(false, 'Expected exception');
}
catch (DMLException e)
{
  System.assertEquals(1, e.getNumDml());
  System.assertEquals(
    'Contestants can only be added to Scheduled Races.',
    e.getDmlMessage(0));
  System.assertEquals(
    StatusCode.FIELD_CUSTOM_VALIDATION_EXCEPTION,
    e.getDmlType(0));
  }
  Test.stopTest();
}
```

The preceding error is a record-level error; the DMLException class also allows you to assert field-level information for field-level errors. The following code shows such a test assertion; the data setup code is not shown:

```
Test.startTest();
try
{
  contestant.Driver__c = anotherDriver.Id;
  update contestant;
  System.assert(false, 'Expected exception');
}
catch (DmlException e)
{
  System.assertEquals(1, e.getNumDml());
  System.assertEquals(
```

```
          'You can only change drivers for scheduled races',
          e.getDmlMessage(0));
      System.assertEquals(Contestant__c.Driver__c,
        e.getDmlFields(0)[0]);
      System.assertEquals(
        StatusCode.FIELD_CUSTOM_VALIDATION_EXCEPTION,
        e.getDmlType(0));
    }
  Test.stopTest();
```

Test methods using the Domain class methods

In order to test custom Domain class methods, an instance of the Domain class should be created in the test method, using test records created in memory or queried from the database having been inserted as shown in the previous tests.

The following example shows the Contestants.awardChampionShip method being tested. Note that the test creates a temporary Unit Of Work but does not commit the work. This is not strictly needed to assert the changes to the records, as the Records property can be used to access the changes and assert the correct value that has been assigned:

```
@IsTest
private static void testAddChampionshipPoints()
{
  // Test data
  ChampionshipPoints__c championShipPoints =
    new ChampionshipPoints__c(
      Name = '1', PointsAwarded__c = 25);
  insert championShipPoints;
  Season__c season =
    new Season__c(Name = '2014', Year__c = '2014');
  insert season;
  Driver__c driver =
    new Driver__c(
      Name = 'Lewis Hamilton', DriverId__c = '42');
  insert driver;
  Race__c race =
    new Race__c(
      Name = 'Spa', Status__c  = 'Scheduled',
      Season__c = season.Id);
  insert race;
  Contestant__c contestant =
```

```
    new Contestant__c(
      Driver__c = driver.Id, Race__c = race.Id);
  insert contestant;
  race.Status__c = 'Finished';
  update race;
  contestant.RacePosition__c = 1;
  update contestant;

  Test.startTest();
  Contestants contestants =
    new Contestants(new List<Contestant__c> { contestant });
  contestants.awardChampionshipPoints(
    Application.UnitOfWork.newInstance());
  System.assertEquals(25, ((Contestant__c)
    contestants.Records[0]).ChampionshipPoints__c);
  Test.stopTest();
}
```

Performing SOQL and DML in tests is expensive in terms of CPU time and adds to the overall time it takes to execute all application tests, which becomes important once you start to consider **Continuous Integration** (covered in a later chapter), for example, whether it is always necessary to commit data updates from the Domain layer, as Service layer tests might also be performing these types of operations and asserting the results.

Calling the Domain layer

The Domain layer is positioned with respect to visibility and dependency below the Service layer. This in practice means that Domain classes should not be called directly from the execution context code, such as Visualforce Controllers or Batch Apex, as it is the Service layer's responsibility to be the sole entry point for business process application logic.

That being said, we saw that the Domain layer also encapsulates an object's behavior as records are manipulated by binding Apex Trigger events to methods on the Domain class. As such, Apex Triggers technically form another point of invocation.

Finally, there is a third caller type for the Domain layer, and this is another Domain class. Restrict your Domain class callers to the following contexts only:

- **Apex Triggers**: This calls via the `fflib_SObjectDomain.handleTrigger` method.

- **Service layer**: This layer directly creates an instance of a Domain class via the new operator or through the Domain factory approach seen earlier in this chapter. Typically, the Domain class custom methods are called in this context.

- **Domain layer**: Other Domain classes can call other Domain classes, for example, the `Races` Domain class can have some functionality it implements that also requires the use of a method on the `Contestants` Domain class.

> Note that it is entirely acceptable to have a Domain class with no Service class code referencing it at all, such as in the case where the Domain class solely implements the code for use in an Apex Trigger context and doesn't contain any custom Domain methods. Then, the only invocation of the Domain class will be indirect via the trigger context.

Service layer interactions

While implementing the compliance framework earlier in this chapter, we saw how a Domain class can be dynamically created within a generic service method. Typically, Domain classes are created directly. In this section, we will see a couple of examples of these.

The following code shows the Domain class constructor being passed records from a Selector class, which returns `List<Contestant__c>` for the purposes of this chapter. Notice that the Unit Of Work is created and passed to the Domain class custom method so that this method can also register work of its own to be later committed to the database:

```
public class ContestantService
{
  public static void awardChampionshipPoints(
    Set<Id> contestantIds)
  {
    fflib_SObjectUnitOfWork =
      Application.UnitOfWork.newInstance();
```

```
    // Apply championship points to given contestants
    Contestants contestants =
      new Contestants(
        new ContestantsSelector().selectById(contestantIds));
    contestants.awardChampionshipPoints(uow);

    uow.commitWork();
  }
}
```

You might have noticed that this example reworks the Service example from the previous chapter by refactoring the code and calculating the points closer to the object, for which the code directly applies, by basically moving the original code to the Domain class.

This following second example also reworks the code from the previous chapter to leverage the Domain layer. In this case, the RaceService class also implements an awardChampionshipPoints method. This can also benefit from the Contestants Domain class method. Note how easy it is to reuse methods between the Service and Domain layers, as both ensure that their methods and interactions are bulkified:

```
public class RaceService
{
  public void awardChampionshipPoints(Set<Id> raceIds)
  {
    fflib_SObjectUnitOfWork uow =
      Application.UnitOfWork.newInstance();

    List<Contestant__c> contestants =
      new List<Contestant__c>();
    for(Race__c race :
      new RacesSelector().selectByIdWithContestants(raceIds))
        contestants.addAll(race.Contestants__r);

    // Delegate to Contestant Domain class
    new Contestants(contestants).awardChampionshipPoints(uow);

    // Commit work
    uow.commitWork();
  }
}
```

Domain layer interactions

In the following example (also included in the sample code for this chapter), a new Custom Object is created to represent the teams that participate in the races. The **Driver** object has gained a new **Lookup** field called **Team** to associate the drivers with their teams.

Leveraging the compliance framework built earlier, a **Verify Compliance** button for the **Team** records is also added to provide a means to check certain aspects of the team that are compliant (such as the maximum distance cars can cover during testing) as well as whether all the drivers in this team are also still compliant (reusing the existing code).

 This will be done by adding the compliance verification code in the new Teams Domain class call or delegating the Drivers Domain class method to implement the same for this object.

The following components have been added to the application to support this example:

- A new **Team** object and tab
- A new **Testing Distance** number field with a length of **6** on the **Team** object
- A new **Team** lookup field on the **Driver** object
- A new Teams Domain class

 You don't always have to create an Apex Trigger that calls the fflib_SObjectDomain.triggerHandler method if you don't plan on overriding any of the Apex Trigger event handler methods.

Being able to call between the Domain layer classes permits the driver compliance-checking code to continue to be reused at the **Driver** level as well as from the **Team** level. This Domain class example shows the Teams Domain class calling the Drivers Domain class:

```
public class Teams extends fflib_SObjectDomain
  implements ComplianceService.ICompliant
{
  public List<ComplianceService.VerifyResult>
    verifyCompliance()
  {
```

```
    // Verify Team compliance
    List<ComplianceService.VerifyResult> teamVerifyResults =
      new List<ComplianceService.VerifyResult>();
    for(Team__c team : (List<Team__c>) Records)
    {
      ComplianceService.VerifyResult testingDistance =
        new ComplianceService.VerifyResult();
      testingDistance.ComplianceCode = '22.5';
      testingDistance.RecordId = team.Id;
      testingDistance.passed = team.TestingDistance__c!=null ?
        team.TestingDistance__c <= 15000 : true;
        testingDistance.failureReason = testingDistance.passed ?
          null : 'Testing exceeded 15,000km';
      teamVerifyResults.add(testingDistance);
    }

    // Verify associated Drivers compliance
    teamVerifyResults.addAll(
      new Drivers(
        new DriversSelector().selectDriversByTeam(
          new Map<Id, SObject(Records).keySet()))
          .verifyCompliance());

    return teamVerifyResults;
  }
}
```

The following screenshot shows the new **Team** object and the **Verify Compliance** button with an invalid **Testing Distance** value greater than **15,000 km**. The **FIA Super License** field on the **Driver** record for **Lewis Hamilton**, which is unchecked, is not shown.

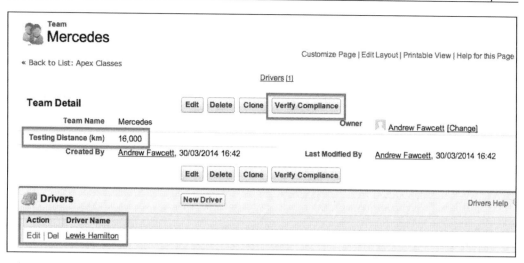

The following errors are shown, confirming that the **Team** and its **Driver** have some compliance issues to be resolved:

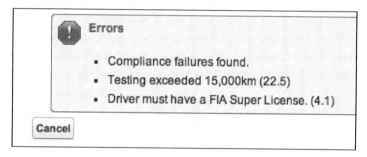

The bulkification guideline applied to the Domain layer is being leveraged here, as the `Drivers` Domain class logic was reused directly from the `Teams` Domain class. Also note that the implementation of the `Drivers` Domain class was and is still unaware of the split of drivers by team.

Updating the FormulaForce package

As before, utilize the source code provided with this chapter to update your packaging org and upload a new version of the package. Make sure that you check for any components not automatically added to the package, such as Apex classes, objects, and tabs.

Only a portion of the installation summary page is shown in the following screenshot, which shows new Custom Objects, fields, and pages added in this chapter:

▼ Tabs (2)

Action	Component Name	Parent Object	Component Type	Installation Notes
Create	Team		Tab	This is a brand new component.
Create	Car		Tab	This is a brand new component.

▼ Objects (2)

Action	Component Name	Parent Object	Component Type	Installation Notes
Create	Team		Custom Object	This is a brand new component.
Create	Car		Custom Object	This is a brand new component.

▼ Fields (7)

Action	Component Name	Parent Object	Component Type	Installation Notes
Create	FIA Super License	Driver	Custom Field	This is a brand new component.
Create	Car	Contestant	Custom Field	This is a brand new component.
Create	Short Name	Driver	Custom Field	This is a brand new component.
Create	Status	Race	Custom Field	This is a brand new component.
Create	Weight	Car__c	Custom Field	This is a brand new component.
Create	Team	Driver	Custom Field	This is a brand new component.
Create	Testing Distance	Team__c	Custom Field	This is a brand new component.

▼ Pages (3)

Action	Component Name	Parent Object	Component Type	Installation Notes
Create	compliancedriver		Visualforce Page	This is a brand new component.
Create	compliancecar		Visualforce Page	This is a brand new component.
Create	complianceteam		Visualforce Page	This is a brand new component.

> Note that the new **Verify Compliance** button has been added to the **Driver** layout as the last release of the package in the previous chapter. As layouts are non-upgradable components, this will need to be added manually after installation in the test org when upgrading, as will any new custom fields added throughout this chapter. You would typically notify users of these steps through your upgrade and installation guide.

Summary

In this chapter, you've seen a new way to factor business logic beyond encapsulating it in the Service layer; one that aligns the logic, implementing the validation changes, and interpretation of an object's data through a Domain class named accordingly. As with the Service layer, this approach makes such code easy to find for new and experienced developers working on the code base.

A Domain class combines the traditional Apex Trigger logic and custom Domain logic—such as the calculation of championship points for a contestant or the verification of compliance rules against the cars, drivers, and teams, while also providing common functionality, such as security requirements need to pass the **Salesforce Security Review**.

By utilizing Apex classes, the ability to start leveraging **OOP** practices emerges, using interfaces and factory methods to implement functional subsystems within the application to deliver not only implementation speed, consistency, and reuse, but also help support a common user experience. Domain classes can call between each other when required to encompass the behavior of related child components, such as drivers within a team.

Finally, when testing the Domain layer, keep in mind the best practice used for unit testing to test as much of the code in isolation with varied use cases and data combinations, despite the fact that other tests, such as those from the Service layer, and other callers will also exercise the code paths, though likely with less variation.

In the next chapter, we will complete the trio of patterns from Martin Fowler, by taking a deeper look at the Selector pattern. This has been utilized a few times in this chapter when reading data from the various Custom Objects used in the application.

7
Application Selector Layer

Apex is a very expressive language to perform calculations and transformations of data entered by the user or records read from your Custom Objects. However, **SOQL** also holds within it a great deal of expressiveness to select, filter, and aggregate information without having to resort to Apex. SOQL is also a powerful way to traverse relationships (up to five levels) in one statement, which would otherwise leave developers in other platforms performing several queries.

Quite often, the same or similar SOQL statements are required in different execution contexts and business logic scenarios throughout an application. Performing these queries inline as and when needed can rapidly become a maintenance problem as you extend and adapt your object schema, fields, and relationships. Salesforce also requires through its **Security Review** that object and field level security be enforced in code, thus further burdening inline queries with additional boilerplating.

This chapter introduces a new type of Apex class, the **Selector,** based on **Martin Fowler's Mapper pattern**, which aims to **encapsulate** the SOQL query logic, making it easy to access, maintain, and reuse such logic throughout the application.

The following aspects will be covered in this chapter:

- Introducing the Selector layer pattern
- Implementation design guidelines
- The Selector class template
- Implementing the standard query logic
- Implementing the custom query logic
- Introducing the Selector factory
- Writing tests and the Selector layer
- Calling the Domain layer

Introducing the Selector layer pattern

The following is Martin Fowler's definition of the **Data Mapper layer** from which the **Selector layer** pattern is based (`http://martinfowler.com/eaaCatalog/dataMapper.html`):

> *"A layer of Mappers (473) that moves data between objects and a database while keeping them independent of each other and the Mapper itself."*

In Martin's definition, he is referring to objects as those resulting from the instantiation of classes within an OO language such as Java or Apex. Of course, in the Force.com world, this has a slightly ambiguous meaning, but is more commonly thought of as the Standard or Custom Object holding the record data.

One of the great features of the Apex language is that it automatically injects object types in the language that mirror the definition of the Custom Objects you define. These so-called **SObjects** create a type-safe bond between the code and the database schema, though you can also leverage **Dynamic Apex** and **Dynamic SOQL** to change these references at runtime if needed.

Essentially, SObjects are the native in-memory representation of the data read from the database. Thus, a traditional **Plain Old Java Object (POJO)** approach in Apex is not strictly required to expose the record field data. Additionally, through relationship fields such as `Race__c.Drivers__r`, related records can be accessed without the need for the usual POJO relationship accessor methods or properties.

For this reason, the role of **Apex classes** that represent the Selector layer code described in this chapter is much more focused on encapsulating the application's SOQL queries, promoting **reuse**, **security compliance**, and **data consistency** rather than mapping information from the database into memory.

 One might consider the Domain classes as data wrappers around `SObject`, as they contain a list of SObjects. However, this is not the intent; the Domain class methods purely expose behavioral methods. The `Records` property exposes the `SObject` list so that callers can access the field data in the usual manner.

The following diagram illustrates where Apex classes implementing the Selector layer fit in terms of its interaction and reuse within the Service and Domain layers as well as other execution contexts such as **Batch Apex**. For the most part, it is a layer that exists conceptually below the Service layer (under the Service boundary), though it can be reused from execution contexts that perform database queries, such as Batch Apex and Controllers.

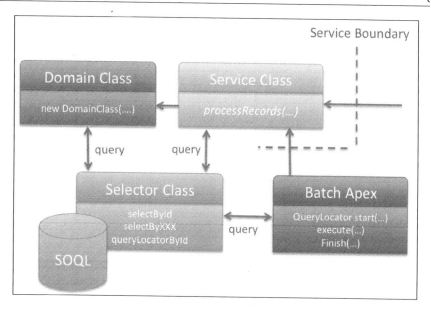

Implementing design guidelines

The methods in the Selector classes encapsulate common SOQL queries made by the application, such as `selectById`, as well as more business-related methods, such as `selectDriversByTeam`. This helps the developers who consume the Selector classes identify the correct methods to use for the business requirement and avoids replication of SOQL queries throughout the application.

Each method also has some standard characteristics in terms of the `SObject` fields populated, regardless of the method called and the security checks implemented. The overall aim is to allow the caller to focus on the record data returned and not how it was read from the database.

Naming conventions

By now, you're starting to get the idea about naming conventions. The Selector classes and methods borrow guidelines from other layers with a few tweaks. Consider the following naming conventions when writing the Selector code:

- **Class names**: In naming a Selector class, it follows the same convention as a Domain class, taking the plural name of the object it is associated with and appending the word `Selector` at the end:

    ○ Some bad examples are `RaceSOQLHelper` and `SOQLHelper`

    ○ Some good examples are `RacesSelector` and `DriversSelector`

- **Method names**: The `select` prefix is a good way to express the shared purpose of the Selector methods, followed by a description of the primary criteria and/or relationships used. As with the Service and Domain methods, avoid repeating terms already used in the class name:

  ○ Some bad examples are `getRecords`, `getDrivers`, `loadDrivers`, `selectDriversById`, and `selectRacesAndContestants`

  ○ Some good examples are `selectById`, `selectByTeam`, `selectByIdWithContestants`, and `selectByIdWithContestantsAndDrivers`

- **Method signatures**: Selector methods typically return a `Map`, `List`, or `QueryLocator` exposing the resulting SObjects, thus supporting the bulkification needs of the platform and other layers such as the Domain class constructors and Batch Apex. Method parameters reflect the parameterized aspects of the `WHERE` clause; again, these should also be bulkified where applicable to do so:

  ○ Some bad examples are:

  ```
  selectById(Id recordId)
  DriverSelector.select(Set<Id> teamIds)
  Database.QueryLocator queryForBatch(Set<Id> ids)
  ```

  ○ Some good examples are:

  ```
  selectById(Set<Id> raceIds)
  selectByTeam(Set<Id> teamIds)
  ```

Bulkification

As you can see, based on the method naming and signature convention examples, as with the Service and Domain layers, it's important to consider that in most cases the caller will want to honor bulkifciation best practices. Make sure that the method return types and parameter types are list types; those such as `Set`, `List`, `Map`, `QueryLocator`, or `Iterator` can be used.

Record order consistency

Quite often, the `order by` clause is overlooked when writing SOQL queries, and this can lead to client/controller developers implementing this themselves. The default ordering of the platform is non-deterministic, though it sometimes appears to reflect the insert order, so the absence of an `order by` clause can often go unnoticed in testing. By using a Selector, you can apply a default ordering to all Selector methods.

Returning `Map<SObject, Id>` instead of `List<SObject>` might seem like a good way to help callers process the information. However, information held in a map is not ordered, so the `order by` clause usage in the Selector is nullified. Given the ease in which maps by SObject ID are created by passing the list into the Map constructor, it's often best to leave this option up to the calling code to wrap or not wrap the list returned.

Querying fields consistently

It is a good practice to avoid requerying the same record(s) more than once within the same Apex execution if it can be avoided. Rather than repeating queries for the same record solely to query different fields, it becomes desirable to factor code such that it can pass the queried data as parameters from one method to another, for example from a Service method to a Domain method.

However, this practice can become problematic, as when using SOQL, the developer must explicitly list the fields needed at the time the statement is executed, typically stating only the fields needed by the most immediate code path ahead.

Later, as the code evolves, the `SObject` data is passed between methods, particularly shared code. Runtime exceptions can occur if an attempt is made to read from a field that was not originally included in the initial SOQL. This results in the same code executing successfully in one scenario but failing in another, due to SOQL statements for the same data being inconsistently expressed.

For example, consider that the `Contestants.awardChampionshipPoint` Domain class method is updated to utilize the `RaceTime__c` field as well as the `RacePosition__c` field. This method is called from the `ContestantsService` and `RaceService` classes. Ignoring the Selector concept for a moment, the following change to `ContestantService` will work just fine to meet this new requirement:

```
Contestants contestants =
    new Contestants(
        [select Id, RacePosition__c, RaceTime__c
          from Contestant__c order by RacePosition__c]);
contestants.awardChampionshipPoints(uow);
```

However, if left unchanged, the following code from the `RaceService` class will cause the same method to fail with an `SObject row was retrieved via SOQL without querying the requested field: Contestant__c.RaceTime__c` exception:

```
List<Contestant__c> contestants = new List<Contestant__c>();
for(Race__c race :
```

```
      [select Id,
          (Select RacePosition__c from Contestants__r)
      from Race__c where Id in :ids])
    contestants.addAll(race.Contestants__r);
  new Contestants(contestants).awardChampionshipPoints(uow);
```

Note that also the order by clause is missing from this example, which means that the **Contestants** objects returned by this second query will be in a different order when passed to the Domain class compared to the first example. There are two possible ways to fix these inconsistencies, though neither is ideal:

- Update the awardChampionshipPoints method to have it perform its own SOQL query to ensure that it always gets the information it needs regardless of what was initially passed into the Domain class constructor. While this is arguably more contained, it is wasteful in regards to SOQL queries and performance.

- Search for SOQL statements across the application code and update the corresponding SOQL logic in each area (including relationship subselects).

Of course, ensuring that both areas have adequate unit and integration testing also somewhat reduces the risk, but neither really helps increase the performance or encourage SOQL reuse. One of the benefits of the Selector pattern is to encapsulate a list of commonly used fields such that all of the methods on the Selector return SObjects populated with a consistent set of fields that can be relied on throughout the application code, as long as the Selector is used to query the records.

 Querying more fields can generally be at odds with the desire to maintain a low **heap** and/or **viewstate size** when querying a large number of records in a single execution context, particularly if the Selector is returning queried data for display on a Visualforce page. In a later section of this chapter, we will see how it is possible to use an Apex data class to represent only the field data queried.

The Selector class template

A Selector class such as the Domain class utilizes inheritance to gain some standard functionality, in this case, the base class delivered through the **FinancialForce.com Enterprise Apex Patterns** library, fflib_SObjectSelector.

A basic example is as follows:

```
public class RacesSelector extends fflib_SObjectSelector
{
    public List<Schema.SObjectField> getSObjectFieldList()
    {
      return new List<Schema.SObjectField> {
          Race__c.Id,
          Race__c.Name,
          Race__c.Status__c,
          Race__c.Season__c,
          Race__c.FastestLapBy__c,
          Race__c.PollPositionLapTime__c,
          Race__c.TotalDNFs__c };
    }

    public Schema.SObjectType getSObjectType()
    {
      return Race__c.sObjectType;
    }
}
```

> The base class uses **Dynamic SOQL** to implement the features described
> in this chapter. One potential disadvantage this can bring is that
> references to the fields are made without the Apex compiler knowing
> about them, and as such, when you attempt to delete or rename fields,
> no warning is given that the given field is already referenced. To avoid
> this, the SObjectField reference to the field is used, which is obtained
> by stating the SObject name followed by the field name separated by a
> period. This is somewhat like a static property on the SObject type. This
> approach ensures that the platform knows the class is referencing the
> fields, even though they are being used in a dynamic SOQL context.

With this minimal example, the following standard query can be made by leveraging
the selectSObjectsById base class method. This method takes the information
provided by the preceding methods and constructs a SOQL query dynamically
and executes it via Database.executeQuery:

```
List<Race__c> races = (List<Race__c>)
    new RacesSelector().selectSObjectsById(raceIds);
```

Note that the `fflib_SObjectSelector.selectSObjectsById`
base class method performs a number of features, described later in
this chapter, including checking the user object security for read access
to the object and throwing an exception if they don't have access. Also,
note that an instance of the Selector was created but was not actually
stored using an instance permits base class behavior to be inherited.
Additional benefits of using instances of Selectors is covered later in
this chapter when we discuss **Selector factories** and testing.

The preceding Selector method example dynamically creates the following SOQL.
As we progress through this chapter, how this is done will become more clear:

```
SELECT
   Name, TotalDNFs__c, Status__c, Season__c, Id,
   PollPositionLapTime__c, FastestLapBy__c
FROM Race__c
WHERE id in :idSet ORDER BY Name
```

The following screenshot shows the base class methods of the `fflib_`
`SObjectSelector` class available to your Selector methods and also those that can be
overridden. Note that the `getSObjectType` and `getSObjectFieldList` methods are
abstract and thus must be implemented as minimum, as per the previous example.

```
▼ ⨀ˣ fflib_SObjectSelector
    ▲ᴬ getSObjectType()
    ▲ᴬ getSObjectFieldList()
    ●ᶜ fflib_SObjectSelector()
    ●ᶜ fflib_SObjectSelector(Boolean)
    ●ⱽ getSObjectFieldSetList()
    ●ⱽ getOrderBy()
    ● getFieldListBuilder()
    ● setFieldListBuilder(fflib_StringBuilder.FieldListBuilder)
    ● getFieldListString()
    ● getRelatedFieldListString(String)
    ● getSObjectName()
    ● selectSObjects ById(Set<Id>)
    ● queryLocator ById(Set<Id>)
    ● assertIsAccessible()
```

Implementing the standard query logic

The previous Selector usage example required a cast of the list returned to a list of `Race__c` objects, which is not ideal. To improve this, you can easily add a new method to the class to provide a more specific version of the base class method, as follows:

```
public List<Race__c> selectById(Set<Id> raceIds)
{
    return (List<Race__c>) selectSObjectsById(raceIds);
}
```

Thus, the usage code now looks like this:

```
List<Race__c> races =
    new RacesSelector().selectById(raceIds);
```

Standard features of the selectSObjectsById method

In addition to forming the field list used in the SOQL query, the base class and the `selectSObjectById` method used also provide additional functionality that would normally have to be replicated each time this section outlines these features. Some of these are also available to custom Selector methods you write.

You can, of course, extend the standard features of this base class further. Perhaps there is something you want all your queries to consider, a common field or aspect to your schema design, or a feature that is common to most of your selectors. In this case, create your own base class and have your selectors extend that, as follows.

```
public abstract class ApplicationSelector
    extends fflib_SObjectSelector
{
    // Add your common methods here
}
public class RacesSelector
    extends ApplicationSelector
{
    // Methods using methods from both base classes
}
```

Security

The `selectSObjectsById` method automatically calls the `assertIsAccessible` method, which despite its name, does not perform a `Test.assert` call, but checks the user's object security settings to determine whether they are permitted to read records from the object if the `fflib_SObjectDomain.DomainException` exception is not thrown. You are required to call the `assertIsAccessible` method if you implement custom Selector methods as described in the upcoming sections.

 The use of this feature ensures that queries comply with the Salesforce Security Review process with respect to **Object Read Security** only.

Ordering

As mentioned in the conventions, having a default order to records is important to avoid the random non-deterministic behavior of the platform SOQL engine. The `selectSObjectById` base class method calls the `getOrderBy` method to determine which field(s) to use to order the records returned from the Selector.

The default behavior is to use the `Name` field (if available, otherwise `CreatedByDate` is used). As such, the previous usage is already ordering by `Name` without further coding. If you wish to change this, override the method as follows. This example is used by the `ContestantsSelector` class to ensure that contestants are always queried in the order of season, race, and their race position:

```
public override String getOrderBy()
{
  return
    'Race__r.Season__r.Name, Race__r.Name, RacePosition__c';
}
```

Later in this chapter, you will see how custom Selector methods can be constructed; these have the option of using the `getOrderBy` method. This allows some methods to use a different `order by` clause other than the default if you wish to do so.

Field Sets

As was discussed in a previous chapter, utilization of the Field Sets platform feature is the key to ensure that your application is strongly aligned with the customization capabilities that your application's users expect. However, you might be wondering what it has to do with querying data? Well, even though most of our discussions around this feature will focus on the use of it in a Visualforce context, the additional custom fields added in the subscriber org still need to be queried for them to be displayed; otherwise, an exception will occur just the same as if you had failed to query a packaged field.

To use this feature, you need to override the `getSObjectFieldSetList` method and construct the Selector with the `includeFieldSetFields` parameter. The default constructor sets this parameter to false so that in general, the **FieldSet** fields are not included. The following example assumes a Field Set on the **Race** object called `SeasonOverview` (included in the code of this chapter):

The following code illustrates the configuration of this feature (note that the logic in the base class also ensures that if the subscriber adds your own packaged fields to the Field Set, such fields are only added to the SOQL statement field list once):

```
public RacesSelector()
{
    super();
}
public RacesSelector(Boolean includeFieldSetFields)
{
    super(includeFieldSetFields);
}

public override List<Schema.FieldSet> getSObjectFieldSetList()
{
  return new List<Schema.FieldSet>
    { SObjectType.Race__c.FieldSets.SeasonOverview };
}
```

Multi-Currency

As discussed in *Chapter 2, Leveraging Platform Features,* enabling and referencing certain platform features can create dependencies on your package that require your customers to also enable those features prior to installation, and this might not always be desirable. One such feature is **Multi-Currency**. Once this is enabled, every object gains a `CurrencyISOCode` field; it then also appears on layouts, reports, and so on. Salesforce ensures that subscribers are fully aware of the implications before enabling it.

If you want to leverage it in your application (but do not think it will be something that all your customers will require), you have the option to reference this field using Dynamic Apex and Dynamic SOQL. It is in this latter area that the `fflib_SObjectSelector` base class provides some assistance.

 You might want to consider the approach described here when working with Personal Accounts, as certain fields on the **Account** object are only present if this feature is enabled.

If you explicitly listed the `CurrencyISOCode` field in your `getSObjectFieldList` method, you will therefore bind your code and the package that contains it to this platform feature. Instead, what the base class does is use the `UserInfo.isMultiCurrencyOrganization` method to dynamically include this field in the SOQL query that it executes. Note that you still need to utilize Dynamic Apex to retrieve the field value, as shown in the following code:

```
List<Team__c> teams = (List<Team__c>)
    new TeamsSelector().selectSObjectsById(teamIds);
for(Team__c team : teams)
{
    String teamCurrency =
        UserInfo.isMultiCurrencyOrganization() ?
            (String) team.get('CurrencyIsoCode') :
            UserInfo.getDefaultCurrency();
}
```

You might want to put a common method in your own Domain base class that encapsulates the preceding turnery operation into a single method, for example, by creating methods such as `Map<Id, String> getCurrencyCodes()`, which can be used as follows:

```
public override onBeforeInsert()
{
    Map<Id, String> currencies = getCurrencyCodes();
    for(Team__c team : (List<Team__c>) Records)
    {
        String teamCurrency = currencies.get(team.Id);
    }
}
```

Implementing the custom query logic

If we take a look at the implementation of the `fflib_SObjectSelector.selectSObjectById` base class method (at the time of writing this book), it is quite simple and gives a template as to the way we can implement custom Selector methods; it also highlights other base class methods we can use:

```
public List<SObject> selectSObjectsById(Set<Id> idSet)
{
    assertIsAccessible();
    return Database.query(buildQuerySObjectById());
}

private String buildQuerySObjectById()
{
    return String.format(
        'SELECT {0} FROM {1} WHERE id in :idSet ORDER BY {2}',
        new List<String>
            {getFieldListString(),getSObjectName(),getOrderBy()});
}
```

The `getFieldListString` method calls the `getSObjectFieldList` and `getSObjectFieldSetList` methods implemented in the preceding code. It basically takes the `SObjectField` lists that result from these methods and builds a single comma-delimited list of fields ready to be inserted into the SOQL query string. Also, note that the `assertIsAccessible` method is called before making the query.

The FinancialForce.com Apex Enterprise Patterns library used in this book has been enhanced around the Selector pattern since this chapter was written. This enhancement introduces a powerful new way to build dynamic SOQL statements, using the new `fflib_QueryFactory` class (sadly outside the current scope of this chapter). The `fflib_SObjectSelector` class has been updated to leverage this new approach to provide the developer writing their custom Selector methods with an instance of this factory. This provides an alternative option to using the `String.format` approach shown in the following examples. However, the following examples and best practices are still valid and are backwards compatible with these new enhancements.

A basic custom Selector method

Let's look first at a basic example, which queries `Driver__c` based on the team they are assigned to. As per the guidelines, the parameters are bulkified and allow you to query for drivers across multiple teams if needed (something that is likely in a Team Apex Trigger context):

```
public List<Driver__c> selectByTeam(Set<Id> teamIds)
{
  assertIsAccessible();
  return Database.query(
    String.format(
      'SELECT {0} FROM {1} WHERE Team__c in :teamIds ' +
      'ORDER BY {2}',
        new List<String
          {getFieldListString(),
           getSObjectName(),
           getOrderBy()}));
}
```

The `assertIsAccessible` method is called to perform the security check needed. The SOQL query is constructed using the `String.format` method parameter replacement; this helps to keep the SOQL query readable but allows for the dynamic aspects to be introduced at runtime.

By using the base class methods for the field list, object name, and `order by` clause, this Selector method behaves consistently in terms of the fields populated and the order of the records returned.

A custom Selector method with sub-select

In the following example, the querying being made uses a **sub-select** to also include child records (in this case, **Contestants** within **Race**). The key thing here is that the `RacesSelector` method (shown in the following code) reuses an instance of the `ContestantsSelector` class to access its field list and perform the security checking:

```
public List<Race__c>
    selectByIdWithContestants(Set<Id> raceIds)
{
    assertIsAccessible();
    ContestantsSelector contestantSelector =
        new ContestantsSelector();
    contestantSelector.assertIsAccessible();

    return (List<Race__c>) Database.query(
        String.format(
            'select {0}, ' +
                '(select {1} ' +
                'from Contestants__r order by {2})' +
            'from {2} ' +
            'where id in :raceIds ' +
            'order by {3}',
                new List<String>{
                    getFieldListString(),
                    contestantSelector.getFieldListString(),
                    contestantSelector.getOrderBy(),
                    getSObjectName(),
                    getOrderBy()}));
}
```

 Note that the `Contestants__r` reference in the preceding example is dependent on the developer, considering an appropriate name when creating the Lookup field initially. This can sometimes get overlooked as Salesforce defaults this field. The default, however, is not always a valid description of the relationship, especially if multiple lookups to the same object exist. Relationship names cannot be changed once the package has been uploaded in the release mode.

This approach ensures that no matter how a list of `Contestant__c` records are queried (directly or as part of a sub-select query), the fields are populated consistently. The `getOrderBy` method on `ContestantSelector` is also used to ensure that even though the records are being returned as part of a sub-select, the default ordering of **Contestant** records is also maintained.

Let's take another look at the example used earlier to illustrate how this pattern has avoided the dangers of inconsistent querying. Although the `Contestant__c` records are queried from two different selectors, `RacesSelector` and `ContestantsSelector`, the result in terms of fields populated is the same due to the reuse of the `ContestantsSelector` class in the preceding implementation.

The following example shows the standard `selectById` method being used to query **Contestants** to pass to the `Contestants` Domain class constructor, as part of the Service layer implementation to award championship points:

```
List<Contestant__c> contestants =
    new ContestantsSelector().selectById(contestantIds);
new Contestants(contestants).awardChampionshipPoints(uow);
```

The following alternative example shows the custom `selectByIdWithContestants` method on `RaceSelector` being used to query **Races** and **Contestants** to pass to the `Contestants` Domain class constructor to achieve the same result:

```
List<Contestant__c> contestants = new List<Contestant__c>();
for(Race__c race :
  new RacesSelector().selectByIdWithContestants(raceIds))
    contestants.addAll(race.Contestants__r);
new Contestants(contestants).awardChampionshipPoints(uow);
```

In either of these two examples, the fields and ordering of the records are consistent, despite the way in which they have been queried, either as a direct query or sub-select. This gives the developer more confidence in using the most optimum approach to query the records needed at the time.

The `selectByIdWithContestants` method generates the following SOQL:

```
select
  Name, TotalDNFs__c, Status__c, Season__c, Id,
  PollPositionLapTime__c, FastestLapBy__c,
  (select
    Qualification1LapTime__c, ChampionshipPoints__c,
    Driver__c, GridPosition__c, Qualification3LapTime__c,
    RacePosition__c, Name, DNF__c, RaceTime__c,
    Id, DriverRace__c, Qualification2LapTime__c, Race__c
  from Contestants__r
  order by Race__r.Season__r.Name, Race__r.Name,
    RacePosition__c)
  from Race__c where id in :raceIds order by Name
```

A custom Selector method with related fields

In addition to querying child records, related records can also be queried using the SOQL field dot notation. This provides an additional way to optimize the querying of additional record information, along with having to make an additional query.

The following is an example of a custom Selector method for the ContestantsSelector class, where **Contestant** records are queried along with the related **Driver** record. The resulting Contestant__c objects expose the Driver__r field, which provides an instance of Driver__c populated with the Driver__c fields specified in DriversSelector:

```
public List<Race__c> selectByIdWithDriver(Set<Id> driverIds)
{
  assertIsAccessible();

  DriversSelector driversSelector = new DriversSelector();
  driversSelector.assertIsAccessible();

  return Database.query(
    String.format(
      'SELECT {0},{1} FROM {1} WHERE Id in :driverIds ' +
      'ORDER BY {2}',
        new List<String>{
      getFieldListString(),
      driversSelector.getRelatedFieldListString('Driver__r'),
      getSObjectName(),
      getOrderBy()}));
}
```

Thus, the following DriversSelector and ContestantsSelector usage examples return consistently populated Driver__c records, which is important to the logic contained with in the Domain class's Drivers.verifyCompliance method. This flexibility allows for the most optimum way of querying Driver__c records and safer reuse of the Domain class method, regardless of how the records where queried.

This first example constructs the Drivers domain class with results from the standard selectById method on the DriversSelector class:

```
List<Driver__c> drivers =
  new DriversSelector().selectById(driverIds);
List<ComplianceService.VerifyResult> results =
  new Drivers(drivers).verifyCompliance();
```

This second example achieves the same, but queries the **Drivers** records via the custom Selector method, `selectByIdWithDriver`, on the `ContestantsSelector` class:

```
List<Driver__c> drivers = new List<Driver__c>();
List<Contestant__c> contestants =
  new ContestantsSelector().selectByIdWithDriver(contIds);
for(Contestant__c contestant : contestants)
  drivers.add(contestant.Driver__r);
List<ComplianceService.VerifyResult> results =
  new Drivers(drivers).verifyCompliance();
```

Again, both of these examples have shown that even when using related fields in SOQL, the resulting records can be kept in alignment with the desired fields as expressed by the selectors. The `selectByIdWithDriver` method generates the following SOQL:

```
SELECT
  Qualification1LapTime__c, ChampionshipPoints__c, Driver__c,
  GridPosition__c, Qualification3LapTime__c, RacePosition__c,
  Name, DNF__c, RaceTime__c, Id, DriverRace__c,
  Qualification2LapTime__c, Race__c,
  Driver__r.FIASuperLicense__c, Driver__r.Name,
  Driver__r.Id, Driver__r.Team__c
FROM Contestant__c
WHERE Id in :driverIds
ORDER BY Name
```

A custom Selector method with a custom data set

SOQL has a very rich dot notation to traverse relationship (lookup) fields to access other fields on related records within a single query. To obtain the following information in a tabular form, it needs to traverse up and down the relationships across many of the objects in the **FormulaForce** application object schema:

- The season name
- The race name
- The race position
- The driver's name
- The car name

First, let's consider the following SOQL and then look at how it and the data it returns can be encapsulated in the `ContestantsSelector` class. Note that the common `order by` clause is also applied here as was the case in the previous example:

```
select
    Race__r.Season__r.Name,
    Race__r.Name,RacePosition__c,
    Driver__r.Name,
    Driver__r.Team__r.Name,
    Car__r.Name
from
    Contestant__c
where
    Race__c in :raceIds
order by
    Race__r.Season__r.Name, Race__r.Name, RacePosition__c
```

This query will result in partially populated `Contestant__c` objects, not only that, but relationship fields will also expose partially populated `Season__c`, `Car__c`, and `Driver__c` records. Thus, these are highly specialized instances of records to simply return into the calling code path.

The following code shows an alternative to the preceding query using a new `ContestantsSelector` method. The biggest difference from the previous ones is that it returns a **custom Apex data type** and not the `Contestant__c` object. You can also see that it's much easier to see what information is available and what is not:

```
for(List<ContestantsSelector.Summary> summaries :
        new ContestantsSelector().
        selectByRaceIdWithContestantSummary(raceIds).values())
    for(ContestantsSelector.Summary summary : summaries)
        System.debug(
            summary.Season + ' ' +
            summary.Race + ' ' +
            summary.Position + ' ' +
            summary.Driver + ' ' +
            summary.Team + ' ' +
            summary.Car);
```

Depending on your data, this would output something like the following debug:

```
USER_DEBUG|[26]|DEBUG|2014 Spa 1 Lewis Hamilton Mercedes MP4-29
USER_DEBUG|[26]|DEBUG|2014 Spa 2 Rubens Barrichello Williams FW36
```

The Selector method returns a new **Apex inner class** that uses Apex properties to explicitly expose only the field information queried, thus creating a clearer contract between the Selector method and the caller. It is now not possible to reference the information that has not been queried and would result in runtime errors when code attempts to reference fields that are not queried. The following shows an Apex inner class that the Selector uses to explicitly expose only the information queried by a custom Selector method:

```
public class Summary
{
  private Contestant__c contestant;
  public String Season {
    get { return contestant.Race__r.Season__r.Name; } }
  public String Race {
    get { return contestant.Race__r.Name; } }
  public Decimal Position {
    get { return contestant.RacePosition__c; } }
  public String Driver {
    get { return contestant.Driver__r.Name; } }
  public String Team {
    get { return contestant.Driver__r.Team__r.Name; } }
  public String Car {
    get { return contestant.Car__r.Name; } }
  private Summary(Contestant__c contestant)
    { this.contestant = contestant; }
}
```

The `Summary` class contains an instance of the query data privately, so no additional heap is used up. It exposes the information as read only and makes the constructor private, indicating that only instances of this class are available through the `ContestantsSelector` class.

Shown in the following code is the Selector method that performs the actual query, utilizing as before other Selectors for the related objects, but this time only so far as to confirm that the security requirements are met by the running user:

```
public Map<Id, List<Summary>>
  selectByRaceIdWithContestantSummary(Set<Id> raceIds)
{
  assertIsAccessible();
  new DriversSelector().assertIsAccessible();
  new CarsSelector().assertIsAccessible();
  new TeamsSelector().assertIsAccessible();
  Map<Id, List<Summary>> summariesByRaceId =
    new Map<Id, List<Summary>>();
  for(Contestant__c contestant :
```

```
Database.query(
  String.format(
    'select {0} from {1} '   +
    'where Race__c in :raceIds order by {2}',
      new List<String>{
        String.join(
          new List<String> {
            'Race__r.Season__r.Name',
            'Race__r.Name',
            'RacePosition__c',
            'Driver__r.Name',
            'Driver__r.Team__r.Name',
            'Car__r.Name' }, ','),
        getSObjectName(),
        getOrderBy()})))
{
  List<Summary> summaries =
    summariesByRaceId.get(contestant.Race__c);
  if(summaries==null)
    summariesByRaceId.put(contestant.Race__c,
      summaries = new List<Summary>());
  summaries.add(new Summary(contestant));
}
return summariesByRaceId;
}
```

Combining Apex data types with SObject types

It is possible to combine Apex data types with SObject data types in responses from Selector methods. So long as when you return SObject data types, they are populated according to the fields indicated by the corresponding Selector.

For example, let's say we want to return an entire Driver__c record associated with the **Contestant** object, instead of just the **Driver** name. The change to the Summary Apex class will be to expose the queried Driver__c record, which is safe as it has been populated in accordance with the DriversSelector. The following code shows how the Summary class can be modified to expose the Driver__c record as queried in the custom Selector method:

```
public class Summary
{
  public Driver__c Driver {
    get { return contestant.Driver__r; } }
  ...
}
```

Now a `DriversSelector` instance is retained in order to obtain the field list, which is injected into the generated SOQL query in place of the `Driver__r.Name` field:

```
Database.query(
  String.format(
    'select {0}, {1} from {2} '  +
    'where Race__c in :raceIds order by {3}',
      new List<String>{
        String.join(
          new List<String> {
            'Race__r.Season__r.Name',
            'Race__r.Name',
            'RacePosition__c',
            'Driver__r.Team__r.Name',
            'Car__r.Name' }, ','),
        driversSelector.
          getRelatedFieldListString('Driver__r'),
        getSObjectName(),
        getOrderBy()}})))
```

SOSL and Aggregate SOQL queries

SOQL is not the only way to query information from the database. Force.com also provides a power **Salesforce Object Search Language (SOSL)** facility. Like SOQL, this returns SObjects. While this chapter has not covered this variation in depth, the use of Selector methods encapsulating SOSL is appropriate and in fact provides a good abstract from the caller, allowing the developer of the Selector to use SOQL or SOSL in future without impacting the callers.

Likewise, **Aggregate SOQL** queries are also good candidates to encapsulate in Selector methods. However, in these cases, consider using Apex native data types (for example, a list of values) or lists of custom Apex data types to expose the aggregate information.

 The consolidated source code for this book, available in the `master` branch of the GitHub repository, contains a `RaceDataSelector` class. Within this class is a custom Selector method, `selectAnaysisGroupByRaceName`, that demonstrates the use of a SOQL aggregate query.

Introducing the Selector factory

The last chapter introduced the concept of a **Domain factory**, which was used to dynamically construct Domain class instances implementing a **common Apex Interface** in order to implement the compliance framework.

The following code is used in the `ComplianceService.verify` method's implementation, making no reference at all to a Selector class to query the records needed to construct the applicable Domain class:

```
fflib_SObjectDomain domain =
    Application.Domain.newInstance(recordIds);
```

So, how did the Domain factory retrieve the records in order to pass them to the underlying Domain class constructor? The answer is that it internally used another factory implementation called the **Selector factory**.

As with the Domain factory, the Selector factory resides within the `Application` class as a static instance, exposed via the `Selector` static class member, as follows:

```
public class Application
{
    public static final SelectorFactory Selector =
        new SelectorFactory(
            new Map<SObjectType, Type> {
                Team__c.SObjectType => TeamsSelector.class,
                Race__c.SObjectType => RacesSelector.class,
                Car__c.SObjectType => CarsSelector.class,
                Driver__c.SObjectType => DriversSelector.class,
                Contestant__c.SObjectType =>
                    ContestantsSelector.class });
}
```

As with the `DomainFactory` class, a full description of the `SelectorFactory` class is beyond the scope of this chapter, though you can explore the code for yourself afterwards to learn more about how it works.

SelectorFactory methods

The SelectorFactory class has two methods on it: newInstance and selectById.
The following code illustrates both these methods by showing two equivalent usage
examples to retrieve records given a set of IDs:

```
List<Contestant__c> contestants =
    Application.Selector.selectById(contestantIds);

List<Contestant__c> contestants =
    Application.Selector.newInstance(Contestant__c.SObjectType)
        .selectSObjectsById(contestantIds);
```

As you can see from the preceding code, the selectById method provides a
shortcut to access the generic selectSObjectById method from the fflib_
SObjectSelector base class for a given Selector class. It offers a cleaner way of
querying records in the standard way without having to know the Apex class name
for the Selector.

 The method internally uses Id.getSObjectType (on the
first ID that is passed in) to look up the Selector class through
the map defined previously and instantiate it (via Type.
newInstance).

So, you might ask why would you use the newInstance method instead of just
instantiating directly via the new operator in the Selector class as per the examples
earlier in this chapter? The following section goes into the use and use cases around
this method in more detail, followed by an example using the Selector factory in a
testing scenario.

Usage and reasons for the newInstance method

The newInstance method returns an fflib_SObjectSelector instance that needs
to be cast to the desired Selector class before any custom methods can be called.
However, as you can see in the following example, making the cast can look a little
ugly compared to the more direct approach that we have seen used throughout this
chapter so far:

```
List<Contestant__c> contestantsWithDriver =
    ( ( ContestantsSelector )
        Application.Selector.
        newInstance(Contestant__c.SObjectType) ).
    selectByIdWithDriver(contestantIds);
```

A better approach is to put a factory helper method on the Selector class itself:

```
public static ContestantsSelector newInstance()
{
   return (ContestantsSelector)
     Application.Selector.
       newInstance(Contestant__c.SObjectType);
}
```

With this method in place, the preceding example now looks cleaner and less ugly, as follows:

```
List<Contestant__c> contestantsWithDriver =
   ContestantsSelector.newInstance().
     selectByIdWithDriver(contestantIds);
```

So far, the examples in this chapter have been constructing Selector classes using the new operator in Apex, by explicitly referencing the class to be constructed. This has worked quite well so far, so why would you want to use the indirection of the Selector factory newInstance method? You might want to consider the following:

- **Caching**: The factory implementation used in this chapter exposes a newInstance method. However, a getInstance method can also be written to effectively cache in the execution scope of the Selector instance. This will allow the Selector author to cache SOQL query results between Selector method calls. However, be careful with this kind of strategy though as cache implementations are not simple; you must consider your cache invalidation logic carefully. Do not use caching as a workaround to poorly bulkified code.

- **Mocking**: You can often feel that Apex tests are more like **integration tests** as they typically require all application data to be in place on the database before invoking the desired class behavior to be tested. Using a Selector factory is an alternative to this; in much the same way the Test.setMock method provides a means to mock responses from HTTP callouts, a mocking implementation around Selectors can be applied in certain use cases to mock the results from SOQL queries and allow developers to focus on testing the immediate class, such as an Apex custom controller.

In the final section of this chapter, we will explore further how the Selector factory can be used to register mock implementations of Selector classes to make writing tests for areas of the application that consume Selectors less complex in terms of the traditional record data setup required.

Writing tests and the Selector layer

When writing tests specifically for a Selector class method, the process is almost as per the standard Apex testing guidelines; insert the data you need to support the queries, call the Selector methods, and assert the results returned. You can review some of the Selector tests included in this chapter.

If you have implemented Selector methods that return `QueryLocator` instances (for use by Batch Apex callers), you can still assert the results of these methods. Use the `iterator` method to obtain `QueryLocatorIterator`, then call the `next` and `hasNext` methods to return the results to pass to your assert statements.

Of course, other Apex tests around the **Controllers**, **Batch Apex**, **Domain**, and **Service** layers might also invoke the Selector methods indirectly, thus providing code coverage, but not necessarily testing every aspect of the Selector classes.

Try to ensure that your Apex tests test the layers and functional components of the application as much as possible in isolation to ensure that the existing and future callers don't run into issues.

As highlighted previously, often writing more isolated Apex tests can be made harder due to the fact that the code being tested often requires records to be set up in the database. By leveraging the Selector factory option described earlier, a **mocking** approach can be taken to the Selector methods, which can help make writing more isolated and varied component or class level tests easier.

If you're not familiar with the mocking approach when developing the test code, this `http://en.wikipedia.org/wiki/Mock_object` link is a useful introduction, though there are many other sites on the Internet describing its benefits. The following is an extract from the Wikipedia page:

> *"In object-oriented programming, mock objects are simulated objects that mimic the behavior of real objects in controlled ways. A programmer typically creates a mock object to test the behavior of some other object, in much the same way that a car designer uses a crash test dummy to simulate the dynamic behavior of a human in vehicle impacts.*
>
> *In a unit test, mock objects can simulate the behavior of complex, real objects and are therefore useful when a real object is impractical or impossible to incorporate into a unit test. If an actual object has any of the following characteristics, it may be useful to use a mock object in its place."*

Mocking Selectors

In this section, we will write a test for an **Apex Visualforce Controller** that invokes the `ContestantsSelector.selectByRaceIdWithContestantSummary` method. Ordinarily, this method requires all the current custom objects in the application to be populated with records. Assuming that we have other tests covering the broader integration of the layers and components in the system, testing the Domain logic for these objects is not something these more focused test methods for this controller should be interested in.

By creating a mock implementation of the Selector method to return the test data defined in memory, we can test the behavior of the controller without having to insert the data physically into the custom objects. The process is as follows:

1. Ensure that the code to be tested is using the `Application.Selector.newInstance` approach to obtain instances of the required Selector classes.

2. Apply the `virtual` keyword and the `@TestVisible` attribute to the class and methods you want to mock or access from the test context.

3. In the test class, create an inner class that extends the Selector class and overrides the virtual methods.

4. Before invoking the code to be tested, call the `Application.Selector.setMock` method.

Step 1 – using the Application.Selector.newInstance approach

The following Visualforce Controller action method uses the factory helper method, `ContestantsSelector.newInstance`, as described earlier in this chapter. Note that, as this examples shows, Selectors can be useful outside the Domain and Selector layers when querying information in Batch Apex or Controllers:

```
public PageReference loadSummary()
{
  try {
    // Query summaries for this race
    Id raceId = standardController.getId();
    Map<Id, List<ContestantsSelector.Summary>>
      summariesByRaceId =
        ContestantsSelector.newInstance().
          selectByRaceIdWithContestantSummary(
            new Set<Id> { raceId });

    // Populate view state
```

```
        if(summariesByRaceId.containsKey(raceId))
          Summary = summariesByRaceId.get(raceId);
        else
          ApexPages.addMessage(
            new ApexPages.Message(ApexPages.Severity.Info,
              'No summaries for this race'));
      }
    catch (Exception e)
    {
      ApexPages.addMessages(e);
    }
    return null;
  }
```

Step 2 – applying virtual and @TestVisible

By applying the `virtual` keyword to the Selector class, it allows your mock class, created here, to override the behavior of the methods, replacing them with whatever you like within a test context:

```
public virtual class ContestantsSelector
  extends fflib_SObjectSelector
{
  public virtual Map<Id, List<Summary>>
    selectByRaceIdWithContestantSummary(Set<Id> raceIds)
  {
```

Depending on the Selector method you're mocking, the following step might not be necessary. In this case, however, we need to expose the private constructor for the `Summary` class using the `@TestVisible` annotation, which ensures that it becomes accessible to the test code but continues to remain inaccessible to non-test code. Only the portion of the class that has changed is shown as follows:

```
public class Summary
{
  @TestVisible
  private Summary(Contestant__c contestant) {
    this.contestant = contestant; }
```

Step 3 – creating a mock Selector class

The following mock test class (residing as an inner class within the applicable test class) extends the `ContestantSelector` class and overrides the appropriate Selector method used by the controller. As this is the test code, it has access to the private `Summary` class constructor:

```
public class ContestantsSelectorMock
    extends ContestantsSelector
{
    public override Map<Id, List<ContestantsSelector.Summary>>
        selectByRaceIdWithContestantSummary(Set<Id> raceIds)
    {
        // Assert this is our test Race ID
        Id raceId = (Id) raceIds.iterator().next();
        System.assertEquals(TEST_RACE_ID, raceId);
        // Create mock database record
        Contestant__c contestant = new Contestant__c();
        contestant.RacePosition__c = 1;
        contestant.Race__r =
            new Race__c(Name = 'Spa',
                Season__r =
                    new Season__c(Name = '2014'));
        contestant.Driver__r =
            new Driver__c(Name = 'Lewis Hamilton',
                Team__r =
                    new Team__c(Name = 'Mercedes'));
        contestant.Car__r =
            new Car__c(Name = 'MP4-29');
        // Return mock response
        return new Map<Id, List<ContestantsSelector.Summary>>
            { raceId => new List<ContestantsSelector.Summary> {
                new ContestantsSelector.Summary(contestant) } };
    }
}
```

Note that the following mock implementation takes the opportunity to assert that the ID of the race passed into the method by the caller (the controller logic being tested) is in fact the same ID used in the test and that TEST_RACE_ID is defined as a static variable in the test with a dummy static ID.

Step 4 – writing a test with Application.Selector. setMock

Finally, let's write the test method in the `RaceSummaryControllerTest` class, which starts by registering a mock instance of the `ContestantSelectorMock` inner class defined previously. This instructs the **Selector factory** to utilize this instance of the Selector rather than create a new one using the `ConestantSelector` class, which would normally execute a SOQL query, thus requiring the physical creation of test records this type of testing is not interested in.

After the mock has been set, the test method and the execution of the code that follows is according to the normal Apex testing principles. Notice that `TEST_RACE_ID` is passed into the controller and is also asserted within the mock Selector method, thus testing the controller's ability to interact with the Selector. Also, note that the following test code has no DML statements inserting test data records:

```
private static Id TEST_RACE_ID = 'a01b00000051mgk';

@IsTest
private static void testLoadSummaries()
{
    // Set mock implementation of ContestantsSelector
    Application.Selector.setMock(new ContestantsSelectorMock());

    // Invoke controller method to load summaries
    RaceSummaryController controller =
        new RaceSummaryController(
            new ApexPages.StandardController(
                new Race__c(Id = TEST_RACE_ID)));
    PageReference pageRef = controller.loadSummary();

    // Assert view state from controller
    System.assertEquals(null, pageRef);
    System.assertEquals(1, controller.Summary.size());
    System.assertEquals('2014', controller.Summary[0].Season);
    System.assertEquals('Spa', controller.Summary[0].Race);
    System.assertEquals(1,  controller.Summary[0].Position);
    System.assertEquals('Lewis Hamilton',
        controller.Summary[0].Driver);
    System.assertEquals('Mercedes', controller.Summary[0].Team);
    System.assertEquals('MP4-29', controller.Summary[0].Car);
}
```

Which type of Selector methods cannot be mocked?

Most Selector methods can be mocked using this approach, even those mentioned previously, returning fields that are populated on related records through dot-notation. Mocking Selectors provides a powerful way to write more focused and varied tests without the database overhead around Apex Controllers, Service classes, and Domain classes.

However, sadly it is currently not possible to mock `QueryLocator`, so Selector methods returning these are not compatible with mocking. Also, Selector methods that return child records via child relationship fields are currently not compatible either, such as the `RacesSelector.selectByIdWithContestants` method.

This is because the child relationship fields on SObjects are read only to Apex and are currently only populated by SOQL, so it is not possible to populate them in memory. The following example demonstrates this limitation:

```
Race__c testRace = new Race__c();
testRace.Contestants__r = new List<Contestant__c>();
```

If you try this, it gives the `Field is not writeable: fforce__Contestants__r` error when you attempt to save the code.

Updating the FormulaForce package

Review the updated code supplied with this chapter and update your **packaging** org. Perform another upload and install the package in your testing org. The following screenshot highlights the new Field Set component added in this chapter:

▼ Resources (1)

Action	Component Name	Parent Object	Component Type	Installation Notes
Create	Season Overview	Race	Field Set	This is a brand new component.

Summary

The Selector pattern provides a powerful layer of encapsulation for some critical logic in your application. It also enforces best practices around security and provides a more consistent and reliable basis for code dealing with the `SObject` data.

Selectors can also take on the responsibility and concern for platform features such as **Multi-Currency** and **Field Sets**. Ultimately allowing the caller, be that the Service, Domain, or even Apex Controllers, or Batch Apex to focus on their responsibilities and concerns, this leads to cleaner code that is easier to maintain and evolve.

With the introduction of the Selector factory, we provide a shortcut to access this layer in the form of the `Application.Selector.selectById` and `Application.Selector.newInstance` methods, opening up potential for other patterns such as caching. Also, a mocking framework was demonstrated that permitted additional, more focused, and varied tests to be written around the consumers of the Selector layer without the need for complex test data set up on the database.

I'd like to close this set of chapters with a simple but expressive diagram that shows how the Service layer code turns with the help of the Domain and Selector layers. These three patterns on Force.com help add value to the developer through consistency and also support best practices around bulkification and code reuse.

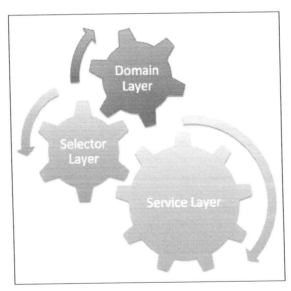

While this is the last chapter focusing on a Force.com implementation of Martin Fowler's Enterprise Application Architecture patterns, we will revisit the role of the Selector in a later chapter and focus on Batch Apex as well as continue to leverage our Service layer in later chapters that discuss the application integration.

8
User Interface

If I was to list all the technologies that have come and gone more often in my career, I would say it has to be those that impact the end user experience. Being a UI technology developer is a tough business; the shift from desktop to web to mobile to device agnostic has shaken things up, and this situation is still ongoing! This means that the investment in this part of your application architecture is important, as is the logic you put in it. Putting the wrong kind of logic in your client tier can result in inconsistent behavior and, at worst, expensive rework if you decide to shift client technology in the future.

This chapter discusses the various user interface options for Force.com-based applications, including the Salesforce standard UI, Visualforce, and also using third-party-rich client frameworks, contrasting their architecture's pros and cons with respect to platform features and performance. Also covered is how to use the **Service layer** and the **Domain layer** patterns, to ensure that your users' interaction with your application is consistent, regardless of the user interface approach.

We will look at general best practices for developing scalable Visualforce pages and the types of technologies available as part of this, before highlighting an upcoming UI device-agnostic technology from Salesforce known as **Aura**. We will cover the following topics in this chapter:

- What devices should you target?
- Leveraging the Salesforce standard UI
- Translation and localization
- Client communication layers
- Visualforce
- Chatter and Publisher Actions
- Creating websites
- Mobile and Salesforce1
- Custom Reporting and the Analytics API

What devices should you target?

One of the first questions historically asked when developing a web-based application is *What desktop browsers and versions shall we support?* These days, you should not be thinking so much about the software installed on the laptops and desktops of your users, but rather the devices they own.

The answer might still likely include a laptop or desktop, though no longer is it a safe assumption that these are the main devices your users use to interact with your application. Mobile phones, tablets, and even wearable devices such as watches are becoming more popular. Depending on your target market, this might be larger devices such as cars or a vending machine! So, make sure that you think big and understand all the types of devices your customers and their customers might want to interact with your application.

For your desktop and laptop users interacting with your Force.com application, it is a combination of using the standard Salesforce UI and any custom UIs you might have built with Visualforce. Given this fact, it is a good idea to base your supported browser matrix on that supported by Salesforce. You can find this by searching for **'Salesforce supported browsers'** in Google. At time of writing this, the PDF listing supported browsers can be found at `https://help.salesforce.com/apex/HTViewHelpDoc?id=getstart_browser_overview.htm&language=en`.

Developing against multiple devices can be expensive, not only to develop the solution but also to perform the testing across multiple devices. In this chapter, we will take a look at a range of options, ranging from those provided by Salesforce at no additional development cost to building totally customized user interfaces using Visualforce and other technologies.

Leveraging the Salesforce standard UI

Salesforce puts a lot of effort into its desktop and Salesforce1-based mobile UI. These declarative UIs are the first to see advancements, one recent example being the ability to embed reporting charts. These standard user interfaces are also the primary method by which your subscribers will customize your application's appearance. Furthermore, with Salesforce's frequent updates, the UI will evolve even without you updating and releasing changes to your application.

For these reasons, you should ensure that, for all objects in your application, you make the best use of the standard UI by ensuring that your packaged layouts are highly polished and make use of every last drop of declarative features. It is even worth considering this practice for those objects that might be typically accessed through Visualforce pages. Considering the standard UI as a kind of primary or default UI also ensures that the validation in your Domain classes is complete, which ensures that it is not possible to enter invalid data regardless of how that data is entered, through Visualforce, Standard UI, or API.

Ensure that you apply the same UI review processes you undertook on your Visualforce pages to the standard UI layouts. Take care to review field labels, sections, button names, and general layout, while also looking for options to add more related information through report charts or embedded Visualforce pages. Also, consider making use of record types and different layouts to help reduce the number of fields a user has to enter.

 Keep in mind that Salesforce layouts packaged in your application are not upgradable, as they can be edited by the subscriber. So, no matter what improvements you make to your layouts in subsequent releases, these will only be available to new customers and not those who are upgrading to newer versions of the application. New aspects to layouts are typically expressed in your install/upgrade documentation.

Overriding the standard Salesforce UI

You can override the Salesforce standard UI for the following actions: **Accept, Tab, Clone, Delete, Edit, List, New**, and **View** for an object with your own Visualforce pages, completely replacing the standard UI pages.

Be aware that, if you take this option, you're taking on the responsibility of not only ensuring that new fields added to the your application are added to such pages but also that new platform features of the standard UI appear in your page as Salesforce evolves the platform. So, make sure to review the standard UI page functionality before taking the decision to package and override for the applicable action and also consider a hybrid approach described in the next subsection.

If you decide to override, the best way to keep your Visualforce pages inline as much as possible is to stick to the standard Visualforce components where possible; at the very least, utilize `apex:inputField` and `apex:outputField`. Using Visualforce components is not however a 100-percent solution; for example, **Chatter** does not automatically appear on pages unless a developer enables it. Another significant consideration is that custom fields or related lists subscribers added to your objects need special consideration in your page code to ensure that these are surfaced, through the use of the **Field Sets** and the `apex:relatedList` component, for example.

Finally, note that, although the **Custom Object Action overrides** (defined by you) can be packaged, they are nonupgradable, so changes will not apply to existing subscribers. Also, the subscriber can remove them post-installation if they prefer to access the custom object through the standard UI, so this is another reason to make sure that you consider the standard UI for all of your objects as a standard practice.

As an alternative to overriding an existing standard action, consider creating **Custom Buttons**, placing them on the object's **Detail page** and/ or **List View** layouts, and naming the button something like **Enhanced Edit** or **Enhanced New**. Note that it is a requirement that the pages behind such buttons use the Standard Controller; so, if the subscriber wished, they could opt in themselves to override Standard Actions (by passing the Custom Buttons). Providing a facility like this allows your subscribers to balance the benefit of both UIs for themselves.

Hybrid standard and Visualforce UIs

Having discussed pure Visualforce UI's, let's look at an example on how to customize the standard UI by embedding a Visualforce page in a detail page layout as shown in the following screenshot for the `Race` object. The following Visualforce page reuses the **Extension Controller** created in the previous chapter:

```
<apex:page standardController="Race__c"
    extensions="RaceSummaryController" action="{!loadSummary}">
  <apex:pageBlock >
    <apex:pageBlockTable value="{!Summary}" var="summaryRow">
      <apex:column value="{!summaryRow.Position}"/>
      <apex:column value="{!summaryRow.Driver}"/>
      <apex:column value="{!summaryRow.Team}"/>
      <apex:column value="{!summaryRow.Car}"/>
    </apex:pageBlockTable>
  </apex:pageBlock>
</apex:page>
```

As the page uses `StandardController`, it appears in the layout editor and can be positioned on the layout.

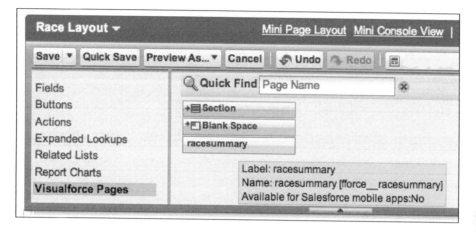

You can then drag and drop it into an existing or new section on the layout. The result will look something like the following screenshot:

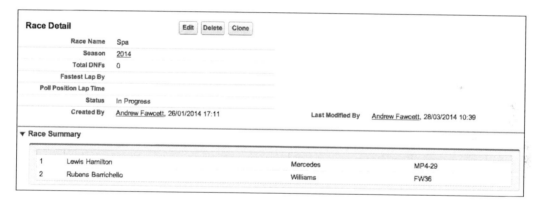

This approach only applies to the layouts when users are viewing records. You can, however, provide a means for users to edit the information through such Visualforce pages, even though they are rendered on the view page for the record. There is, however, no way to refresh the main page when you do so. While the width of the Visualforce page will adjust automatically, the height is fixed, so be sure to set accordingly to common data volumes.

Custom Buttons and Related lists

You are probably aware that Custom Buttons can be added to the **Detail** page and **Listview** layouts. However, what you might not know is they can also be added to the buttons displayed on **Related lists** for a given layout.

In the following example, an **Out of Race** button has been added to the contestant's related list on the **Race object layout**. To support this, the following modifications have been made to the **FormulaForce** application; you can find these changes in the code samples included with this chapter:

1. The **Retirement Reason** field has been added to the **Contestant** object.

2. The `ContestantSelector` class was updated to include the new field in queries.

3. The `OutOfRaceController` class was created to set the `DNF__c` field to true on page load for the selected records.

4. The `outofrace` Visualforce page has been created.

Notice that `outofrace` uses the `StandardSetController` class's `save` and `cancel` methods to directly update the records. As this is essentially a simple database operation, no Service class is needed. However, your **Domain layer logic** will be invoked during the **Apex Trigger** execution. The Visualforce page, `outofrace`, looks like this:

```
<apex:page standardController="Contestant__c"
    extensions="OutOfRaceController"
    recordSetVar="Contestants" action="{!markAsDNF}">
  <apex:sectionHeader title="Drivers out of Race"/>
    <apex:form>
      <apex:pageBlock>
        <apex:pageBlockTable value="{!Selected}"
          var="Contestant">
          <apex:column value="{!Contestant.DriverRace__c}"/>
          <apex:column value="{!Contestant.DNF__c}"/>
          <apex:column headerValue="
            {!$ObjectType.Contestant__c.fields.
              RetirementReason__c.Label}">
            <apex:inputField
              value="{!Contestant.RetirementReason__c}"/>
          </apex:column>
        </apex:pageBlockTable>
      </apex:pageBlock>
      <apex:commandButton value="Save" action="{!save}"/>
      <apex:commandButton value="Cancel" action="{!cancel}"/>
    </apex:form>
</apex:page>
```

We can now create a **Custom Button** on the **Contestants** object as shown in the following screenshot. Note that the **Display Checkboxes (for Multi-Record Selection)** checkbox has been selected.

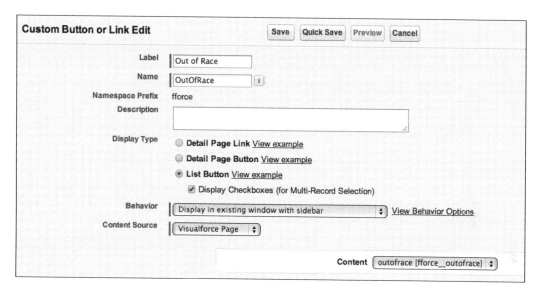

With this created, the list related to **Contestants** on the **Race** layout can be edited to include the button on the layout. Note that this button can also be added to **Contestant List View Layout** as well.

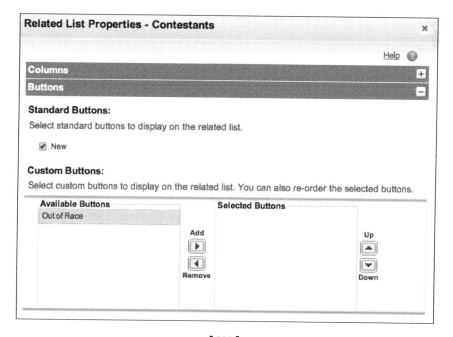

With the **Race** layout updated, the button displays as follows:

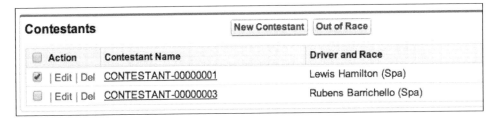

The user selects the contestants and clicks on the **Out of Race** button to display the Visualforce page as shown in the following screenshot:

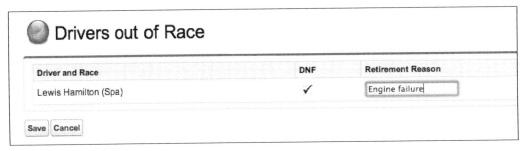

Rendering the standard UI within a Visualforce page

Although the `apex:detail` tag can be used on a Visualforce page to render most of the look and feel of the standard UI, the component is not very granular; for example, you cannot add your own buttons alongside the standard buttons it renders. This means that your page buttons need to be rendered elsewhere on the page, making the UI look inconsistent and confusing. In most cases, the hybrid approach described earlier in the chapter provides a better solution to most requirements like this.

Translation and localization

Chapter 2, Leveraging Platform Features, covered this topic, so we will not be revisiting it in further detail here. Just to reiterate, it is important to consider translation and localization requirements from the outset, as they can be expensive to retrofit afterwards.

Also, note that in the preceding example, the $ObjectType global variable was used in the Visualforce page to access the **Custom Field** label for the column title. Ensuring that you leverage approaches like this will reduce the number of **Custom Labels** you need to create and, ultimately, your translation costs.

Client communication layers

Fundamentally, any communication between the user's chosen device (client) and the data and logic available on the Salesforce server occurs using the **HTTP** protocol. As a Force.com developer, you rarely get involved with the low-level aspects of forming the correct **HTTP POST** or **HTTP GET** request to the server and parsing the responses.

For example, the Visualforce apex:commandButton and apex:actionFunction (AJAX) components do an excellent job of handling this for you, resulting in your Apex code being called with very little effort on your behalf apart from simply using these components. Salesforce also takes care of the security aspects for you, ensuring that the user is logged in and has a valid session to make the request to the server.

Depending on the context your client code is running in, Force.com offers a number of communication options to either perform **CRUD** operations on Standard or Custom Objects and/or invoke your application's Apex code to perform more complex tasks.

It is important that you correctly place the logic in your Domain and Service layers to make sure that, regardless of the client communication options, the backend of your application behaves consistently and that each client has the same level of functionality available to it. The sections in this chapter will show how to ensure that, regardless of the communications approach utilized, these layers can be effectively reused and accessed consistently.

Client communication options

Although the upcoming sections discuss the various communications in further detail, a full walk-through of them is outside the scope of this book. The Salesforce documentation and developer site offer quite an extensive set of examples on their use.

The aim of this chapter is to understand the architecture decisions behind using them, related limits, and how each interacts with the Apex code layers introduced in the previous chapters.

This table lists the various client communication options available along with the types of user interface they are typically utilized by. It also indicates whether the API calls are governed (see the following subsection on what this means).

Communication option	Visualforce Pages 1	Custom Button or link	Public websites	Native device UI (refer to step 3 in the following list)	API governor
Visualforce Components (inc. AJAX Support, for example, apex:commandButton and apex:actionFunction)	Yes	No	Yes (refer to step 1 in the following list)	No	No
Visualforce JavaScript Remoting (Access Apex code)	Yes	No	Yes (refer to step 1 in the following list)	No	No
Visualforce JavaScript Remote Objects (CRUD operations)	Yes	No	Yes (refer to step 1 in the following list)	No	No
Salesforce REST/SOAP API's(CRUD API, also including access to custom Apex SOAP and REST API's)	No	No	Yes (refer to step 2 in the following list)	Yes	Yes
Salesforce Streaming API (Read access to standard and custom objects)	Yes	No	Yes (refer to step 2 in the following list)	Yes	Yes
AJAX Toolkit (refer to step 4 in the following list)	Yes	Yes	Yes (refer to step 2 in the following list)	No	Yes
Analytics API	Yes	Yes	Yes	Yes	Yes

1. As Visualforce pages are essentially dynamically rendered HTML pages output by Salesforce servers, these can also be used to build public-facing websites and also pages that adapt to various devices such as mobile phones and tablets (given the appropriate coding by the developer). The Salesforce Streaming API is currently only accessible via JavaScript.

2. Websites built using traditional off-platform languages, such as .NET, Java, Ruby, or PHP, are required to access Salesforce via the REST/SOAP and Streaming API's only.

3. A client is built using a device-specific platform and UI technology, such as a native mobile application using Xcode, Java, or a natively wrapped HTML5 application.

4. The AJAX Toolkit is a JavaScript library used to access the Salesforce SOAP API from a Visualforce or HTML page. It is the oldest way in which you can access Salesforce objects and also Apex Web Services from JavaScript. Though it is possible to utilize it from Custom Buttons and Visualforce pages, my recommendation is to utilize one of the more recent Visualforce communication options (by associating Visualforce pages to your Custom Buttons rather than JavaScript). Salesforce only supports the very latest version of this library, which is also quite telling in terms of their commitment to it.

API governors and availability

As shown in the preceding table, for some communication methods, Salesforce currently caps the amount of API requests that can be made in a rolling 24-hour period (though this can be extended through Salesforce support). This can be seen on the **Company Information** page under **Setup** and the **API Requests, Last 24 Hours** and **Streaming API Events, Last 24 Hours** fields.

Note that these are not scoped by your application's namespace unlike other governors (such as the SOQL and DML ones). As such, other client applications accessing the subscriber org can consume, and thus compete with, your application for this resource. If possible, utilize a communication approach that does not consume the daily API usage, such as **JavaScript Remoting** or **Remote Objects**. If you cannot avoid this, ensure that you are monitoring how many requests your client is making and where aggregating them using relationship queries and/or Apex calls is possible.

If you are planning on targeting **Professional Edition**, be sure to discuss your API usage with your **Partner Account Manager**. The accessibility within this edition of Salesforce when using API's such as the Salesforce SOAP/REST API, Streaming API, and AJAX Toolkit is different from other editions. For the latest information, you can also review the *API Access in Group and Professional Editions* section in the *ISVforce Guide*, available at `https://na1.salesforce.com/help/pdfs/en/salesforce_packaging_guide.pdf`.

Database transaction scope and client calls

As discussed in *Chapter 4, Apex Execution and Separation of Concerns*, the transaction context spans the execution context for a request made to the Salesforce server from a client. When writing the client code in JavaScript, be careful when using the CRUD-based communication options such as **Remote Objects** and Salesforce API, as the execution scope in the client does not translate to a single execution scope on the server.

Each CRUD operation that the client makes is made in its own execution scope and, thus, its own transaction. This means that, if your client code hits an error midway through a user interaction, prior changes to the database are not rolled back. To wrap several CRUD operations in a single database transaction, implement the logic in Apex and expose it through one of the previous means, such as Remote Actions. Note that this is generally a good practice anyway from a service-orientated application design perspective.

Visualforce

Visualforce is not only a powerful way to create entirely new pages for your application but also augments the Salesforce user interface in multiple places. As we've seen so far, you can use it to extend the standard UI layouts and Custom Buttons. Here is a list of platform areas that accept Visualforce pages:

- Layout sections
- Custom Buttons
- Custom Tabs
- Custom Tab Splash page
- Chatter Custom Publisher Actions

- Sidebar component
- Dashboard component
- Force.com sites

Profiles and Permission Sets also reference Visualforce pages; users must be given access to a page before they can use it from these areas.

What can I do within a Visualforce page?

While Salesforce provides many components to use within the Visualforce pages, the only component that is strictly required is the `apex:page` component. That's it!

```
<apex:page>Anything I like in here!</apex:page>
```

When studying the attributes of the `apex:page` component, it's clear that this is a powerful way to communicate with the browser, returning content other than HTML. You also have access to various HTTP headers returned to the browser when your page is rendered.

Before we go any further, it is worth understanding more about the powerful attributes on the `apex:page` component and what situations you might want to use them in.

 If you have the need to capture a snapshot of a page for storage as a file or attachment, the `PageReference.getContent` and `getContentAsPDF` methods are a headless way of invoking your Visualforce page from Apex and returning the resulting page content as either a string or a PDF. Currently, these methods can only be called from an interactive Apex context.

Executing the code on page load with the action attribute

The `action` attribute allows you to specify an Apex method in your controller to execute before the page is returned to the browser, as follows:

```
<apex:page controller="MyController" action="{!OnPageLoad}">
```

You might think that the Apex controller's constructor is the best place to do this. However, the Visualforce page rendering engine has not completed its initialization (including that of Standard Controllers) until the custom controller is constructed. So, best practice is to place the page load logic in an action method referenced by this attribute.

Such a method could query for information to display, check the status of a record, and/or emit Apex Page Message's via the `apex:pageMessages` component to display dynamic messages to the user to direct them once the page has loaded. It is also possible to use this method as a page redirector, as it returns `PageReference`. The preceding example used it to preset the `DNF__c` field to `true` on the selected records. The page described earlier to select which drivers are out of the race used the following controller and action method code during page load to preselect the DNF field:

```
public with sharing class OutOfRaceController
{
  private ApexPages.StandardSetController
    standardSetController;

  public OutOfRaceController(ApexPages.StandardSetController
      standardSetController)
  {
    this.standardSetController = standardSetController;
  }

  public PageReference markAsDNF()
  {
    for(Contestant__c contestant : (List<Contestant__c>)
        standardSetController.getSelected())
      contestant.DNF__c = true;
    return null;
  }
}
```

Do not perform DML in this method; while this will work, it will not pass the Salesforce Security Review, as doing so represents a **Cross-site Request Forgery (CSRF)** security risk. If you want to know more about CSRF, look it up on Wikipedia at `http://en.wikipedia.org/wiki/Cross-site_request_forgery`.

Caching content with the cache and the expires attributes

By default, Force.com-generated pages will not be cached by your browser, unless served from a Force.com site. It determines whether the browser should cache the page or not. By using the `expires` attribute, you can control how long the page content is cached in the browser. For Force.com site pages, it defaults to 600 seconds. Use page caching to improve response times for data that changes infrequently, such as a page that lists **Teams** and **Drivers** with some bio information. As drivers rarely move teams in a given season, an hour delay would be acceptable.

Creating a Download button with the contentType attribute

The contentType attribute allows you to control how the browser interprets the page output; with this attribute, you can, for example, output some CSV, JSON, or XML content. Using a controller binding, this can be dynamically generated output. This can be useful to generate content to download. The following changes have been made to the FormulaForce application and are included in the code for this chapter:

- Added a new method, generateSummaryAsCSV, to RaceService
- Added a new getCSVContent method to RaceSummaryController
- Added a new racesummaryascsv Visualforce page
- Added a new Custom Button, **Download Summary**, to the **Race** layout

The new method is added to the existing RaceSummaryController class but is only used by the new page. Feel free to review the new Service method; note that it also uses the ContestantsSelector.selectByRaceIdWithContestantSummary method introduced in the previous chapter. Here is the new controller method calling it:

```
public String getCSVContent()
{
   return RaceService.generateSummaryAsCSV(
     new Set<Id> { standardController.getId() });
}
```

 The RaceService class contains the logic to generate the CSV file and not the controller class. Although at first you might consider this controller logic, if you think about it from a general data export perspective, there could equally be an API requirement in the future for external developers wanting to automate the CSV export process; thus, placing this logic in the Service layer facilitates this.

The new Visualforce page utilizes the contentType attribute as follows:

```
<apex:page
   standardController="Race__c"
   extensions="RaceSummaryController"
   contentType="application/csv#{!Race__c.Name} Race
Summary">{!CSVContent}
</apex:page>
```

As this page uses a Standard Controller, a Custom Button can be created; once it has been clicked, instead of the page opening, the browser prompts you to download the file.

Pressing the **Download Summary** button results in the following prompt to download the resulting CSV file:

 If you put a # symbol after the content type, you can specify a default filename to be presented to the user when the file downloads. Also, note that the Visualforce formula can also be used in attribute values, and this is how the **Race** name appears in the filename. This also allows you to vary contentType dynamically if required.

 While this example works quite well to illustrate the contentType attribute, it should be noted that the platform-reporting engine also supports CSV exports. As such, if you are considering CSV export facilities, it is worth first considering asking users to leverage reports; thus, they have more freedom to control the output.

Overriding the language of the page with the language attribute

By default, the Visualforce page looks up translated text for Custom Field labels and Custom labels that you reference on your page or in your Apex code through the user's locale. However, if you wish to override this, you can specify this attribute, for example, if you wish to use a Visualforce page to generate a newsletter in different languages and wish to preview them before sending them out.

This does not apply to any descriptive field values such as Name or any custom description fields that you add to your objects. In order to provide translation for the data entered by a user, you must develop such a feature yourself. There is no platform support for this.

HTML5 and the docType attribute

This attribute was mainly introduced to support the growing trend towards using Visualforce pages to deliver a UI for mobile devices and applications. The latest features of HTML5 such as offline and device access can be accessed through the use of the docType attribute. Typically, this attribute is used with others in this context, to disable the output of the standard Salesforce content into the page, especially in cases where you might be using client frameworks such as **Sencha**. The following code illustrates the use of this attribute with other related attributes:

```
<apex:page
  docType="html-5.0"
  sidebar="false"
  showHeader="false"
  standardStylesheets="false">
```

Offline Visualforce pages with the manifest attribute

The manifest attribute is part of the HTML5 standard to support offline web pages. While a full discussion on its use is outside the scope of this book, one thing to keep in mind is that any information you store in the browser's local offline storage is not secure. This attribute requires the use of the docType attribute to indicate that the page output is HTML5-compliant.

Salesforce, however, introduced this feature mainly to support **hybrid** mobile applications, wanting to utilize Visualforce pages within a native mobile application container that supports the offline mode. In this case. the offline content is stored within the mobile application's own private store.

> Hybrid mobile applications in the context of Salesforce Mobile SDK's are those that use a small native to the mobile device application that hosts a mobile browser that then utilizes the Salesforces login and Visualforce pages to deliver the application. In general, this would require a network connection; however, with the help of the manifest attribute, offline support can be achieved.

Generating PDF content with the renderAs attribute

Salesforce has a built-in PDF generation engine that can take your HTML markup and turn it into a PDF. This is a very useful feature to generate more formal documents such as invoices or purchase orders. You can access it using the renderAs attribute and setting it to pdf. Note that you would typically dedicate a specific Visualforce page for this purpose rather than attempt to use this attribute on one used for other purposes.

Make sure that you use as much vanilla HTML and CSS as possible; the Visualforce standard components do not always render well in this mode. For this reason, it is also useful to use the `standardStylesheets` attribute to disable Salesforce CSS as well. Note that you can programmatically access this capability by using the `PageReference.getContentAsPDF` method and attach the PDF generated to records for future reference (this method, however, does not currently work in asynchronous contexts).

Visualforce SOQL, iterator limits, and the readOnly attribute

Normally, the total number of records retrieved within a single controller execution context is 50,000 records (in total across all **SOQL** queries executed). In addition, Visualforce components such as `apex:dataTable` and `apex:repeat` can only iterate over 1000 items before a runtime exception is thrown.

At the time of writing this, the `readOnly` attribute (specified on the `apex:page` component) changes this to 1 million records and 10,000 iterations within Visualforce components on the page (refer to the Salesforce documentation for the latest update). As the name suggests, no updates to the database can occur, which basically means no DML at all. Note that queries are still governed by timeouts.

If you require a more granular elevation of the SOQL query rows governor, you can apply the `@ReadOnly` Apex attribute to a JavaScript Remoting method in your controller, and not at the page level as described previously. Again, this method will not be able to use DML operations to update the database, but you will gain access to querying a higher number of query rows. Note that the iterator limit increase is not applicable in this context, as JavaScript Remoting and Visualforce iterator components cannot be used together.

Field-level security

Visualforce pages exposing the SObject information (either via Standard, Custom, or Extension Controllers) can leverage built-in **field-level security enforcements** when using components or expressions that reference SObject fields directly; such usage will honor the user's field-level security. However, Visualforce expressions referencing SObject fields by way of a controller property are not affected, as the Visualforce engine cannot tell whether the controller property in turn refers to an SObject field.

For example, when using the `apex:inputField` and `apex:outputField` components, fields (including the label if present) will be hidden or made read only accordingly. A less well-known fact is that direct SObject field expressions are also affected by field-level security; for example, `{!Race__c.Status__c}` will not be evaluated (no output emitted to the page) if the user has no read access to the `Status__c` field. This behavior is particularly subtle and not well documented.

The documentation states that when using components such as `apex:inputText` and `apex:ouputText`, these will not enforce field security. While this is correct, security is always applied to SObject field expressions as well. So, if a field is not visible (as opposed to just read only), even the `apex:outputText` component will not display a value. However, if a field is read only and is used with `apex:inputText` (for example), it will render as an editable field. Thus, the general guideline here is that, if you have an SObject field expression, use the recommended `apex:inputField` and `apex:outputField` components.

A common confusion point is the use of the `with sharing` and `without sharing` keywords on the associated controllers. These keywords have no effect at all on the enforcement of field-level security; they purely determine record visibility, and thus effect only SOQL queries made within the controller.

In addition to using Apex described within your controller code, you can also determine directly a field's accessibility, using the `$ObjectType` global variable. For example, you can use the following expression to hide an entire section based on a given field's security, `{!$ObjectType.Race__c.fields.Status__c.Accessible}`.

The following Visualforce page and associated custom controller illustrates field-level security. In the use case shown here, two users are used, one has full access and the other has been given the following permissions via their profile:

- Read-only access to the `Status__c` field
- No access at all to the `FastestLapBy__c` field

First, review the Visualforce page; each section shows the following use case:

- **Use Case A** shows the use of `apex:inputField`
- **Use Case B** shows the use of `apex:outputField`

- **Use Case C** shows the use of `apex:inputText`
- **Use Case D** shows the use of `apex:outputText`
- **Use Case E** shows the use of an SObject field expression
- **Use Case F** shows the use of a controller property expression

To make it easier to compare, messages are shown on the page to confirm the level of field access. The `FLSDemoController` is included in the sample code for this chapter; it simply reads the first `Race__c` record in your org. It exposes two string properties indirectly exposing the `Status__c` and `FastestLapBy__c` field values. The following shows the Visualforce page used to illustrate the effects of using different Visualforce bindings and components against the permissions of the current user:

```
<apex:page controller="FLSDemoController" tabStyle="Race__c">
  <apex:form>

    <apex:pageMessage summary="Race__c.Status__c Accessible is
        {!$ObjectType.Race__c.fields.Status__c.Accessible}"
        severity="info"/>
    <apex:pageMessage summary="Race__c.Status__c Updatable is
        {!$ObjectType.Race__c.fields.Status__c.Updateable}"
        severity="info"/>
    <apex:pageMessage
        summary="Race__c.FastestLapBy__c Accessible is
          {!$ObjectType.Race__c.fields.
            FastestLapBy__c.Accessible}"
        severity="info"/>
    <apex:pageMessage
        summary="Race__c.FastestLapBy__c Updatable is
          {!$ObjectType.Race__c.fields.
            FastestLapBy__c.Updateable}"
        severity="info"/>
    <apex:pageBlock>

    <apex:pageBlockSection
      title="Use Case A: Using apex:inputField">
      <apex:inputField value="{!Race.Status__c}"/>
      <apex:inputField value="{!Race.FastestLapBy__c}"/>
    </apex:pageBlockSection>

    <apex:pageBlockSection
      title="Use Case B: Using apex:outputField">
```

```
        <apex:outputField value="{!Race.Status__c}"/>
        <apex:outputField value="{!Race.FastestLapBy__c}"/>
      </apex:pageBlockSection>

      <apex:pageBlockSection
          title="Use Case C: Using apex:inputText">
          <apex:inputText value="{!Race.Status__c}"/>
          <apex:inputText value="{!Race.FastestLapBy__c}"/>
      </apex:pageBlockSection>

      <apex:pageBlockSection
          title="Use Case D: Using apex:outputText">
          <apex:outputText value="{!Race.Status__c}"/>
          <apex:outputText value="{!Race.FastestLapBy__c}"/>
      </apex:pageBlockSection>

      <apex:pageBlockSection
          title="Use Case E: Using SObject Field Expressions">
          <apex:pageBlockSection>
            The value of Status__c is '{!Race.Status__c}'
          </apex:pageBlockSection>
          <apex:pageBlockSection>
            The value of FastestLapBy__c is
            '{!Race.FastestLapBy__c}'
          </apex:pageBlockSection>
       </apex:pageBlockSection>

      <apex:pageBlockSection
          title="Use Case F: Using Controller
          Property Expressions">
          <apex:pageBlockSection>
            The value of Status__c is '{!Status}'
          </apex:pageBlockSection>
          <apex:pageBlockSection>
            The value of FastestLapBy__c is '{!FastestLapBy}'
          </apex:pageBlockSection>
       </apex:pageBlockSection>
    </apex:pageBlock>

  </apex:form>
</apex:page>
```

For a user with full access, this page displays as follows:

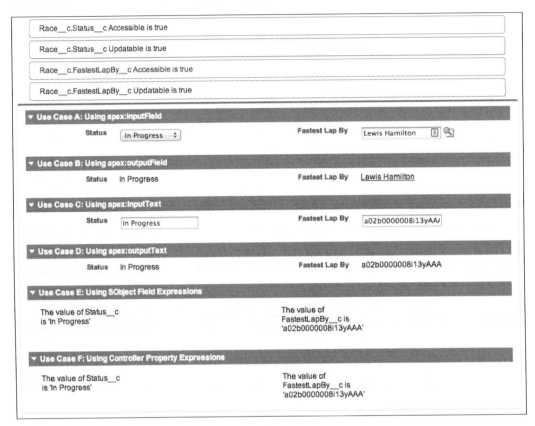

The following screenshot and explanations confirm how the page reacts and displays to the user with limited access; this page shows that some information is hidden or read-only as expected, but not all, the exceptions being use cases C and F:

- For **Use Case C**, the field is read only, so its value is accessible and placed in the input field. As it is a `apex:inputText` field, it does not honor the field-level security status of the field and the field is editable when it should not be.

- For **Use Case F**, the `FastedLapBy__c` field value is shown because it is not using a SObject field binding; it is using a binding to controller property, which is indirectly exposing the field value. In this case, the responsibility lies with the developer to check the field-level security in the controller code.

Race__c.Status__c Accessible is true

Race__c.Status__c Updatable is false

Race__c.FastestLapBy__c Accessible is false

Race__c.FastestLapBy__c Updatable is false

▼ **Use Case A: Using apex:inputField**

> Status   In Progress

▼ **Use Case B: Using apex:outputField**

> Status   In Progress

▼ **Use Case C: Using apex:inputText**

> Status   [In Progress]

▼ **Use Case D: Using apex:outputText**

> Status   In Progress

▼ **Use Case E: Using SObject Field Expressions**

The value of Status__c
is 'In Progress'

The value of
FastestLapBy__c is "

▼ **Use Case F: Using Controller Property Expressions**

The value of Status__c
is 'In Progress'

The value of
FastestLapBy__c is
'a02b0000008i13yAAA'

Page response time and components

Visualforce Developer's Guide has a section within it entitled *Best Practices for Improving Visualforce Performance*, in which it outlines some excellent ways to ensure that your pages remain responsive. I highly recommend that you take the time to read through it. There is, however, one point in that topic that I want to elaborate further on in this section:

> *"If your view state is affected by a large component tree, try reducing the number of components your page depends on."*

This symptom can result in poor response times, even for pages that are properly optimized in all other regards described in the documentation. The cause stems from the internal overhead of the Salesforce Visualforce components, known as **internal view state**, which increases when you have many such components on the page, typically in tabular or `apex:repeat` scenarios.

Depending on your Visualforce page design, it can often represent proportionally more than the data the developer explicitly places in the view state through controller properties and member variables. Together, they both contribute to reaching the 145 Kb limit on view state size, though before this is reached larger view states can effect response times.

Demonstrating a large component tree

This section is intended to help you understand the impact of large component trees in your Visualforce pages and some considerations for managing it.

We will be using the `outofrace` Visualforce page created earlier in this chapter to illustrate how to observe the increase in Viewstate. First, run the following Apex script to create some test data in the FormulaForce application objects:

```
TestData.createVolumeDataForViewStateTest();
```

Salesforce provides an excellent tool called **View State debugger tool** that allows you to look within the view state through a tree view, determine which areas are taking up space, and then take measures to remove them, such as using the `transient` keyword, as described in the Salesforce documentation.

This tool is accessed in two ways, through the **Developer Mode** when the page is displayed normally or through the **Developer Console Preview** feature. At the time of writing this, I could not find a way to preview a page from using a `StandardSetController` within **Developer Console**; as such, we will be using the traditional approach.

1. On your **User** settings, enable **Development Mode**.
2. Also enable **Show View State in Development Mode**.
3. Save and then navigate to the desired Visualforce page.

The previous script inserted a **Season** called **Volume Test**, with a **Race** called **Big Race**. By varying the number of selected **Contestants** and then clicking on the **Out of Race** button, it is possible to observe the incremental increase in view state that arises.

First, select 10 contestants from the list (use the **Show x More** link to load more contestants into the related list) and click on the **Out of Race** button.

 The View State debugger is also available to ISV's when logging into a subscriber org via the **Subscriber Support** tab, which enables you to debug large view state issues in your customer orgs.

The **View State** tab at the bottom of the page should show something like the following:

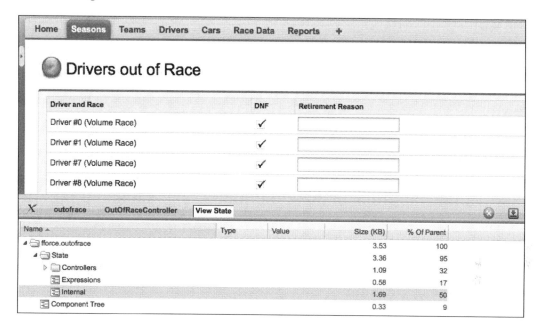

Next, perform the same test with 50 contestants, as follows:

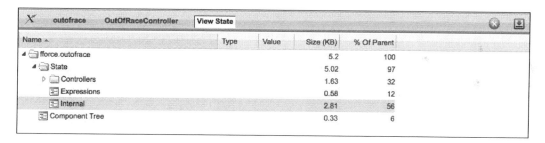

The results of these two tests show that the **Internal** section goes from 1.69 Kb to 2.81 Kb (66-percent growth), compared to the **Controllers** size, which went from 1.09 Kb to 1.63 Kb (49-percent growth, reflecting additional records being selected). This confirms that it is not only the information in your controller that contributes to the view state.

The **Internal** view state is generated by the use of Visualforce components such as `apex:column` and `apex:outputField` and is increased by the use of them repeatedly in a table (or equally through the `apex:repeat` tag).

Clearly, however, these components provide good functional value in terms of field-level security and enhanced UI features such as date and record selection (for lookup fields). That being said, depending on your needs there are other alternative HTML components and/or strategies you can apply to manage this situation and keep your Viewstate lean.

Considerations for managing large component trees

Here are a few considerations when designing Visualforce pages utilizing tables or repeated sections that contain the native Visualforce components:

- View state is only generated if you have a `apex:form` tag on the page; if you don't need one remove it, for example in view only pages.

- Consider if you need to use Visualforce components such as `apex:outputField` or if using HTML elements directly with a Visualforce expression would suffice. Be careful to consider localization features the standard components provide when doing this, such as formatting dates and numbers, you might need to perform this in the Apex code and bind to the formatted values.

- Avoid nested `apex:repeat` tags that contain Visualforce components. If possible, flatten a nested structure with the Apex logic in your controller and expose a single iterable list property that results in the same output.

- Consider moving to a stateless controller mode as described in the following section.

- Consider implementing pagination in your page.

For example, by applying **consideration 2** to the `outofrace` page for the **DNF** column resulted in a reduction of internal view state on the page from 2.81 kb to 2.51 kb (10-percent reduction). This reduction can be obtained by applying the following change to render the **DNF** checkbox using a HTML component instead of the `apex:column`:

```
<apex:column
    headerValue="
        {!$ObjectType.Contestant__c.fields.DNF__c.Label}">

    <input type="checkbox"
        checked="{!Contestant__c.DNF__c}"
        disabled="true"/>

</apex:column>
```

For a further analysis, search `http://salesforce.stackexchange.com/` for '*How to reduce a large internal view state / what is in the internal view state?*'.

Client-managed state versus server-managed state

State refers to either the data held in members and properties of an Apex Controller class and that then gets included in the view state, or the data held in the HTML components or JavaScript objects of the page itself within the browser.

Thus, a statefull controller is one that depends upon the data held in its members and properties to retain the information entered by the user. In contrast, a stateless controller depends solely on the information held in the HTML page within the browser client. In this architecture, the controller methods must pass all the information they need every time they are called. The following points expand on this distinction further:

- Stateless controllers leverage JavaScript Remoting to make calls from JavaScript embedded in the page back to a `static` Apex Controller method, for example, `@RemoteAction public static myRemoteMethod()`. Once the methods are declared in this way, it is as easy as calling a JavaScript function (of the same name). The communications are still handled for you, and there is no need to get into the HTTP protocol in any depth. Further, the JavaScript code is required to handle the results of the call.

- Statefull controllers utilize the action method convention, for example, `public PageReference myActionMethod()`. Such methods are instance methods on the controller and can access a member's variables from previous method calls. Action methods can be invoked from a page without JavaScript via `apex:commandButton` and `apex:actionSupport`, additionally via JavaScript using `apex:actionFunciton`.

So, given the previous discussion around **Viewstate** limits and potential page response time issues, you might be thinking that a stateless controller sounds like a good thing! Well, as always, there are pros and cons depending on the type of page you are building and also your skills as a client HTML and JavaScript developer.

Action methods versus JavaScript Remoting

The following table provides some insight into the pros and cons based on the technical challenges, page performance, user experience, and skills that are to be considered when reviewing action methods (the traditional Visualforce development) versus JavaScript Remoting. Following this table is the discussion on options for combining these technologies.

 The Salesforce Spring'14 release has introduced JavaScript Remote Objects, which offers a JavaScript CRUD API through a similar approach to JavaScript Remoting, except that no Apex Controller code is required. For the purposes of this section, the following comparison also applies to the use of JavaScript Remote Objects. A more detailed discussion about this latest addition to Visualforce communications is discussed in the following section.

	Visualforce action methods	Visualforce JavaScript Remoting and Remote Objects
State management, performance, and communications	State data is maintained in the member variables of the Apex Controllers and is transmitted, encoded, and decoded by the platform between method calls automatically. The response times of this data being sent and received is related to its size, and it can thus affect page response times. There is a limit of 145 kb, and some of this state can be used up by excessive use of certain Visualforce components, as per the examples earlier.	State data is maintained within the HTML and JavaScript objects stored in the browser client DOM. There is a 3-MB limit on data sent and received per call to the underlying Apex Controller methods via their parameters and return types. As the data being transmitted is pure data and does not contain component details, performance is improved. Note that the excessive amount of data stored in the browser page can also make the page run slowly; ultimately, it depends on the browser, desktop speed, and resources. Some pages can scale to several megabytes with today's browsers and hardware.

	Visualforce action methods	**Visualforce JavaScript Remoting and Remote Objects**
Access to Visualforce components and features	Visualforce provides many data output and input components that bind directly to the Viewstate and SObject fields and automatically provide the platform with the look and feel similar to that of the standard UI, with features such as localization, date format, and currency conversion while also enforcing Field Level Security.	While Visualforce components that deal with initial page output can be used, if there is no Viewstate, the data entry components cannot be used. As such, on the whole, pages that utilize JavaScript Remoting also have to implement custom HTML components in JavaScript; thus, it must take on significant responsibilities related to security, validation, prompting (for example, lookup fields), and formatting in their code.
Developer skills	On some occasions, basic JavaScript skills might be needed. Visualforce provides powerful features when it comes to refreshing selective parts of the page based on user navigation or selection, all without any JavaScript code. The ability to do so via JavaScript is also supported.	Typically, medium to advanced level JavaScript skills are required here. Although calling the Apex Controller method is straightforward, handling the response and updating the page accordingly requires deeper knowledge of HTML, CSS, and JavaScript, as the standard Visualforce components are not available. Familiarity with a well-known JavaScript framework would be a bonus in helping to replace some of the work done by the Visualforce components.

	Visualforce action methods	**Visualforce JavaScript Remoting and Remote Objects**
Building data entry UI pages	My personal feeling is that Visualforce pages designed for single-record data entry or wizard step-by-step scenarios are most suited here as opposed to tabular data. Unless paging solutions are implemented, the resulting costs of the component internal Viewstate can easily grow and impact the performance of the page. Even then, if a given page has many fields/components on it (considering user-added fields via Field Sets), a single page of data can still generate a high Viewstate size. Ensure that you monitor the Viewstate size carefully in tabular data entry scenarios.	Using JavaScript Remoting, you can build rich client experiences that can perform well regardless of the amount of data within reason. The trade-offs are the developer skills and components required to get to the point where you start to build your client rather than functionality. The rewards in terms of usability, look and feel, and responsiveness are great however.
Client logic unit and automated testing	Apex Controllers can be tested using Apex tests, as the state is accessible through accessing the properties and action methods exposed on the controller class. The existing Salesforce Apex test framework can be used here.	Salesforce does not provide a client-side test harness as yet; as such, you must approach third-party tool vendors to write automated tests that invoke the HTML elements and assert the state of the DOM. Tests are written in JavaScript typically or a point-and-click style language. Such tests must be run outside the Salesforce test execution facilities.

	Visualforce action methods	Visualforce JavaScript Remoting and Remote Objects
Mobile and device-agnostic UI strategies	While it is possible to use the standard Visualforce components in a mobile client context, the styling and behavior are not currently tailored towards this type of device; for example, the lookup and date fields.	Such UI's are typically built using JavaScript client frameworks designed for mobiles, such as **JQuery Mobile** or **Sencha Touch**, both of which assume that the state is managed in the browser. Such libraries also play better with the JSON data exchange format used. Salesforce plans to roll out a new component library that is device-agnostic called Aura. It is currently available as open source through a local installation for developer feedback.

Mixing the use of action methods and JavaScript Remoting

Both action methods and JavaScript Remoting offer different advantages. It is not given that you have to pick one and use one exclusively on a single page. Certainly some hybrid use cases can make more sense than others. The following points outline some use cases you should consider:

- **Action methods for update and JavaScript Remoting for query support**: Leveraging JavaScript Remoting to perform some querying or autocomplete type functionality that helps the user complete the data on the page could make sense on a page that utilizes traditional Visualforce components and Viewstate as its main means to track and capture data entry and activity.

- **Action methods and JavaScript Remoting methods for update and query**: I feel that using both approaches to transmit data back to the database will most certainly lead to confusion for the user and poor transaction integrity, as some updates are done by action methods based on Viewstate and others when JavaScript Remoting methods are called based on the page state. There is a probability that the Viewstate will become out-of-date due to updates happening around it. Use this combination with care.

Applying JavaScript Remoting to the Service layer

As with the Apex controller action methods you've seen in the earlier chapters, the **Service** layer is also designed to be called from JavaScript Remoting methods, as follows:

```
public with sharing class RaceResultsController
{
  @RemoteAction
  public static List<RaceService.ProvisionalResult>
    loadProvisionalResults(Id raceId)
  {
    return RaceService.calculateProvisionResults(
      new Set<Id> { raceId }).get(raceId);
  }

  @RemoteAction
  public static void saveConfirmedResults(
    Id raceId, List<RaceService.ProvisionalResult> results)
  {
    RaceService.applyRaceResults(
      new Map<Id, List<RaceService.ProvisionalResult>>
        { raceId => results});
  }
}
```

In this case, however, there is no `try`/`catch` block, as error handling is done by the client code and there is no `apex:pageMessages` component to render the messages. When exceptions are thrown, the platform takes care of catching the exception and passing it back to the calling JavaScript code for it to display accordingly. In short, there is no need to invent your own error message handling system; just let the platform handle pass it back to the client JavaScript code for you.

Considerations for client-side logic and Service layer logic

With the addition of more complex logic in the client via JavaScript, more attention needs to be given to **Separation of Concerns**. The following points provide some guidelines for this:

- **Single service method per remoting method**: A single Service layer method invocation rule should still be observed when developing remoting methods on the controller. If multiple Service layer methods are being called, this becomes a sign that a new aggregate Service layer method should be created and called instead.

- **Avoid remoting client bias**: Do not be tempted to design your Service layer solely around your JavaScript Remoting controller method needs (the needs of your JavaScript client). Always consider the Service layer as client-agnostic; this becomes particularly important if you want to also later expose your Service layer as an API to your application.

- **Apex Enum types**: If you utilize Enum types in your Service layer design (to be honest, why would you not?), they are very expressive and self-documenting! However, they unfortunately at this time are not supported by the JavaScript Remoting JSON de-serializer, which means that you can return Apex data structures containing them, but cannot receive them from the client (a platform exception occurs).

  The workarounds are to either not use Enum's and drop back to using string data types or create Apex class data types within the controller class and perform your own marshaling between these types and service types (leveraging the `Enum.name()` method to map Enum's to string values). The choice is between your desire to protect your Service layer's use of Enum's (especially if it is your public-facing API) and the effort involved. Hopefully, at some point, Salesforce will fix this issue.

When should I use JavaScript Remote Objects?

JavaScript Remote Objects are designed to expose a 'SOQL- and DML-like' API for use by the JavaScript code embedded within a page. Providing a way to query and update the database without having to go through the traditional AJAX Toolkit or Salesforce REST API's that incur charges to the daily API limit.

Visualforce Developer's Guide has an excellent topic that describes the best practices around using this feature, entitled *Best Practices for Using Remote Objects*, which I highly recommend that you read and digest fully. The main aspect from this topic I'd like to highlight is the one that relates to transactional boundaries in close conjunction with maintaining a good Separation of Concerns.

Resist the temptation to invoke multiple JavaScript Remote Object operations within a single JavaScript code block as each will be executed in its own Salesforce execution context and thus transaction. This means that, if an error occurs in your JavaScript code, previous operations will not be rolled back.

If you find yourself in this situation, it is also likely that you should be positioning such code in your application's Service layer and thus using JavaScript Remoting to call that Service layer method, which will then occur within a single transactional scope.

That said, if you have use cases that result in a single database operation then you can of course consider using this feature, safely assured that your Apex Trigger and Domain layer code will continue to enforce your data validation and integrity.

Client-side alternatives to Visualforce UI components

As discussed, the more you move towards a stateless controller and JavaScript Remoting client architecture, the more you need to invest in providing or obtaining client-side components not presently provided by Salesforce.

Consider this decision carefully on a per-case basis (not all of your application UI has to use the same approach) and make sure that you appreciate the value of the platform features that you are leaving behind. Expect to adjust your expectations around your client developer's velocity more in alignment with those on other platform developers.

Libraries such as JQuery provide a great deal of convenience, flexibility, and components available in the community to provide some alternatives and improvements over the Visualforce components, in addition to larger components such as grids and trees. Taking things a step further, larger commercially available libraries such as **Sencha ExtJS** are also usable from within a Visualforce page, including mobile variants such as JQuery Mobile and Sencha Touch.

All of these libraries require a good deal of JavaScript programming knowledge, including its OOP style of programming. Some provide the **Model View Controller** (**MVC**) frameworks as well, such as **AngularJS**. If you search on Google for Salesforce. you will find many examples and articles from the community and the Salesforce Developer Evangelists team.

Here are some aspects of developing with such libraries you should consider:

- **Developer flow**: What is the process from storing the client code in source control, pushing it into an org for development, editing code, debugging it, and pushing it back into Source Control? Likewise when it comes to packaging, consider whether you should compress your JavaScript or not. The Developer flow has to be fast; editing JavaScript files, rebuilding zip files, and uploading new static resources is not fast. Consider whether you can support a loose file development flow for client developers, such as using Visualforce components, page, or static resources for each file (**MavensMate** has good support to this), and then combine these into a single static resource for packaging and deployment.

- **Security**: Salesforce takes a great deal of care with their Visualforce components to ensure that the escape values are displayed by the components to prevent attacks such as HTML injection for example. Check your components' escape values that they inject into the DOM from your database records, or you could find yourself open to attack and delays getting through the Salesforce Security Review.

- **Testing frameworks**: There are a number of approaches when testing rich clients, ranging from unit testing frameworks that have the developer write a JavaScript code to testing commercial applications that actually drive the web browser and assert the state of the page. Make sure that you invest according to the amount of JavaScript code your application contains.

Salesforce Aura

Salesforce themselves are also working on a rich client framework and related component library known as **Aura**. If you have been using the Salesforce1 mobile application, you have already been using an application built with it. Eventually, you will be able to use it as an alternative to Visualforce pages by creating Aura pages and components in the developer console and various IDE's such as Force.com IDE and MavensMate.

One of Salesforce's goals when creating this library was to produce something that would be completely device-agnostic, not targeted at browser clients or mobile clients, but both. Time will tell whether they will truly succeed in this; if you want to see what they are up to and even try it out on a local web server for yourself, you can find it here. `https://github.com/forcedotcom/aura`:

> *"Aura is a UI framework for developing dynamic web apps for mobile and desktop devices, while providing a scalable long-lived lifecycle to support building apps engineered for growth. It supports partitioned multi-tier component development that bridges the client and server."*

Custom Publisher Actions

In a previous chapter, we created a **Publisher Action** to mark a **Contestant** as a **DNF (Did not Finish)** object easily from a Chatter feed. This leveraged the declarative approach to creating Publisher Actions, based on creating or updating a related record. If your use case does not fit into this type of operations, you can use Visualforce page to develop a Custom Publisher Action. Keep in mind that these are also available to your users through the Salesforce1 mobile application.

At the time of writing this, there is no API support to determine what context the page is running in, other than sensing the HTTP User Agent header value and adjusting the layout and styling accordingly. As Salesforce continues to improve their API's around Salesforce1, hopefully, this will be improved soon.

Certainly, Custom Publisher Actions and Salesforce1 mobile is an area that requires further development by Salesforce compared to the more declarative aspects of the application. As Salesforce1 is developed using Aura already, we can expect the Aura technology once available on the platform to developers to help address some of the current challenges found when working with Visualforce pages in this environment.

Creating websites

Salesforce provides the following two ways to create public facing web content:

- **Force.com**: This offers a means to create public-facing authenticated websites using Visualforce pages. Due to this, it can access Standard and Custom objects using the approaches described in this chapter, reusing components and services from your application as needed. The Force.com site configurations cannot be packaged, though the pages and controllers you create to support them can be. This feature is available in the **Enterprise** and **Developer Edition** orgs.

- **Sites.com**: This is a declarative website product that is targeted at nontechnical users. Visualforce pages cannot be used directly with Site.com though components available with Site.com can access your application's Custom Objects and as such will invoke your Apex Trigger and thus Domain logic code.

Mobile strategy

Mobile application development using Salesforce has been a hot topic for the last few years, starting with the use of various well-known mobile frameworks such as jQuery mobile, AngularJS along with Salesforce's own API's, including oAuth for authentication, and **Salesforce REST API** to access Standard and Custom Object records, leading up to the current development around the latest Salesforce1 mobile application.

The interesting thing about this is that it has evolved in a different way to the browser UI, which started with the standard declarative-driven UI and could then be augmented with a more developer-driven solution such as Visualforce. For a mobile UI, up until the release of Salesforce1, we only had the option of building something with a developer.

As things stand today, we now have both options available for building mobile UI's. As such, make sure that you understand first and foremost the capability of the Salesforce1 mobile application and its ability to surface your objects through its standard UI. **Publisher Actions** provide an excellent way to enhance the **Chatter feed** presence of your application and also add the same actions to your users' Salesforce1 experience.

Salesforce1's user interface model is not for everyone; it is, like the browser UI, mostly data-centric if you wish to expose a more fine-tailored process-driven user experience for a very specific mobile application. If this is something you feel you need, you can review Salesforce Mobile Packs to choose the architecture and API's that suite your needs the best (`https://developer.salesforce.com/mobile`).

Custom Reporting and the Analytics API

Sometimes, the standard output from the **Salesforce Reporting** engine is just not what your users are looking for. They require formatting or a layout not supported by Salesforce, but the way in which they have defined the report is appealing to them.

The **Salesforce Analytics API** allows you to build a Visualforce page or mobile application that can execute a given **tabular**, **summary**, or **matrix report** and return its data into your client code to be rendered accordingly. The API is available directly to Apex developers and as a **REST API** for native mobile applications.

You might want to consider using a report to drive an alternative approach to selecting records for an additional process in your application by leveraging the flexibility of the **Report Designer** as a kind of record selection UI.

Updating the FormulaForce package

Apply the code included in this chapter into your package org. Apart from the `RaceResultsController` Apex class, all components provided with the sample code for this chapter will be included in the package automatically as they are additions to or referenced from components that are already packaged. The following screenshots show a partial view of what the package installation summary should look like:

▼ Pages (3)

Action	Component Name	Parent Object	Component Type	Installation Notes
Create	outofrace		Visualforce Page	This is a brand new component.
Create	racesummaryascsv		Visualforce Page	This is a brand new component.
Create	racesummary		Visualforce Page	This is a brand new component.

▼ Fields (1)

Action	Component Name	Parent Object	Component Type	Installation Notes
Create	Retirement Reason	Contestant	Custom Field	This is a brand new component.

Summary

Salesforce provides a great standard UI experience that is highly customizable and adaptable to new features of the platform without you necessarily releasing new revisions of your application. At its core, it is a data-centric user experience, which means that most tasks come down to creating, editing, or deleting records of some kind. Having a strong focus on your Domain layer code ensures that it protects the data integrity of your application. **Publisher Actions** help turn these actions into smaller tasks that are more business-like in their name and usage.

If you want to express a more complex process or a series of tasks, Visualforce allows you to be more expressive using Visualforce components or other HTML libraries to create the user experience needed for the task at hand. While this is very powerful, it is important to always consider the standard U, and, wherever possible, augment or complement it with the Visualforce page rather than making this the only way of interacting with your application.

Equally important is to observe best practices around engineering Visualforce pages for performance and security. Consider carefully and choose wisely the degree to which you depart from the standard UI and/or standard Visualforce components, as the further you move away from these, the more responsibility and complexity you have to deal with as a developer. Look for opportunities to create hybrid standard UI and Visualforce combinations to get the best of both worlds.

Reporting can be a personal thing for your users; the Salesforce Analytics API allows you to harness the power of the Salesforce Report Designer and engine with a more tailored rendering of the reporting data returned.

At present, there are numerous combinations of technologies and approaches to build a mobile user experience for your users. As with the standard UI in the browser, start with what Salesforce provides you and your users with out of the box as standard. The Salesforce1 mobile application is effectively a platform feature that users expect to be able to use with your application objects like any other.

Building custom Visualforce pages for use within Salesforce1 mobile is still an emerging approach given the lack of API's. Certainly, the declarative aspects offer a more stable option at the time of writing this. However, if you choose to build your own mobile application, you can choose to develop it using one of the Salesforces Mobile SDK's as a starting point; alternatively, if you have the skills and experience, use them as a guide on how to call the various Salesforce API's.

Finally, keep a close eye on the emergence of the new Salesforce Aura UI framework!

Providing Integration and Extensibility

9

Enterprise businesses have complex needs involving many human, device, and increasingly machine interactions, often distributed across the globe. Allowing them to work together in an efficient and secure manner is no easy task, and as such, it is no great surprise that utilizing cloud-based software over the Internet has become so popular. High-grade security, scalability, and availability is high on checklists when choosing a new application, often followed by API needs and the ability to customize.

By developing on the Force.com platform, your application already has a good start. The http://www.trust.salesforce.com/ site provides a wide selection of industry strength, compliance, and encryption standards that are equally applicable to your applications. With this comes a selection of standard APIs offered in the SOAP and REST forms as well as the ability to create your own application APIs. In my view there is not a more integration-ready cloud platform available today than Force.com.

In this chapter, we will review the integration and extensibility options provided as standard on the platform and how your application can get the most from them, in addition to developing custom application APIs. Once again the Application Enterprise Patterns will come into play, supporting the need for APIs and UIs to have a strong functionality parity, through the use of the Domain and Service layers described in earlier chapters.

This chapter will cover the following topics:

- Reviewing integration and extensibility needs
- Force.com platform APIs for integration
- Application-specific APIs
- Alignment with Force.com extensibility features
- Extending the application logic with Apex Interfaces

Reviewing your integration and extensibility needs

Before diving into the different ways in which you can provide APIs to those integrating or extending your application, let's review these needs through the eyes of *Developer X*. This is the name I give to a persona representing a consumer of your APIs and general integration and extensibility requirements. Much like its use in designing a user interface, we can use the persona concept to sense check the design and interpretation of an API.

Defining the Developer X persona

Asking a few people (internal and external to the project) to represent this persona is well worth doing, allow them to provide use cases and feedback to the features and functions of your application's API strategy. As it is too easy to design an API you think makes sense, but others with less knowledge of the application do not agree with. A good way to develop a developer community around your API is to publish designs for feedback. Keep in mind the following when designing your API for *Developer X*:

- *Developer X* is skilled in many platforms and programming languages these days, which might not always be Force.com. Increasingly *Developer X* is also creating Mobile, JavaScript, and Heroku applications around your API.

- As the **Internet of Things** (**IoT**) continues to expand, there is also a shift towards device integration from consumer devices such as watches, fridges, cars, and jet engines. So, APIs that work well on-platform and off-platform are a must.

- *Developer X* might not have an in-depth knowledge of the application domain, thus it's important for them to be able to communicate with those that do, meaning that your API and application functionality terminology has to be well aligned.

The upcoming sections outline general considerations and needs around providing both an integration API and general extensibility of your application's functionality.

Versioning

As your product functionality grows, it is important to manage the impact this has on developers and partners who have already adopted your APIs in earlier releases of your application and not force them to make code changes unless needed. Where possible, maintain backwards compatibility such that even after your application has been upgraded in a subscriber org, existing integrations and extensions continue to work without modification (multiple versions of your application code are not stored in a subscriber org).

Without backwards compatibility you can inhibit upgrades to your application within your customer base, as the time spent by *Developer X* addressing API issues can delay upgrades and be expensive. Some subscribers might have utilized consulting services to affect the original work or be dependent on one of your partners for add-on solution using your API.

Versioning falls into two categories: versioning the definition (or contract determined input and output of data) and the functionality (or behavior) each API represents.

Versioning the API definition

Once you have published a specific version of an API, do not change its definition, for example the Custom Objects, fields, Apex classes, methods, or members, or equivalent REST or SOAP constructs. Even though the platform will help avoid certain changes, additions can be considered a breaking change, especially new required fields. Anything that changes the definition or signature of the API can be considered a potential breaking change.

Developer X should be able to modify and redeploy their existing integrations or extensions without having to recode or adjust their code using your API and without forcing them to upgrade to the latest version of your API, unless, of course, they want to access new functionality only accessible by completing new fields. Note that this is different from upgrading the package itself within the subscriber org, which must be allowed to happen.

The standard Salesforce APIs and platform help provide versioning when *Developer X* interacts with your Custom Objects and Application APIs. Versioning is implemented as follows:

- In an Apex code context, the platform retains the version of your package installed when the Apex code was first written by *Developer X*, and then only ensures that Apex classes, methods, members, Custom Objects, and fields visible in this packaged version are visible to the code. This feature is something that we will explore in further detail later in this chapter.

- In the case of the SOAP and REST APIs, by default the latest version of your Custom Objects is visible. When using the SOAP API, header values can be passed in such calls to lock a particular package version if needed (search for `PackageVersionHeader` in *Apex Developer's Guide*). Alternatively the packaged version used by these APIs can be set at an org-configuration level.

Versioning application access through the Salesforce APIs

Under the **Setup** menu, search for **API**. You will find a setup page that allows you to download the WSDLs for one of the many Salesforce SOAP APIs. In the next section there are some versioning settings that determine which installed package version should be assumed during interactions with your packaged objects.

For example, when performing a `describeSObject` web service operation via the Salesforce Enterprise or Partner APIs, these APIs will return different custom fields depending on when new fields were added, as new versions of the package have been released over time. The default behavior will return all fields as the default is the current package version.

If this is important to *Developer X* or third-party solutions when using these Salesforce APIs, the subscriber administrator can specify an explicit previous version. If they do this, new fields available in future package versions will not be available unless this is changed. The following screenshot shows how these settings can be accessed on the API page under **Setup**:

Package Version Settings

Enterprise Package Version Settings
These version settings are used if an API call doesn't include version information for an installed package. This ensures backwards compatibility.

Configure Enterprise Package Version Settings

Partner Package Version Settings
These version settings are used if an API call doesn't include version information for an installed package.

Configure Partner Package Version Settings

Versioning the API functionality

When offering new versions of your application to users through the UI, new features are accessed by the user—either by opting into the feature by configuration using a new page or button, or sometimes just seamlessly such as a new type of calculation, optimization, or improvement to existing behavior with added benefits.

As the API is just another way into your application's logic, you should think about enabling these new features through the API in conceptually the same way. If it is seamlessly available through the UI to users, it becomes so in the API regardless of the API version, and thus, solutions built around your application's API will also benefit automatically without changes to the integration or extension code. However, if there is some new field or button needed, then a new API parameter or operation will be needed to enable the new feature. It is reasonable for this to be exposed in a new version of your API definition. Thus, *Developer X* will have to modify the existing code, test it, and deploy it before the solution can leverage it.

Trying to be sophisticated in your code by providing exactly the same behavior to older callers of your API will depend on the Service and Domain layers understanding the concept of API versus UI contexts and package versioning, which will rapidly become complex for you to develop, test, support, and document.

Agree and communicate to your customers and partners clearly how many versions of your API you will support and give warning on retirements. Always be sure to test your APIs at different versions to ensure the lack of fields that arrive later in your package, which are not provided by older callers, does not cause errors or unwanted behavior in these cases. Try to avoid adding new required fields to your applications without a way to default them.

If in your regression testing of older API versions, you notice reduction in data volume throughput due to governors, it can be acceptable to condition newer logic (such as checks for newer fields). Again, be careful with how often you implant this type of conditional logic in your code base.

Translation and localization

As with the guidelines around the Service layer, which can be used as a means to form your application API later in this chapter, you should ensure that any error or status messages are translated according to your use of **Custom Labels**, as described in *Chapter 2*, *Leveraging Platform Features* (the Apex runtime will ensure that the user locale determines the translation used).

It is not possible to override the language used to look up the appropriate Custom Labels through Apex. However, if the API is called from a Visualforce page utilizing the language attribute as described in the previous chapter, your API code will also honor this.

Some APIs expose error codes to provide a language-neutral way to recognize a certain error use case programmatically (parsing the message text is not reliable in a translated environment). As such, one approach is to use an Apex **enum** and a custom Apex **exception** class, which captures both the translated error message and the exception code. The following enum and exception types are defined in the `Application` class contained within the sample code for this chapter. Note the use of the `global` keyword in Apex; this will be discussed later in this chapter in more detail:

```
global Application
{
  global enum ExceptionCode
  {
    ComplianceFailure,
    UnableToVerifyCompliance
  }
```

```
global virtual class ApplicationException extends Exception
{
    global ExceptionCode ExceptionCode {get; private set;}

    public ApplicationException(
        ExceptionCode exceptionCode, String message)
    {
        this(message);
        this.exceptionCode = exceptionCode;
    }
}
}
```

While the preceding `ApplicationException` class can be used as it is, the following `ComplianceService` class has its own custom exception that can then extend this:

```
global class ComplianceException
    extends Application.ApplicationException
{
    global List<VerifyResult> failures {get; private set;}

    public ComplianceException(
        Application.ExceptionCode exceptionCode,
        String message, List<VerifyResult> failures)
    {
        super(exceptionCode, message);
        this.failures = failures;
    }
}
```

This code can then raise exceptions specifying the enum value related to the message as follows:

```
throw new ComplianceException(
    Application.ExceptionCode.ComplianceFailure,
    Label.ComplianceFailuresFound,
    failedCompliances);

throw new ComplianceException(
    Application.ExceptionCode.UnableToVerifyCompliance,
    Label.UnableToVerifyCompliance,
    null);
```

As with the Service layer guidelines, the API should be client agnostic, and thus you cannot assume whether the data values accepted or returned should be formatted or not. Thus, it is best to use the native Apex types for date, date/time, and number and allow the caller to decide whether or not to format the values. Returning formatted values is useful for UI callers, but for headless or automated solutions, this is not ideal.

Terminology and platform alignment

If you're following the guidelines of the Service layer when defining your classes, methods, parameters, and interfaces (as discussed later in this chapter), then any API based on this layer should already mirror the functional terms used in your application. Having a good alignment with your application terms makes your API easier to map to functional concepts in your application and thus for *Developer X* to navigate around and understand and discuss with those that know the application in more functional depth.

In addition, like the Service layer, your API should support platform concerns such as bulkification and not inhibit *Developer X* from calling your API in a bulkified way to make optimum use of the platform resources. This also includes *Developer X* utilizing Apex DML statements and thus then raises the importance of bulkified Domain layer logic as well as bulkified Service layer logic.

What are your application's integration needs?

Typically an integration need arises from a controlling process or application that consumes the functionality of your application, effectively invoking the functionality within your application automatically on behalf of a user, or as part of an event or scheduled background process. Both, the standard Salesforce APIs and any additional application APIs that you create can support this need. The following diagram shows a controlling system driving your application through either the standard Salesforce API and/or application APIs that you have provided as part of the managed package:

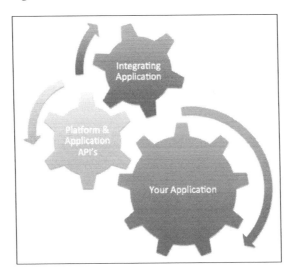

Although integrations are much easier when all applications are built based on the same platform, it is a good practice to have an API strategy that covers both, on-and off-platform, *Developer X* scenarios, ideally exposing the same functionality consistently.

Developer X calling your APIs on-platform

A Force.com Apex developer can manipulate the data stored in your application through Apex DML statements. You can think of Apex DML as your free Apex API to your application data, as this approach avoids the need for you to build your own application APIs to purely manage record data, particularly for those Custom Objects that you are already exposing through the standard Salesforce UI.

 It can be a useful aid to these developers to browse your Custom Object schema through Salesforce Schema Builder, as highlighted earlier in this book. Try to avoid inconsistencies between your **Field Labels** and **Field API** names (though the Schema Builder does permit toggling of these), as this can make it harder for developers and those expressing the requirements to collaborate.

Just because Apex is being used does not mean that *Developer X* can bypass logic in your managed Apex Triggers. However, take note that they can also write Apex Triggers of their own, which can execute before yours (as the Apex Trigger order is nondeterministic). To avoid *Developer X* triggers making invalid changes to record data, ensure that you follow the best practice when you're writing the validation logic to place it in the after-phase of your application triggers. As discussed in the previous chapter, utilizing the Domain pattern will ensure this.

Later in this chapter we will discuss application APIs that expose functionality not directly related to manipulating your Custom Object records, but one that is more business logic related, for example exposing the `ComplianceService.verify` method. In this case, by making the Service class and methods `global` as opposed to `public`, you can make this same method available to *Developer X*. As an extension to your Apex API strategy, allow them to consume it in the same manner as you do within your application.

The motivation behind this approach, described further in this chapter, is to ensure that the maximum amount of your application functionality is available through your API as your application evolves. However, if you do not want to expose your full Service layer directly as your application API, you can elect to create separate Apex classes that define your API which delegate to the Service layer or selectively apply the `global` keyword to your Service methods.

Developer X calling your APIs off-platform

The approach for *Developer X* using languages such as Java, .NET, or Ruby is much the same except that the HTTP protocol is used to connect between the two platforms. Salesforce provides APIs to log in and authorize access for you as well as APIs to manipulate the data in your Custom Objects much like using Apex DML. Salesforce currently chooses to expose both SOAP- and REST-based variants of its HTTP-based APIs. So again, you need not develop your own APIs for this type of data integration.

 Many third-party Salesforce integration applications leverage platform APIs and as such will also work with your application data; this fact is a key platform benefit for you and *Developer X*.

When it comes to exposing application APIs, to support SOAP and REST, you will need to develop separate Apex classes in each case for each API that you want to expose. This is because the definition and design of these types are different, though the functionality your exposing is the same. We will discuss this further later in this chapter.

SOAP versus REST

If you have been following the debate over SOAP versus REST or just simply Google for it, you'll know that there is currently a general trend towards REST. As it's easier to code against and consume in mobile and JavaScript-based scenarios, most major cloud services such as Facebook and LinkedIn only provide REST versions of their APIs.

There is an emerging standard called **Web Application Definition Language (WADL)** that aims to provide a WSDL-like definition that can be used by code generators that provide precompiled libraries to help in building and consuming JSON data structures used by REST APIs. A WADL to Apex tool to generate Apex native types reflecting the JSON structures would be the next obvious step in my view, much like the WSDL to Apex tool we have today.

What are your applications extensibility needs?

So far we have been discussing providing facilities to build custom solutions around your application, which is one type of integration. Another is providing ways to make extensions to its existing business logic. In an extensibility use case, *Developer X* or an administrator is happy for your users to consume your application UI and functionality directly but wants to extend it in some way to add additional functionality or updates to other Custom Objects. Some examples of the type of extensions you might want to consider are as follows:

- Adding subscriber-created **Custom Fields** to **Visualforce Pages** and **Field Sets** is an easy way to achieve this

- Providing alternatives to hardcoded **Email messages** via **Email Templates**

- Extending the application Apex code logic with the subscriber-written Apex logic

In this chapter we will explore the preceding extensions in further detail. The following diagram shows your application making use of what I am referring to as **Application Callouts** to access **Application Extensions** written by *Developer X*. Later in this chapter we will see an example of how you can implement these through the use of Apex interfaces and custom settings.

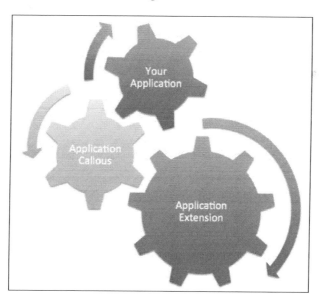

Force.com platform APIs for integration

Chapter 2, Leveraging Platform Features, provided a good overview of the many platform APIs available to those integrating with your application from outside of the Force.com platform, from environments such as Java, .NET, PHP, and Ruby. It also provided the best practices to ensure that your application and developers using these APIs have the best experience.

As stated in that chapter, these APIs are mostly focused on record data manipulation and querying, often known as CRUD. Leveraging the Salesforce APIs means developers wishing to learn how to integrate with your application objects can leverage the standard Salesforce API documentation and websites such as https://developer.salesforce.com/.

 Although the Enterprise API provides a strongly typed SOAP API for Java or .NET developers, its larger size can be problematic to load into development environments (as it includes all Custom Objects and fields present in the org). As such, more general Partner API is often a better recommendation to make to *Developer X*. Most developers are used to generic data access layers such as JDBC and ADO, and in essence to them the Partner API is similar and a lot smaller to embed in their applications. If however, you are recommending an API for mobile or JavaScript integration, the Salesforce REST APIs are even lighter, though come at the added responsibility of the developer to parse and form the correct JSON responses and requests without the aid of generated class types provided via the WSDLs of the SOAP APIs. Typically, languages that prefer more strongly typed programming principles prefer the SOAP variants over the REST variant.

For Java developers, Salesforce provides an excellent **Web Service Connector (WSC)** framework, which offers an efficient way to consume the SOAP and REST APIs without the need for any other web service stacks. They provide compiled versions of their popular Partner and Metadata APIs, with plenty of examples online. If you're familiar with it, the easiest way to download and start using this API is to use Apache Maven. You can also download WSC from https://github.com/forcedotcom/wsc:

> *"The Force.com Web Service Connector (WSC) is a high performing web service client stack implemented using a streaming parser. WSC also makes it much easier to use the Force.com API (Web Services/SOAP or Asynchronous/BULK API)."*

For .NET developers, Salesforce has recently started an open source initiative to build precompiled assemblies providing access to their APIs, much in the same spirit as the WSC Java library described earlier. You can download the toolkit for .NET from `https://github.com/developerforce/Force.com-Toolkit-for-NET`:

> *"The Force.com Toolkits for .NET provides an easy way for .NET developers to interact with the Force.com & Chatter REST APIs using native libraries."*

Application integration APIs

This section describes ways in which you can expose your application's business logic functionality encapsulated within your Service layer.

In some cases, *Developer X* is able to achieve such functionality through the standard Salesforce APIs. However, depending on the requirement, it might be easier and safer to call an API that exposes an existing business logic within the application. You can decide to do this for the same reasoning you would create a custom Visualforce page rather than expect the end users to utilize solely the standard UI (as using your objects directly requires them to understand the application's object schema in more detail).

Providing Apex application APIs

If your Service layer is developed and tested as robustly as possible following the guidelines discussed in the earlier chapter, it is worth considering exposing it to *Developer X* by simply updating the class, methods, members, properties, and any custom Apex types such as `global`. This part of the chapter discusses the approach in more detail, though it can also be applied to dedicated Apex classes built specifically to expose an API that is delegating to your Service layer classes:

```
global class ComplianceService
{
  global static void verify(Set<Id> recordIds)
  {
```

Make sure that you apply the global modifier carefully as it is not easy to deprecate it after your package has been released. Also, be sure to apply `global` to aspects of your Service layer only, avoid exposing Domain or Selector layer classes or types. If you need to expose behavior in these classes, write a Service layer method to do so. Also, note that the `ComplianceService.ICompliant` interface has not had the global modifier applied, as this is an internal aspect to the service.

As shown earlier in this chapter, we have also applied the `global` modifier to the Apex exception class defined within the `ComplianceService` class.

To try out this new application API, we will perform the following steps and execute the sample Apex test code introduced below in your test development org:

1. Apply the sample code for this chapter to your packaging org.

2. Comment out the `ComplianceService.report` method (we will uncomment this shortly before performing another upload).

3. Upload a release of the package and install it in your test development org.

4. Open the **Developer Console** and create an Apex class called `ApplicationAPITest`.

If you inspect the `ComplianceService` class in your test development org from the **Apex Classes** page under the **Setup** menu, you can see the new API methods and types you've just exposed are now visible (without the code). This provides a basic means for *Developer X* to learn about your API, in addition to any documentation you provide. A portion of how this looks for `ComplianceService` is shown in the following screenshot.

You can also see a **Version** drop-down box, which allows *Developer X* to explore different versions of the API definition. Note that the version shown might differ from yours depending on how many uploads of the package you have done at this point in the book.

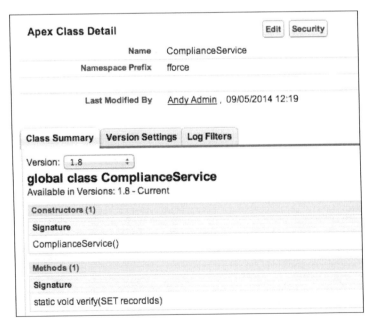

All `global` Apex classes will also show the **Security** link next to them in the list of classes, in the subscriber org. This is so that the subscriber org administrator can control permissions around the execution of the API's through Profiles. Note this only applies to global controller methods custom or extension controller or Web Service calls by Developer X. You can also granted access through appropriate Permission Set's as described in an earlier chapter. Meaning if the user is assigned a Permission Set granting them access to a specific set of features in the application, included is accessing those via API as well. If you want to control API permissions separately, create separate but functionality scoped permission sets.

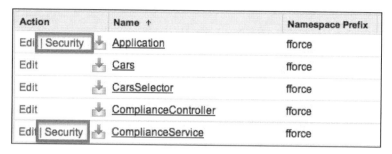

Action	Name ↑	Namespace Prefix
Edit	Security	Application	fforce
Edit	Cars	fforce
Edit	CarsSelector	fforce
Edit	ComplianceController	fforce
Edit	Security	ComplianceService	fforce

Calling an application API from Apex

The code used in this section uses Apex test methods (not included in the FormulaForce application). As an easy way to run API code examples, we will be using to illustrate the use of Apex APIs from the sample code included in this chapter. The two test methods we will look at call the compliance API after calling the season API to create some test data (which, of course, only exists on the database within the scope of the test execution).

In the following examples, the **Driver** records created by the `SeasonService. createTestSeason` API do not indicate that the drivers hold **FIA Super License**. Thus, the expectation is that the `ComplianceService.verify` method will throw an exception reporting this problem. The following example test code asserts this behavior purely for illustration purposes in this chapter:

```
@IsTest
private class ApplicationAPITest
{
    @IsTest
    private static void demoComplianceVerifyAPI()
    {
        // Create some test data via the SeasonService
        fforce.SeasonService.createTestSeason();
```

```
// Query Drivers to test compliance against
Map<Id, fforce__Driver__c> driversById =
    new Map<Id, fforce__Driver__c>(
        [select Id from fforce__Driver__c]);

try
{
    // Invoke the compliance engine for the drivers
    fforce.ComplianceService.verify(
        driversById.keySet());
    System.assert(false, 'Expected failures');
}
catch (fforce.ComplianceService.ComplianceException e)
{
    // Check the results
    System.assertEquals(
        '4.1', e.failures[0].complianceCode);
    System.assertEquals(
        'Driver must have a FIA Super License.',
        e.failures[0].failureReason);
}
}
}
```

The namespace used in this sample is fforce. Your namespace will differ. Replace the namespace to get the code sample to compile (you can also find this class in the sample code for this chapter).

Run the test to confirm whether the API is working as expected.

As you have used the same Service layer method as used by the rest of the application, your existing unit and integration tests around this class should suffice in providing you confidence in the robustness of this as an API to your application. If not, improving your testing around your Service layer benefits both external and internal callers equally.

Notice that when you click on the **Show Dependencies** button in the ApplicationAPITest class, it shows the API and Custom Objects being referenced from the package.

Show Dependencies

Dependency Information for Apex Class ApplicationAPITest

« Back to Apex Class: ApplicationAPITest

A dependency is created when one component references another component, permission, or preferer below have dependencies. In addition, the object-level operational scope, that is, the data manipulatio also listed. To see field-level detail of the operational scope, click Fields next to name of an object.

▼ **Object Operational Scope**

		Insert
Driver (Installed Package: FormulaForce)	[Fields]	☐

▼ **Apex Class, Trigger and Page References**

ComplianceService (Installed Package: FormulaForce)
SeasonService (Installed Package: FormulaForce)

Modifying and depreciating the application API

Once a `global` class method or member has been published by including it in a released package, it cannot be removed or changed. For example, try changing the `ComplianceService.verify` method by renaming it to `verification` (for example). When you attempt to save the class, you will receive the following error:

```
(ComplianceService) Global/WebService identifiers cannot be removed
from managed application: Method: void verify(SET<Id>)   (Line: 1)
```

> If you want to perform some testing or distribute your package while reserving the ability to make changes to your new APIs, upload your package as a beta until you are happy with your API definition. Note that you can of course change the behavior of your API (determined by the Apex code behind it) at any time, though this has to be done with care.

The `@Deprecated` annotation can be used to effectively remove from visibility the class, interface, method, or member that `global` has been applied to from the perspective of subsequent package version consumers. *Developer X* can still access the deprecated items by referencing an earlier version of the package through the class version settings shown via the **Version Settings** tab as described in more detail in the following sections.

At the time of writing this, the @Depricated flag cannot be used in developer orgs that are unmanaged. In a later chapter, we will discuss a team development model that permits the development of your application through managing your code within Source Control system and separately managing developer orgs per developer. While this style of development has a number of benefits, it does exclude the use of the @Depricated flag, as such orgs are effectively unmanaged.

Versioning Apex API definitions

When saved, the ApplicationAPITest class, the **Version Settings** tab, and the **Dependencies** page reflects the fact that code within the class is referencing the ComplianceService and SeasonService classes from the FormulaForce package.

In the following screenshot, the version is shown v1.8 as this was the current version of the package when the Apex class was first created (this might be different in your case, depending on how many times you have uploaded the package so far):

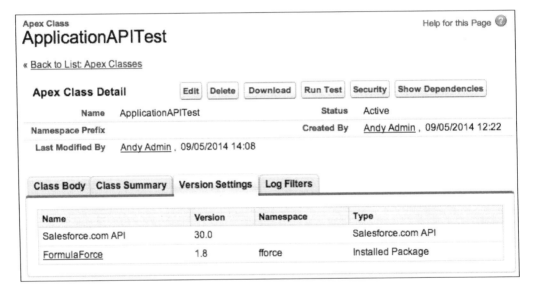

In the following steps, we will release a new version of the package with a new Compliance API to explore how the platform provides Apex API versioning:

1. In the packaging org, uncomment the `ComplianceService.report` method. This method works like the verify method but will not throw an exception; instead, it returns a full list of results including compliance passes and failures.

2. Upload a new release of the package and install it into your test development org.

3. In the test development org, open the Apex class `ApplicationAPITest`.

Attempt to add the following new test method and save the class:

```
@IsTest
private static void demoComplianceReportAPI()
{
    // Create some test data via the SeasonService
    fforce.SeasonService.createTestSeason();

    // Query Drivers to test compliance against
    Map<Id, fforce__Driver__c> driversById =
        new Map<Id, fforce__Driver__c>(
            [select Id from fforce__Driver__c]);

    // Update the licenses for the drivers
    for(fforce__Driver__c driver : driversById.values())
        driver.fforce__FIASuperLicense__c = true;
    update driversById.values();

    // Invoke the compliance engine to verify the drivers
    List<fforce.ComplianceService.VerifyResult>
      reportResults =
        fforce.ComplianceService.report(
          driversById.keySet());

    // Check the results
    System.assertEquals('4.1',
      reportResults[0].complianceCode);
    System.assertEquals(true, reportResults[0].passed);
    System.assertEquals(null,
      reportResults[0].failureReason);
}
```

You should get an error, indicating that the method does not exist:

```
Compile Error: Package Visibility: Method is not visible: fforce.
ComplianceService.report(SET<Id>) at line 21 column 13
```

This is due to the package version information in the Apex class metadata of the test class still referencing the release of the package installed at the time the code was originally written. Upgrading the package does not change this. Open the **Version Settings** tab and change to the release you have just installed to fix this compile problem.

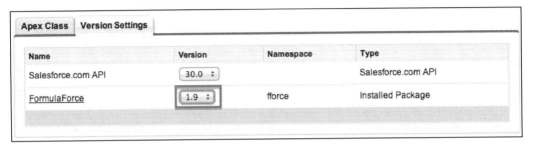

The preceding steps have illustrated how the Apex runtime manages versioning of the Apex APIs you expose from your package. Thus, the requirement of versioning API definition described earlier has been provided by the platform for you. There is no need to manage this yourself, though you do need to be aware of how it works.

Finally, revisit the `ComplianceService` Apex class page from within your test development org and notice that the available versions of this class has also increased to include the version just uploaded. Toggle between them, you can see the changes that the API definition has undergone between the last two package releases we have just performed.

Select **All Versions** to get a full summary of which methods arrived at which package version. You can see in the following screenshot that the `verify` method was first available in v1.8 and the `report` method in v1.9; again, your version numbers might differ:

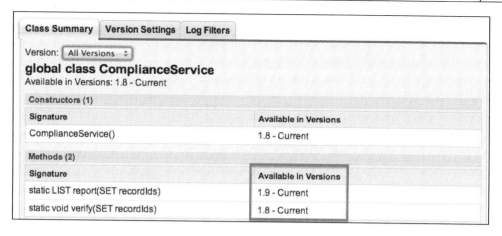

Versioning Apex API behavior

The API definition is not the only aspect that can undergo changes between releases. Even if the definition stays the same, the code behind it can change the behavior of the API. The Apex runtime provides means for the packaged code to determine which version the calling code written by *Developer X* is expecting. This can be obtained by calling the System.requestVersion method. With this information, your packaged code can modify its behavior according to the expectations of the calling code.

As you release more versions of your package and the functionality grows, the management of this type of code becomes more complex. Also note that this feature is only available in the code located within the packaging org or specifically managed code. In the standard developer org, this method will throw a runtime exception. This essentially rules out its use if you plan on relocating your code outside the packaging org, for example, by following the team development model discussed in the last chapter of this book.

Another way of versioning behavior is by considering whether changes in your application logic are something that *Developer X* would want to opt-in to or be immediately available to their existing code once the package was upgraded. Changes to fix bugs or minor improvements in the way information is processed are likely things you wish to be available, regardless of the API version. However, other changes such as the way values are calculated or the addition of significantly new processing would be something that might justify a new API method or a parameter for *Developer X* to modify their code to use. Much like in the UI, you will choose to add a new tab, page, or button.

By considering when to version the API behavior, you have put the choice as to when to accept new API behaviors in the hands of *Developer X*. Critically, by considering backwards compatibility you have not blocked upgrading to the latest version of your package due to integration failures. Spotting backwards compatibility regressions caused by behavior changes will get harder the more versions you release and the more supported versions you have in your customer base. Therefore making sure that you have a strong API-testing strategy becomes all the more critical.

Providing RESTful application APIs

So far we have focused on *Developer X* being an on-platform Apex developer and the ways in which you can provide application APIs via Apex. However, it is also possible that *Developer X* can be coding off-platform, needing to call your application APIs from Java or Microsoft .NET, or a mobile application. Perhaps they want to write a small dedicated mobile application to check the compliance for teams, drivers, or cars.

This part of the chapter will focus on exposing a REST API of the preceding compliance API for use by off-platform developers writing integrations with your application. Don't forget, as with the on-platform scenario Salesforce provides a number of standard Salesforce APIs via SOAP and REST, which by coding off-platform *Developer X* can use to create, read, update, and delete records held in your application's Custom Objects.

> Apex provides support to expose the application logic via web services (SOAP), through the use of the `webservice` keyword placed in your Apex classes. If you want to expose a SOAP API, the platform can generate the appropriate WSDLs once you have applied this keyword to methods on your Service classes. The design of services designed in this book happens to align quite well with the general requirements of web services. Note that the afore mentioned @Depricated attribute cannot be used on Apex code exposed this way One thing to consider though is that the WSDLs generated are not versioned, they are only generated based on the code for the installed version of your package. *Developer X* cannot generate historic versions of it from previous package versions. While Apex methods that use the `webservice` keyword fall under the same restrictions as `global`, you cannot exclude new methods or fields in your web services by version.

Apex also provides support to create your own REST APIs, with some great reference documentation within the *Apex Developer's Guide*. However, what it doesn't cover are REST API design considerations, often referred to as RESTful. Many mistakes are made in exposing REST APIs without first understanding what it means to be RESTful. Before we get into using your Service layer to deliver a REST API, let's learn more about being RESTful.

Key aspects of being RESTful

A full discussion and overview of RESTful API design could easily take up a full chapter. The following is a summary of the key RESTful design goals and how these apply to REST APIs delivered via Apex (some guidelines are handled for you by the platform). As we discuss this topic further, the use of the term *operation* represents the methods in the application's Service layer classes. This will be used to help expose the application's REST API but should not steer it's design.

> There is no one list of guidelines and some are open to interpretation. However, if you enter `Designing a RESTful API` in Google, you're sure to come up with some useful reading. I recommend that you focus on those articles that give insight as to how some of the larger services such as Facebook, LinkedIn, and Salesforce themselves are interpreting RESTful, such as `http://www.apigee.com/`.

What are your application resources?

In the RESTful world, your operations are associated with a resource that is expressed via **Uniform Resource Identifier (URI)**. A resource can be a physical thing in your application such as Custom Object, or a conceptual thing. This is different from the Service layer design that drove the Apex API we have looked at earlier, where operations are expressed by grouping them under functional areas of the application, which are then expressed by Apex Service classes and methods for each operation.

The Salesforce REST API uses Custom Objects to define physical resources the REST URI uses, allowing you to build a URI and use the various HTTP methods to perform the create, read, update, and delete operations. For example, to retrieve a record you can issue the following request via the Developer Workbench tool:

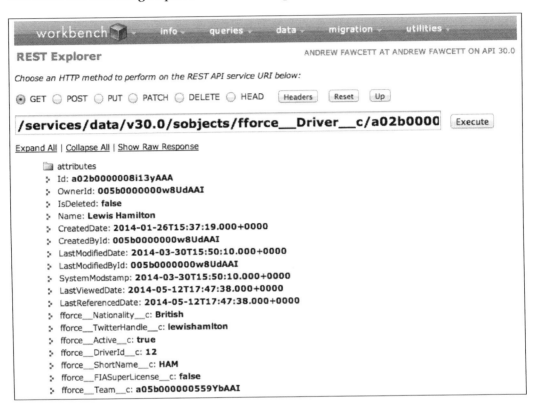

In cases where you are exposing more business process or task-orientated operations that are not data centric, it can be difficult to decide what the resource name should actually be? So it is worth taking the time to plan out and agree with the whole product team what the key REST resources are in the application and stick to them.

One operation that falls into this category in our FormulaForce package is the compliance report. This operates on a number of different Custom Object records to report compliance, such as the driver, car, and team. Should we define a URI that applies it to each of these physical resources individually, or create a new logical compliance resource?

I chose the latter in this chapter because it feels more extensible to do it this way, as it also leverages the compliance service in the application, which already supports adding new object types to the compliance checker. Thus, the REST API will support new object types without future changes to the API, as they are added to the compliance checker.

Salesforce dictates the initial parts of the URI used to define the resource and the developer gets to define the rest. For the compliance REST API, we will use this URI:

```
/services/apexrest/compliance
```

Once you package your Apex code implementing this REST API, you will find that the preceding URI needs to be qualified by your package namespace, so will take on the format, shown as follows, from the point of view of *Developer X*, where `fforce` is my namespace. We will use this format of URI when we test the compliance REST API later in this chapter:

```
/services/apexrest/fforce/compliance
```

Mapping HTTP methods

Your application operations for a given resource URI should be mapped to one of the standard HTTP methods on which REST is based: GET, POST, PUT, PATCH, and DELETE. Choosing which to use and being consistent about its use throughout your REST API is vital. Again, there are many resources on the Internet that discuss this topic in much more detail. Here is a brief summary of my interpretation of those readings:

- GET: This method is typically for operations that query the database and whose parameters are easily expressed in the URI structure and/or whose parameters fit well with this method.

- PUT versus POST: These methods are typically for operations that create, update, or query the database and where parameters are more complex, for example lists or structures of information that cannot be reflected in URI parameters. There is also a consideration around the term **Idempotent** (check out Wikipedia for a full definition of this), which relates to whether or not the request can be repeated over and over, resulting in the same state in the database. As you dig deeper into the RESTful design guidelines, this term typically drives the decision over using PUT versus POST.

- PATCH: This method is typically for operations that solely update existing information, such as a record or some other complex dataset spanning multiple records.

- DELETE: This method is, of course, to delete existing information expressed in the URI.

We will use the POST HTTP method with the `/services/apexrest/compliance` resource URI to implement our REST API for the compliance verify operation, passing the list of records to verify as a part of the HTTP request body using the JSON data format.

Providing REST application APIs

The following Apex class follows the naming convention `[ResourceName]Resource` as the class name and then defines the appropriate methods (whose names are not as important in this case), mapping them accordingly to the HTTP method for the URL mapping. This is included in the sample code of this chapter:

```
@RestResource(urlMapping='/compliance')
global with sharing class ComplianceResource
{
  @HttpPost
  global static List<ComplianceService.VerifyResult>
    report(List<Id> Ids)
  {
    return ComplianceService.report(new Set<Id>(Ids));
  }
}
```

The following are some things to note about the preceding example, and in general about wrapping Service layer methods in Apex REST methods to create Application REST APIs:

- The methods in this class should delegate to one, and only one, applicable method in a Service class, as per general Service layer calling guidelines, to maintain a transaction scope and also Separation of Concerns.

- It is not recommended that you map your Apex resource classes only to a specific Service class, as your earlier RESTful API design might not match your Service class design, though it should still delegate to it.

- Treat these classes like you would treat a Visualforce controller, including only marshaling and error handling logic as required.

- Typically you don't need to catch exceptions from the Service layer (unlike Visualforce controller action method callers), as the Apex REST runtime catches the exception and the returns appropriate REST API error code and message. Avoid implementing your own REST API error handling.

- The `global` modifier is still required. Keep in mind that the same packaging restrictions regarding changes to these methods apply.

- It is possible for the *Developer X* Apex developer to call these methods from Apex, as they are `global`. However, this should be discouraged because these methods might reference the REST API context variables, which will not be initialized in a standard Apex context.

- The `Set` Apex data type is not supported by Apex REST methods.

- The `ComplianceService.verify` method throws an exception with additional information about the specific compliance failures. However, information in a custom Apex exception is not automatically serialized by the platform, only the error message is included. In this case, a custom response would be required to catch the exception and return the information.

Calling your REST application APIs

The Salesforce Developer Workbench can be used to call the preceding REST API. Locate a **Driver** record without the **FIA Super License** field selected and use the following ID. Note that the URI shown in the following screenshot contains the package namespace, `fforce`. To try this out you need to replace this with your chosen package namespace:

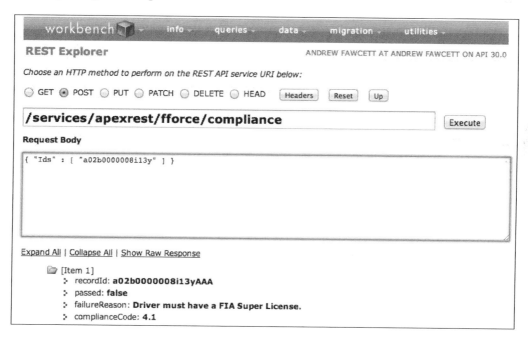

Versioning REST APIs

The generally recognized way in which REST APIs are versioned is to include the version in the URI. Notice that v30.0 (the Salesforce platform version) was included in the standard Salesforce REST API example shown earlier, but no version was included in the URI for the REST API exposing the compliance report operation.

One option to address this is to map a versioned URI to a specific Apex resource class per version, for example, to support version v1.0 and v2.0 of the compliance REST API:

```
@RestResource(urlMapping='/v1.0/compliance')
global with sharing class ComplianceResource_v1_0
{
  @HttpPost
  global static List<ComplianceService.VerifyResult>
    report(List<Id> Ids)
  {
    return ComplianceService.report(new Set<Id>(Ids));
  }
}

@RestResource(urlMapping='/v2.0/compliance')
global with sharing class ComplianceResource_v2_0
{
  @HttpPost
  global static List<ComplianceService.VerifyResult>
    report(List<Id> Ids)
  {
    return ComplianceService.report(new Set<Id>(Ids));
  }
}
```

This approach allows you to know which version of your API the caller is using and thus allows you to do some behavior versioning (perhaps by setting a static variable):

```
/service/apexrest/fforce/v1.0/compliance
/service/apexrest/fforce/v2.0/compliance
```

To version the REST API definition, the preceding classes need to also capture their own copies of the Apex data types used in the Service layer. The main coding overhead here is going to be marshaling between the Apex types defined in the Service layer (which are always the latest version) and those in the class implementing the REST API.

For example, to version the `report` API, we have to capture its types as inner Apex classes at the time the API class is created. The following example illustrates this for v1.0, you can see how the definition of the API can be encapsulated within the specific version of the Apex class denoted by the `v1_0` suffix:

```
@RestResource(urlMapping='/v1.0/compliance')
global with sharing class ComplianceResource_v1_0
{
  global class VerifyResult
  {
    global Id recordId;
    global String complianceCode;
    global Boolean passed;
    global String failureReason;
  }

  @HttpPost
  global static List<VerifyResult> report(List<Id> Ids)
  {
    List<VerifyResult> results = new List<VerifyResult>();
    for(ComplianceService.VerifyResult result :
      ComplianceService.report(new Set<Id>(Ids)))
    results.add(makeVerifyResult(result));
    return results;
  }

  private static VerifyResult
    makeVerifyResult(ComplianceService.VerifyResult verifyResult)
  {
    VerifyResult restVerifyResult = new VerifyResult();
    restVerifyResult.recordId = verifyResult.recordId;
    restVerifyResult.complianceCode = verifyResult.complianceCode;
    restVerifyResult.passed = verifyResult.passed;
    restVerifyResult.failureReason = verifyResult.failureReason;
    return restVerifyResult;
  }
}
```

While the version number you use can be anything you like, you may want to consider following your package version numbering sequence.

Is it worth versioning Apex REST APIs?

Versioning Apex REST APIs this way is not ideal, I would prefer some platform support along the lines of the way the SOAP API allows the caller to embed the package version in the request headers, or being able to specify the package version in the URI just after the namespace, the way Salesforce would have done for its standard Salesforce REST API.

Until this happens, the preceding way is the only way I can currently recommend to support multiple versions of a REST API, if this is important to your callers. Without this, you have to be extra careful about adding new members and items to your responses and requests, as the global modifier will itself help you manage most breaking changes.

Breaking news! Starting with the Winter'15 platform release, API version v31.0, the Salesforce REST API and any Apex REST APIs exposed can receive from a new HTTP header, such as x-sfdc-packageversion-fforce: 1.10. In case of Apex REST APIs, at the time of writing, the prerelease documenation states that this can be used to allow the packaged API code to implement versioning. Initial testing at time of writing indicates that this can be used to set the version returned by System.requestVersion as described earlier in this chapter. However it does not control the REST URIs and HTTP methods available or adjust the JSON accepted or returned. In other words, it appears that it can be used to implement behavior versioning, but not versioning the definition, as per the previous strategy. Nor is the version information as explicit, as requiring it to be present in the URI. Once Winter'15 is fully released this may of course change.

Alignment with Force.com extensibility features

Here are some platform features that can help ensure your application functionality is open to being extended by *Developer X* or subscriber org administrators:

- **Apex Triggers**: *Developer X* can write their own triggers against your application's managed Custom Objects. These will execute in addition to those packaged. This allows *Developer X* to implement defaulting of fields or custom validations, for example. Salesforce does not guarantee that packaged triggers execute before or after *Developer X* triggers in the subscriber org. To ensure that all changes are validated regardless to the trigger execution order, perform your validation logic in the after-phase of your packaged triggers.

- **Field Sets**: As described in earlier chapters, make sure to leverage this feature as often as possible on your Visualforce pages to ensure that regions and tables can be extended with subscriber added fields. These can also be used with JavaScript frameworks if you're developing a mobile UI.

- **E-mail templates**: If you're writing code to emit e-mails, consider providing a means to allow the text to be customized using an e-mail template. These can be referenced through their developer name using a custom setting. Field Sets can also be leveraged here to provide an easy way to include additional custom fields added by the subscriber administrator.

- **Visualforce components**: Consider creating some Visualforce components globally, such that *Developer X* can more easily build alternative custom Visualforce pages without having to re-invent all aspects of your applications pages. Such components can be built to allow dynamic content in e-mail templates.

- **Dynamic Apex type creation**: The `Type.forName` method can be used to create an instance of an Apex type, and from that an instance of that type at runtime. This capability can be used to allow *Developer X* to write the Apex code, which your application code can dynamically call at a specified time. This approach is discussed in further detail in the upcoming section.

Extending the application logic with Apex Interfaces

An **Apex Interface** can be used to describe a point in your application logic where custom code written by *Developer X* can be called. For example, in order to provide an alterative means to calculate championship points driven by *Developer X*, we might expose a global interface describing an application callout that looks like this:

```
global class ContestantService
{
  global interface IAwardChampionshipPoints
  {
    void calculate(List<Contestant__c> contestants);
  }
}
```

We can then reference a custom setting (the **Application** setting has been included in the source code for this chapter) to determine whether *Developer X* has provided an implementation of this interface to call instead of the standard calculation code. The following code uses the `Type.forName` methods to construct at runtime the Apex type and create an instance of the type that can be cast to the interface.

Notice how the code supports *Developer X* providing a class name that is either fully qualified (perhaps from an extension package, for example, fforceext.SimpleCalc) or a local class (defined in the subscriber org), for example, DeveloperXCustomCalc:

```
public void awardChampionshipPoints(fflib_SObjectUnitOfWork uow)
{
    // Custom implementation configured by Developer X?
    String customImplementationClassName =
      Application__c.getInstance().
        IAwardChampionshipPointsApexClass__c;
    if(customImplementationClassName!=null)
    {
        // Attempt to resolve the class?
        Type customImplementationClass =
            // Namespace (managed) qualified e.g. devx.CustomCalc
            Type.forName(customImplementationClassName);
        if(customImplementationClass==null)
            customImplementationClass =
                // Local (unmanaged) namespace e.g. CustomCalc
                Type.forName('',customImplementationClassName);
        if(customImplementationClass!=null)
        {
            // Create instance of Developer X's class
            ContestantService.IAwardChampionshipPoints
                customImplementation =
                    (ContestantService.IAwardChampionshipPoints)
                        customImplementationClass.newInstance();
            // Invoke the custom method
            customImplementation.calculate(Records);
            // Mark dirty on behalf of Developer X
            for(Contestant__c contestant : (List<Contestant__c>) Records)
                uow.registerDirty(contestant);
        }
        return;
    }

    // Continue with standard implementation...
```

In the subscriber org or the test development org, *Developer X* can then implement this interface as follows and configure via the Custom Setting. The next time the award championship points service is called, this custom logic will be called instead.

```
public class SimpleCalc
  implements fforce.ContestantService.IAwardChampionshipPoints
{
  public void calculate(List<fforce__Contestant__c> contestants)
  {
    // Very simple, points equals race position
    for(fforce__Contestant__c contestant : contestants)
      contestant.fforce__ChampionshipPoints__c =
        contestant.fforce__RacePosition__c;
  }
}
```

Some aspects to consider when exposing global Apex interfaces are as follows:

- You cannot modify global interfaces once published by uploading them within a release managed package.

- You can extend a global interface from another global interface, for example `IAwardChampionshipPointsExt extends IAwardChampionshipPoints`.

- Consider carefully what you pass into an Application Callout via your Apex Interface methods, especially if the parameters are objects whose values are later referenced by the application code. Be sure that you are happy for the Application Callout to make any changes to this object or data. If you're not comfortable with this, consider cloning the object before passing it as a parameter to the interface method.

Summary

In this chapter, we have reviewed enterprise application integration and extensibility requirements through the eyes of a persona known as *Developer X*. By using this persona, much like your UI designs, you can ensure that your API tracks real use cases and requirements from the representative and ideally actual users of it.

When defining your API strategy, keep in mind the benefits of the standard Salesforce APIs and how to evangelize those and the significant investment Salesforce puts into them in order to provide access to the information stored in your Custom Objects. When needed, leverage your Service layer to create application APIs either on-and/or off-platform using Apex and REST as delivery mechanisms. Keep in mind that REST requires additional design considerations to ensure that your REST API can be considered properly RESTful and thus familiar to *Developer X* who has been using other REST APIs.

Don't forget that while technologies such as Visualforce and Apex provide you great flexibility as a developer and finely tuned functionality to the user, they can often lead to reduced opportunities for extensibility for the subscriber, by using Field Sets and Apex Application Extensions (leveraging `Type.forName`) you can readdress this balance. Also keep in mind that Field Sets provide a good extensibility tool beyond Visualforce use cases. For example, they can be used to expose subscriber custom fields when building Mobile UIs using JavaScript frameworks.

There is no need to upload a new version of the FormulaForce package in this chapter if you have been following along; if not, take the latest code from the sample code provided with this chapter to update your packaging org and upload a new package.

10

Asynchronous Processing and Big Data Volumes

This chapter covers two important aspects of developing an Enterprise-level application on the Force.com platform. While asynchronous processing and Big Data volumes are not necessarily linked, the greater governor limits and processing power of the platform are mostly to be found in the async processing mode. However, making sure that your interactive user experience is still responsive when querying large volumes of data is also very important.

In this chapter, we will first review how to ensure SOQL queries are as performant as possible by understanding how to profile queries and make use of the standard and custom indexes. This will benefit both interactive and batch (or async) processes in your application as well as how they leverage native platform features such as reporting.

We will then take a look at the options, best practices, design, and usability considerations to move your application processing into the async mode, once again leveraging the **Service** layer as the shared backbone of your application, before finally understanding some thoughts and considerations when it comes to volume testing your application. We will cover the following topics in this chapter:

- Creating test data for volume testing
- Indexes, being selective, and query optimization
- Asynchronous execution contexts
- Volume testing

Creating test data for volume testing

Throughout this chapter, we are going to use the `RaceData__c` object. We will be extending it with additional fields and running a script to populate it with some test volume data, before exploring the different ways of accessing it and processing the data held within it.

In the **Formula1** racing world, a huge amount of data is captured from the drivers and the cars during the race. This information is used to perform real-time or post-race analysis in order to lead to further improvements or troubleshoot issues. Because of the huge volumes of data involved, the FormulaForce application considers ways to summarize this data such that it can be removed and later reloaded easily if required.

The following functionalities will be added to the FormulaForce application to process this information and help demonstrate the Force.com features described in this chapter. The Apex classes and Visualforce page for this functionality is included in the sample code for this chapter.

- A Visualforce page able to perform some *What-If* analysis on the race data
- A Batch Apex process to validate and associate race data with contestants

The sample code for this chapter also contains updates to the **Race Data** object, as follows:

1. The **Type** field represents the type of race data, for example, **Oil Pressure**, **Engine Temperature**, **Sector Time**, **Fuel Level**, **Pit Stop Times**, and so on.

2. The **Value** field is a numeric value dependent on the **Type** field.

3. The **Lap** and **Sector** fields are numeric fields that represent the lap and sector number the data was captured on.

4. The **Year**, **Race Name**, and **Driver Id** fields are text fields whose values, when later combined together, can be used to form a key to link each **Race Data** record with the appropriate **Contestant** record (which has its own relationships with the **Driver**, **Race**, and **Season** objects). In this use case, we assume that the electronic systems generating this raw data do not know or want to understand Salesforce IDs, so the FormulaForce application must correctly resolve the relationship with the **Contestant** record.

5. The **Contestant** lookup field references the applicable **Contestant** record. As the incoming raw data does not contain Salesforce record Ids, this field is not initially populated. The FormulaForce applications logic will populate this later, as will be shown later in this chapter.

6. A new **Race Data ID** external ID field has been added to the **Contestant** object. The Apex code in the `Contestants` Domain class has been updated to ensure that this field is automatically populated as **Contestants** are added and that its value can be used during the processing of new **Race Data** to correctly associate **Race Data** records with **Contestant** records.

The **Race Data** object uses an **Auto Number** field type for its **Name** field. This ensures the insert order for the data is also retained.

> Note that we have added the **Race Data ID** field to an object already released in previous versions of the package, while the `Contestants` Domain class has been updated to populate this field for new records. The records already existing in subscriber orgs will not contain this value. Force.com provides a means to execute the Apex code after installation (and uninstallation) of the package, such that you can include the code to trigger a Batch Apex job to update this field value with the appropriate value on existing records.

Using the Apex script to create the Race Data object

Just like me, I doubt you have a real Formula1 race team or car to provide raw data input. We will be using an Apex script to generate the test data, though in reality race data may be inserted through a CSV file import or through an integration with the car itself via the Salesforce APIs.

This test script will generate 10,000 rows, which is about enough to explore the platform features described in this chapter and the behavior, Force.com SOQL **profiler**, which makes different choices dependent on row count.

Due to the volumes of data being created (and deleted if you rerun the scripts), you must run each of the following Apex statements one by one to stay within the governors via the **Execute Anonymous** prompt from your chosen IDE or developer console:

1. Run `TestData.resetTestSeason();`.
2. Run `TestData.purgeVolumeDataForChapter10(false);`.
3. Run `TestData.purgeVolumeDataForChapter10(true);`.
4. Run `TestData.createVolumeDataForChapter10(2014, 'Spain', 52, 4);`.

Step 1 of the preceding steps will run a script that will clear down all other data from other FormulaForce objects in order to set up test **Season**, **Race**, and **Driver** data for the rest of the chapter. You can repeat step 4 to generate a further 10,000 **Race Data** records for additional races—something we will do later in this chapter. This step might take a few minutes to complete.

Once the script has been executed, go to the **Race Data** tab and review the data. The values shown in the **Value** column are random values, so your results will differ.

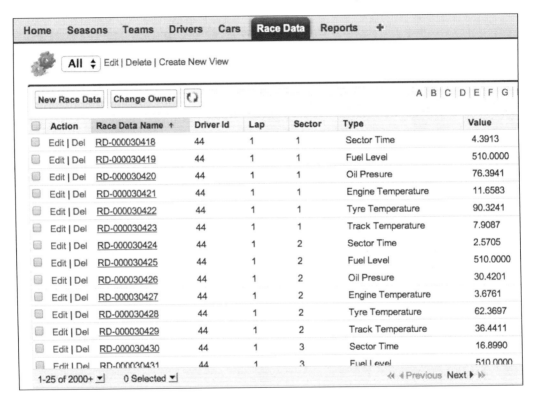

Action	Race Data Name ↑	Driver Id	Lap	Sector	Type	Value
Edit | Del	RD-000030418	44	1	1	Sector Time	4.3913
Edit | Del	RD-000030419	44	1	1	Fuel Level	510.0000
Edit | Del	RD-000030420	44	1	1	Oil Presure	76.3941
Edit | Del	RD-000030421	44	1	1	Engine Temperature	11.6583
Edit | Del	RD-000030422	44	1	1	Tyre Temperature	90.3241
Edit | Del	RD-000030423	44	1	1	Track Temperature	7.9087
Edit | Del	RD-000030424	44	1	2	Sector Time	2.5705
Edit | Del	RD-000030425	44	1	2	Fuel Level	510.0000
Edit | Del	RD-000030426	44	1	2	Oil Presure	30.4201
Edit | Del	RD-000030427	44	1	2	Engine Temperature	3.6761
Edit | Del	RD-000030428	44	1	2	Tyre Temperature	62.3697
Edit | Del	RD-000030429	44	1	2	Track Temperature	36.4411
Edit | Del	RD-000030430	44	1	3	Sector Time	16.8990
Edit | Del	RD-000030431	44	1	3	Fuel Level	510.0000

1-25 of 2000+ 0 Selected « ‹ Previous Next › »

You should also see the following row count if you review the **Storage Usage** page:

Current Data Storage Usage

Record Type	Record Count
Race Data	10,000

Indexes, being selective, and query optimization

In this section, we will review when system and custom indexes maintained by the Force.com platform are used to make queries more performant and, once larger query results are returned, the ways in which they can be most effectively consumed by your Apex logic.

Standard and custom indexes

As with other databases, Force.com maintains database indexes as record data is manipulated to ensure that, when data is queried, such indexes can be used to improve query performance. Due to the design of the Force.com multitenant platform, it has its own database index implementation (instead of using the underlying Oracle database indexes) that considers the needs of each tenant. By default, it maintains standard indexes for the following fields:

- ID
- Name
- OwnerId
- CreateDate
- CreatedById
- LastModifiedDate
- LastModifiedById
- SystemModStamp
- RecordType
- Any Master Detail fields
- Any Lookup fields
- Any fields marked as Unique
- Any fields marked as External Id

Once your application is deployed into a subscriber org, you can also request Salesforce to consider creating additional custom indexes on fields not covered by the preceding list, such as fields used by your application logic to filter records, including custom formula fields and custom fields added to your objects by the subscriber as well.

Formula fields can be indexed so long as the formula result is deterministic, which means that it does not use any dynamic data or time functions such as TODAY or NOW, or leverage-related fields via lookup fields or any other formula fields that are non-deterministic.

As creating indexes and maintaining them consumes platform resources, custom indexes cannot be packaged, as the decision to enable them is determined by conditions only found in the subscriber org.

Though objects can contain millions of records, standard indexes will only index up to 1 million records and custom indexes up to 333,333 records. These limits have a bearing on whether an index is used or not, depending on the query and filter criteria being used. This is discussed in more detail further in this chapter.

With respect to the **Race Data** object, the following fields will be indexed by default by the platform. Only through contacting Salesforce support and enabling in the subscriber org can additional custom indexes be created, for example, on the Type__c field.

Field	Standard Index
Created By	Yes (Lookup Field)
LastModifiedBy	Yes (Lookup Field)
Name	Yes
Contestant__c	Yes (Lookup Field)
DriverId__c	No
Lap__c	No
RaceName__c	No
Sector__c	No
Type__c	No
Value__c	No
Year__c	No

Thus, if a query filters by fields covered by a system or custom index, the index will be considered by the Force.com query optimizer. This means that just because an index exists does not mean it will be used; the final decision is determined by how *selective* the query is.

By default, Salesforce does not include rows (that contain null values) within its indexes for the respective field. In this case, although the **Contestant** field is indexed by default, it initially contains a null value and thus initially the index will be ineffective (this fact relates to why the use of nulls in filter criteria will deter the Force.com query optimizer from using an index, as discussed in the next section). You can, however, get Salesforce Support to discuss enablement of the inclusion of nulls in indexes.

Ensuring queries leverage indexes

The process of selecting an appropriate index applies to queries made via SOQL through APIs and Apex, but also via **Reporting** and **List Views**. The use of an index is determined by the SOQL statement being selective or not. The following provides definitions of being selective and being non-selective:

- Salesforce uses the term **selective** to describe queries filtering record data that are able to leverage indexes maintained behind the scenes by Salesforce, making such queries more efficient and thus returning results more quickly

- Conversely, the term **non selective** implies a given query is not leveraging an index; thus, it will, in most cases, not perform as well; it will either time-out or, for objects with records greater than 100,000, result in a runtime exception

In a nonselective query situation, the platform will scan all the records in the object, applying the filtering to each; this is known as a *full table scan*. However, this is not necessarily the slowest option, depending on the number of records and the filter criteria.

The main goal of this part of the chapter is to explain what it takes for Salesforce to select an index for a given query. This depends on a number of factors, both when you build your application queries and the number of records in your objects within the subscriber org.

Factors affecting the use of indexes

There are two things that determine whether an index is used. Firstly, the **filter criteria** (or the WHERE clause in SOQL terms) of the query must comply with certain rules in terms of operators and conditions used. Secondly, the total **number of records** in the object versus the estimated number of records that will be returned by applying the filter criteria.

The filter criteria must, of course, reference a field that has either a standard or custom index defined for it. After this, the use of unary, AND, OR, and LIKE operators can be used to filter records. However, other operators, such as negative operators, wild cards, and text comparison operators as well as the use of null in the filter criteria, can easily disqualify the query from using an index. For example, a filter criteria that is more explicit in the rows it wants, `Type__c = 'Sector Time'`, is more likely to leverage an index (assuming that this field has a custom index enabled), than say, for example `Type__c != 'Pit Stop Time'`, which will cause the platform to perform a full table scan, as the platform cannot leverage the internal statistics it maintains on the spread of data throughout the rows across this column.

The filtered record count must be below a certain percentage of the overall records in the object for an index to be used. You might well ask how Salesforce knows this information without actually performing the query in the first place? Though they do not give full details, they do describe what is known as a pre-query using statistical data that the platform captures as the standard or custom indexes are maintained. This statistical data helps to understand the spread of data based on the field values. For example, the percentage of rows loaded by the execution of the scripts to load sample data where the `Type__c` field contains the value **PitStop Time** is 0.16 percent, and thus, if a custom index was in place and the queries filter criteria was selective enough (for example, `Type__c = 'PitStop Time'`), an index would be used.

A query for **Sector Time**, such as `Type__c = 'Sector Time'`, will result in 1664 records, which is 16.64 percent of the total rows being selected. So, while the filter criteria are selective, the filtered record count is above the threshold for custom index 10 percent or 333,333 records max. Thus, in this case, an index is not used. This might result in a timeout or runtime exception. So, in order to avoid this, the query must be made more selective, for example, by enabling a custom index and adding either `Lap__c` or `Sector__c` into the filter criteria.

Salesforce provides more detailed information on how to handle large data volumes, such as fully documenting the filter record count tolerances used to select indexes (note that they differ based on standard or custom indexes) and some insights as to how they store data within the Oracle database that help make more sense of things. These are a must-read in my view and can be found in various white papers and Wiki pages. Some of them are as follows:

- *Query & Search Optimization Cheat Sheet*: `http://help.salesforce.com/help/pdfs/en/salesforce_query_search_optimization_developer_cheatsheet.pdf`.

- *Best Practices for Deployments with Large Data Volumes*: `http://www.salesforce.com/docs/en/cce/ldv_deployments/salesforce_large_data_volumes_bp.pdf`.

- *Force.com SOQL Best Practices: Nulls and Formula Fields*: `https://developer.salesforce.com/blogs/engineering/2013/02/force-com-soql-best-practices-nulls-and-formula-fields.html`.

- *Developing Selective Force.com Queries through the Query Resource Feedback Parameter Pilot*: `https://developer.salesforce.com/blogs/engineering/2014/04/developing-selective-force-com-queries-query-resource-feedback-parameter-pilot.html`.

Profiling queries

As you can see, consideration for which indexes are needed and when they are used are very much determined by the rate of data growth in the subscriber org and also the spread of distinct groups of data values in that data. So, profiling is typically something that is only done in conjunction with your customers and Salesforce, within the subscriber org.

In some cases, disclosing the queries your application makes from Apex and Visualforce pages might help you and your subscribers plan ahead as to which indexes are going to be needed. You can also capture the SOQL queries made from your code through the debug logs, once you're logged in through the **Subscriber Support** feature.

Once you have a SOQL query you suspect is causing problems, you will profile it to determine which indexes are being used in order to determine what to do to resolve the issue, create a new index, and/or make the filter criteria select less records by adding more constraints. To do this, you can use a feature of the platform to ask it to explain its choices when considering which index (if any) to use for a given query. Again, it is important to use this in the subscriber org or sandbox itself.

For the purposes of this chapter, the following example utilizes the `explain` parameter on the Salesforce REST API to execute a query within the packaging org we ran the preceding script in, to populate the **Race Data** object with 10,000 records.

 Starting with Summer'14, **Developer Console** now includes **Query Planner Tool**, which can be enabled under the **Preferences** tab. When you run queries via **Query Editor**, a popup will appear with an explanation of the indexes considered. The information shown is basically the same as that described in this chapter via the `explain` parameter.

This section utilizes the `explain` parameter when running SOQL via the **Developer Workbench** tool. Here, you can run the various queries in the explain mode and review the results. The results show a list of query plans that would have been used, had the query been actually executed. They are shown in order of preference by the platform. The following steps show how to login to the Developer Workbench to obtain a query plan for a given query:

1. Log in to **Developer Workbench**.
2. From the **Utilities** menu, select **REST Explorer**.
3. Enter `/services/data/v30.0/query?explain=` and then paste your **SOQL**.
4. Click on **Execute**.

First, let's try the following example without a custom index on the `Type__c` field. Note that the `fforce` prefix is used; as the SOQL query is being executed in the namespace-enabled packaging org, you should replace this with your own chosen namespace.

```
select id from fforce__RaceData__c
  where fforce__Type__c = 'PitStop Time'
```

This screenshot shows the Developer Workbench showing the query plan result for this query:

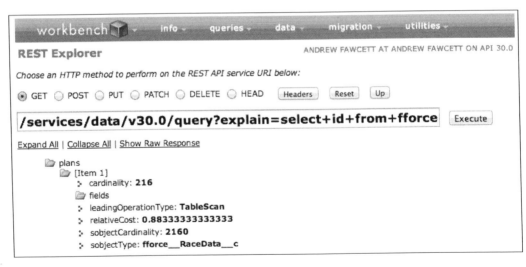

You can see, as expected, the result is **TableScan**, compared to the following query:

```
select id from fforce__RaceData__c
    where CreatedDate = TODAY
```

This screenshot shows the query plan for this query:

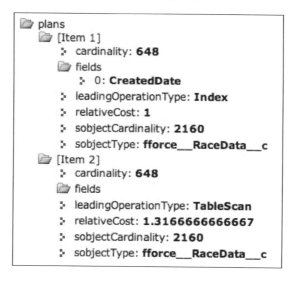

This results in two plans; however, the standard **Index** was selected over **TableScan**.

The `cardinality` and `sobjectCardinality` fields are both estimates based on the aforementioned statistical information that Salesforce maintains internally relating to the spread of records (in this case, distinct records by `Type__c`). Thus, it gives the rows it thinks will be selected by the filter versus the total number of also estimated rows in the sObject.

In this case, we can see that these are just estimates, as we know we have 10,000 records in the `RaceData__c` object; actually, 1,664 of those are **Sector Time** records. In general though, as long as these are broadly relative to the actual physical records, what the platform is doing is looking for the percentage of one from the other in order to decide whether an index will be worth using. It is actually the `relativeCost` field that is most important; basically a value greater than 1 means that the query will not be executed using the associated plan.

Now that you have a general idea of how to obtain this information, let's review a few more samples, but this time with 100,000 RaceData__c records (10 races worth of data using the same distribution of records). I have also asked Salesforce Support to enable a custom index over the Type__c, Lap__c and Sector__c custom fields. The namespace fforce prefix has been removed for clarity.

SOQL	Resulting plans

select id from RaceData__c where Type__c = 'PitStop Time'
 	
The number of records relating to **PitStop Time** is less than 10 percent of the overall record count, so an index was used.
	``
	{
	  "plans" : [{
	    "cardinality" : 160,
	    "fields" : ["Type__c"],
	    "leadingOperationType" : "Index",
	    "relativeCost" : 0.016,
	    "sobjectCardinality" : 100000,
	    "sobjectType" : "RaceData__c"
	  }, {
	    "cardinality" : 160,
	    "fields" : [ ],
	    "leadingOperationType" : "TableScan",
	    "relativeCost" : 0.6701333333333334,
	    "sobjectCardinality" : 100000,
	    "sobjectType" : "RaceData__c"
	  }]
	}
	``

SOQL	Resulting plans

`select id from RaceData__c where Type__c = 'Sector Time'`
 	
A table scan plan was selected as the number of records relating to **Sector Times** was greater than 10 percent of the overall record count.
	``json
	{
	  "plans" : [{
	    "cardinality" : 16640,
	    "fields" : [ ],
	    "leadingOperationType" : "TableScan",
	    "relativeCost" : 1.0272,
	    "sobjectCardinality" : 100000,
	    "sobjectType" : "RaceData__c"
	  }, {
	    "cardinality" : 16640,
	    "fields" : ["fforce__Type__c"],
	    "leadingOperationType" : "Index",
	    "relativeCost" : 1.664,
	    "sobjectCardinality" : 100000,
	    "sobjectType" : "RaceData__c"
	  }]
	}
	``

`select id from RaceData__c where Type__c = 'Sector Time' and RaceName__c = 'Spa'`
 	
Again, a table scan was selected even though the query was made more selective by adding the race name. Adding a custom index over the race name would be advised here, as it is likely to be a common filter criteria.
	``json
	{
	  "plans" : [{
	    "cardinality" : 1000,
	    "fields" : [ ],
	    "leadingOperationType" : "TableScan",
	    "relativeCost" : 0.6883333333333334,
	    "sobjectCardinality" : 100000,
	    "sobjectType" : "fforce__RaceData__c"
	  }, {
	    "cardinality" : 16640,
	    "fields" : ["fforce__Type__c"],
	    "leadingOperationType" : "Index",
	    "relativeCost" : 1.664,
	    "sobjectCardinality" : 100000,
	    "sobjectType" : "fforce__RaceData__c"
	  }]
	}
	``

SOQL	Resulting plans
`select id from RaceData__c where Type__c != 'PitStop Time'` A table scan plan was selected, as a negative operator was used.	```{ "plans" : [{ "cardinality" : 100000, "fields" : [ ], "leadingOperationType" : "TableScan", "relativeCost" : 2.8333333333333335, "sobjectCardinality" : 100000, "sobjectType" : "RaceData__c" }] }```
`select id from RaceData__c where Type__c != 'PitStop' and Lap__c >=20 and Lap__c <=40` Even though a negative operator was used, by adding more selective criteria backed by a custom index, the platform chose to use the index over a table scan.	```{ "plans" : [{ "cardinality" : 10000, "fields" : ["Lap__c"], "leadingOperationType" : "Index", "relativeCost" : 1.0, "sobjectCardinality" : 100000, "sobjectType" : "RaceData__c" }, { "cardinality" : 40000, "fields" : [ ], "leadingOperationType" : "TableScan", "relativeCost" : 1.5333333333333334, "sobjectCardinality" : 100000, "sobjectType" : "RaceData__c" }] }```

Skinny tables

Internally, Salesforce stores Standard Object's field data and custom field data for a given record in two separate physical Oracle tables; so, while you don't see it, when you execute a SOQL query to return a mixture of both standard and custom fields, internally this requires an Oracle SQL query, which requires an internal database join to be made.

If Salesforce Support determines that avoiding this join would speed up a given set of queries, they can create a skinny table. Such a table is not visible to the Force.com developer and is kept in sync with your object records automatically by the platform, including any standard or custom indexes.

A skinny table can contain commonly used standard and custom fields that you, the subscriber, and Salesforce deem appropriate, all in the one Oracle table, and thus, it avoids the join (all at the internal cost of duplicating the record data). If a SOQL, Report, or List View query utilizes the fields or a subset, the platform will automatically use the skinny table instead of the join to improve performance. As an additional benefit, the record size needed internally is smaller, which means that the data bandwidth used to move chunks of records around the platform can be better utilized.

This is obviously quite an advanced feature of the platform, but worth considering as an additional means to improve query performance in a subscriber org.

> Skinny tables are not kept in sync if you change field types or add new fields to the corresponding object in the Force.com world. Also, they are not replicated in sandbox environments. So, you or your subscriber will need to contact Salesforce Support again each time these types of changes occur. Also, note that skinny tables cannot be packaged; they are configurations only for subscriber orgs.

Handling large result sets

In most cases within Apex, it is only possible to read up to 50,000 records, regardless of whether they are read individually or as a part of forming an aggregate query result. There is, however, a context parameter that can be applied that will allow an unlimited number of records to be read. However, this context does not permit any database updates. In this section, we will review the following three ways in which you can manage large datasets:

- Processing 50k maximum result sets in Apex
- Processing unlimited results sets in Apex
- Processing unlimited results sets via the Salesforce APIs

Processing 50k maximum results in Apex

One of the problems with reading 50,000 records is that you run the risk of hitting other governors, such as the **heap governor**, which, although increased in an async context, can still be hit depending on the processing being performed. Take a look at the following contrived example to generate attachments on each **Race Data** record:

```
List<Attachment> attachments = new List<Attachment>();
for(RaceData__c raceData : [select Id from RaceData__c])
  attachments.add(
    new Attachment(
      Name = 'Some Attachment',
      ParentId = raceData.Id,
      Body = Blob.valueOf('Some Text'.repeat(1000))));
insert attachments;
```

 To try out the examples in this chapter, you will need the **Partner Portal Developer Edition** org, which comes with 250 MB of record and document storage.

If you try to execute the preceding code from an **Execute Anonymous** window, you will receive the following error, as the code quickly hits the **6 MB heap size limit**:

```
System.LimitException: Apex heap size too large: 6022466
```

The solution to this problem is to utilize what is known as **SOQL FOR LOOP** (as follows); it allows the record data to be returned to the Apex code in chunks of 200 records so that not all the **Attachment** records will build up on the heap:

```
for(List<RaceData__c> raceDataChunk :
      [select Id from RaceData__c])
{
  List<Attachment> attachments = new List<Attachment>();
  for(RaceData__c raceData : raceDataChunk)
    attachments.add(
      new Attachment(
        Name = 'Some Attachment',
        ParentId = raceData.Id,
        Body = Blob.valueOf('Some Text'.repeat(1000))));
  insert attachments;
}
```

Once this code completes, it will have generated over 80 MB of attachment data in one execution context! Note that in doing so, the preceding code does technically break a bulkification rule, in that there is a DML statement contained within the outer chunking loop. For 10,000 records split over 200 record chunks, this will result in 50 chunks, and thus, this will consume 50 out of the available 100 DML statements (or 200 in async). In this case, the end justifies the means, so this is just something to be mindful of.

Processing unlimited result sets in Apex

In this section, a new **Race Analysis** page is created to allow the user to view results of various calculations and simulations applied dynamically to selected **Race Data**. Ultimately, imagine that the page allows the user to input adjustments and other parameters to apply to the calculations and replay the race data to see how the race might have finished differently.

For the purposes of this chapter, we are focusing on querying the **Race Data** object only. The standard row limits 50,000 records (approximately 5 races' worth of data) to be returned from the SOQL query. The following changes have been made to the FormulaForce application to deliver this page and are present in the code samples associated with this chapter if you wish to deploy them:

- A new `analyizeData` method on the `RaceService` class has been added.

- The `RaceDataSelector` class has been created to encapsulate the query logic.

- `RaceAnalysisController` has been created for the Visualforce page.

- The `raceanalysis` Visualforce page has been created.

- A new **Race Analysis** list Custom Button has been added to the `Race__c` object. This button has been added to the list related to **Races** on the **Season** detail page.

The user can now select one or more **Race** records from the related list to process as follows:

The next display provides a confirmation of the selected races before starting the calculations. This button invokes the `RaceService.analyizeData` method and attempts to query the applicable `RaceData__c` records.

Generating more Race Data

To demonstrate how it is possible to read more than 50,000 records, we will need to generate some more **Race Data**. To do this, we can rerun a portion of the script we ran earlier in this chapter to generate up to 100,000 records (which will nearly fill a Partner Portal Developer Edition org).

From an **Anonymous Apex** prompt, execute the following Apex code for each race; this should result in 100,000 records in the **Race Data** object (which you can verify through the **Data Storage** page under **Setup**):

```
TestData.createVolumeDataForChapter10(2014, 'Monza', 52, 4);
```

Run the preceding code again a further eight times, each time changing the name of the race to `Austin`, `Sochi`, `Singapore`, `Shanghai`, `Spa`, `Suzuka`, `Silverstone`, and `Budapest` (note that **Race Data** for `Spain` was generated earlier).

 Note that to clear down the data for any reason, repeatedly call the following, then go to your **Recycle Bin** and delete all org data:

TestData.purgeVolumeDataForChapter10(false);

Leveraging Visualforce and the Apex read-only mode

The **Start Analysis** button calls the service to query the race data and analyze the data, and for the purposes of this chapter, it outputs the total number of queried rows as follows:

```
ApexPages.addMessage(
  new ApexPages.Message(
    ApexPages.Severity.Info,
    'Just read ' + Limits.getQueryRows() +
    ' rows from RaceData__c'));
```

As per the previous screenshot, select all 10 races (click on the **Show 5 more** link to show more related list records). Click on the **Start Analysis** button to display a message, confirming the number of records processed is above the standard 50,000.

The reason this has been made possible is due to the Visualforce page enabling the read-only mode, via the readOnly attribute on the apex:page element, as follows:

```
<apex:page
   standardController="Race__c"
   extensions="RaceAnalysisController"
   recordSetVar="Races"
   readOnly="true">
```

This mode can also be enabled via the @ReadOnly Apex attribute on an Apex Scheduled class or on an Apex Remote Action method. As the name suggests, the downside is that there can be no DML statements, so we have no means to update the database. For this use case, this restriction is not a problem. Note that, by using **JavaScript Remoting**, you can create a mix of methods with and without @ReadOnly.

 Note that, in this mode, other governors are still active, such as heap and CPU timeout. You might also want to consider combining this mode with the SOQL FOR LOOP approach described earlier. Also, the SOQL Aggregate queries will benefit from this (as these also count against the SOQL query rows governor).

Processing unlimited result sets using the Salesforce APIs

Salesforce does not limit the maximum number of rows that can be queried when using the Salesforce SOAP and REST APIs to retrieve record data, as in these contexts, the resources consuming and processing the resulting record data are off-platform.

One consideration to keep in mind, however, is the daily API limits—although you can read unlimited data, it is still chunked from the Salesforce servers and retrieving each chunk will consume an API call. Although less friendly, the Salesforce Bulk API is more efficient in retrieving more records while using less API calls to the Salesforce servers.

Asynchronous execution contexts

Salesforce is committed to ensuring that the interactive user experience (browser or mobile response times) of your applications and that of its own is as optimal as possible. In a multitenant environment, it uses the governors as one way to manage this. The other approach is to provide a means for you to move the processing of code from the foreground (interactive) into the background (async mode). This section of the chapter discusses the design considerations, implementation options, and benefits available in this context.

As the code running in the background is, by definition, not holding up the response times of the pages the users are using, Salesforce can and does throttle when and how often async processes execute, depending on the load on the servers at the time. For this reason, it currently do not provide an **SLA** on exactly when an async piece of code will run or guarantee exactly when the Apex Schedule code will run at the allotted time. This aspect of the platform can at times be a source of frustration for end users, waiting for critical business processes to complete. However, there are some design, implementation, user interface, and messaging considerations that can make a big difference in terms of managing their expectations.

The good news is that the platform rewards you for running your code in async by giving you increased governors in areas such as Heap, SOQL queries, and CPU governor. You can find the full details in their documentation (attempting to document them in a book is a nonstarter as they are constantly being improved and removed in some cases).

More recently, the `@future` async execution contexts even offers the developer the ability to choose which governors they wish to increase over and above others, depending on the needs of their code.

Understanding Execution Governors and Limits: `http://www.salesforce.com/us/developer/docs/apexcode/Content/apex_gov_limits.htm`.

General async design considerations

The platform provides some straightforward ways in which you can execute code in async. What is often overlooked though is error handling and general user experience considerations. This section presents some points to consider functionally when moving a task or process into async or background to use a more end user-facing term:

- **Type of background work**: I categorize work performed in the background in two ways, application and end user:
  - **Application** is something that the application requires to support future end user tasks, such as periodic recalculation, major data manipulation, or on-boarding of data from an external service, for example.
  - **End user** is something that is related (typically initiated) to an end user activity that just happens to require more platform resources than are available in the interactive (or foreground) context. The latter can be much harder to accept for business analysts and end users, who are constantly demanding real-time response times. If you do find that this is your only route, focus hard on the user interaction and messaging aspects as follows.

- **User experience**: A well-crafted user experience around the execution of background work can make all the difference when the platform is choosing to queue or slow the processing of work. Here are some considerations to keep in mind:

    ○ **Starting the background work**: Decide how the user starts the background process, is it explicit via a button or indirect via a scheduled job or a side effect of performing another task? Starting the background work explicitly from a user interface button gives you the opportunity to set expectations. A critical one being whether the work is queued or it has actually started; if they didn't know this, they might be inclined to attempt to start the work again, thus resulting in potentially two jobs processing in parallel! If you decide to start the process indirectly, make sure that you focus on error handling and recovery to ensure that the user has a way of being notified of any important failures at a later point in time.

    ○ **Progress bar indicators**: These can be used to allow the user to monitor the progress of the job from start to finish. Providing messages during the progress of the work can also help the user understand what is going on.

    ○ **Monitoring**: Ensuring that the user can continue to monitor the progress between sessions or other tasks can also be important. Often, users might close tabs or get logged out, and so consider providing a means to revisit the place where they started the job and have the user interface recognize that the job is still being processed, allowing the user to resume monitoring of the job.

- **Messaging and Logging**: Think about the ways in which your background process communicates and notifies the end user of the work it has done and any errors that occurred. While e-mails can be the default choice, consider yourself how such e-mails can get lost easily, look for alternative notification and logging approaches that are more aligned with the platform and the application environment. Here are some considerations to keep in mind:

    ○ **Logging**: Ideally, persist log information within the application through an associated log (such as a logging Custom Object) with other Custom Objects that are associated with records being processed by the job, such that the end users can leverage related lists to see log entries contextually.

- ○ **Unhandled exceptions**: They are caught by the platform and displayed on the **Apex Jobs** page. The problem with this page is that it's not very user-friendly and also lacks the context as to what the job was actually doing with which records (the Apex class name might not be enough to determine this alone). Try to handle exceptions routing them via your end-user facing messaging. Some Apex exceptions cannot be handled and will still require admins or support consultants to check for these. Your interactive monitoring solutions can also query `AsyncApexJob` for such messages.

- ○ **Notifications**: Notifications that a job has completed or failed with an error can be sent via an e-mail; however, also consider creating a child record as part of the logging alternative. A user-related task or a chatter post can also work quite well. The benefit of options that leverage information stored in the org is that these can also be a place to display Custom Buttons to restart the process.

- **Concurrency**: Consider what would happen if two or more users attempted to run your jobs at the same time or if the data being processed overlaps between two jobs. Note that this scenario can also occur when scheduled jobs execute. You might want to store the Apex job ID during the processing of the job against an appropriate record to effectively lock it from being processed by other jobs until it is cleared.

- **Error recovery**: Consider whether the user needs to rerun the job processing that has only failed records or if the job can simply be designed in a way which is re-entrant, which means that it checks whether executions of a previous job might have already been made over the same data and cleans up or resets as it goes along.

Running Apex in the asynchronous mode

There are two ways to implement the asynchronous code in Force.com; both run with the same default extended governors compared to the interactive execution context.

As stated previously, there is no guarantee when the code will be executed. Salesforce monitors the frequency and length of each execution, adjusting a queue that takes into consideration performance over the entire instance and not just the subscriber org. It also caps the number of async jobs over a rolling 24-hour period. See the *Understanding Execution Governors and Limits* section for more details. Salesforce provides a detailed white paper describing the queuing.

Asynchronous Processing in Force.com: `http://www.salesforce.com/us/developer/docs/async_processing/salesforce_async_processing.pdf`.

 Apex Scheduler can be used to execute code in an async context via its `execute` method. This also provides enhanced governors. Depending on the processing involved, you might choose to start a Batch Apex job from the `execute` method. Otherwise, if you want a one-off, scheduled execution, you can use the `Database.scheduleBatch` method.

@future

Consider the following implementation guidelines when utilizing `@future`:

- Avoid flooding the async queue with many `@future` jobs (consider Batch Apex).

- Methods must execute quickly or risk platform throttling, which will delay the execution.

- It is easier to implement as they require only a method annotation to be added.

- Typically, the time taken to de-queue and execute the work is less than Batch Apex.

- You can express, via a method annotation, an increase in a specific governor to customize the governor limits to your needs.

- Parameter types are limited to simple types and lists.

- Be careful while passing in list parameters by ensuring that you volume test with large lists.

- There is no way to track execution as the **Apex Job ID** is not returned.

- Executing from an Apex Trigger should be considered carefully; `@future` methods should be bulkified, and if there is a possibility of bulk data loading, there is a greater chance of hitting the daily per user limit for `@future` jobs.

- You cannot start another `@future` or Batch Apex job. This is particularly an issue if your packaged code can be invoked by code (such as that written by developer X) in a subscriber org. If they have their own `@future` methods indirectly invoking your use of this feature, an exception will occur. As such, try to avoid using these features from a packaged Apex Trigger context.

Batch Apex

In our scenario, the **Race Data** records loaded into Salesforce do not by default associate themselves with the applicable **Contestant** records. As noted earlier, the **Contestant** record has a **Race Data Id** field that contains an Apex-calculated unique value made up from the **Year, Race Name**, and **Driver Id** fields concatenated together.

The following Batch Apex job is designed to process all the **Race Data** records, calculate the compound **Contestant Race Data Id** field, and update the records with the associated **Contestant** record relationship. The following example highlights a number of other things in terms of the Selector and Service layer patterns usage within this context:

- The `RaceDataSelector` class is used to provide the `QueryLocator` method needed, keeping the SOQL logic (albeit simple in this case) encapsulated in the Selector layer.

- The `RaceService.processData` method (added to support this job) is passed in the IDs of the records rather than the records passed to the `execute` method in the `scope` parameter. This general approach avoids any concern over the record data being old, as Batch Apex serialized all record data at the start of the job.

- As per the standard practice, the Service layer does not handle exceptions; these are thrown to the caller and it handles them appropriately. In this case, a new `LogService` class is used to capture exceptions thrown and log them to a Custom Object, utilizing the Apex job ID as a means to differentiate log entries from others jobs. Note that the use of `LogService` is for illustration only; it is not implemented in the sample code for this chapter.

- In the `finish` method, new `NotificationService` encapsulates logic, which is able to notify end users (perhaps via e-mail, tasks, or Chatter as considered earlier) of the result of the job, passing on the Apex job ID, such that it can leverage the information stored in the log Custom Object and/or `ApexAsyncJob` to form an appropriate message to the user. Again, this is for illustration only.

The following code shows the implementation of the Batch Apex job to process the race data records:

```
public class ProcessRaceDataJob
   implements Database.Batchable<SObject>
{
  public Database.QueryLocator start(
     Database.BatchableContext ctx)
  {
    return
      RaceDataSelector.newInstance().selectAllQueryLocator();
  }

  public void execute(
     Database.BatchableContext ctx, List<RaceData__c> scope)
  {
    try
    {
      Set<Id> raceDataIds =
        new Map<Id, SObject>(scope).keySet();
      RaceService.processData(raceDataIds);
    }
    catch (Exception e)
    {
      LogService.log(ctx.getJobId(), e);
    }
  }

  public void finish(Database.BatchableContext ctx)
  {
    NotificationService.notify(
      ctx.getJobId(), 'Process Race Data');
  }
}
```

Note that even the code to start the Apex job is implemented in a `Service` method; this allows for certain pre-checks for concurrency and configuration to be encapsulated. To run this job, a list view Custom Button has been placed on the **Race Data** object in order to start the process. The controller calls the Service method to start the job as follows:

```
Id jobId = RaceService.runProcessDataJob();
```

Consider the following implementation guidelines when utilizing Batch Apex:

- An exception is thrown if 5 jobs in an org are already enqueued or executing.
- A platform queue of 100 jobs is in pilot (the Summer'14 release) at the time of writing this.
- It is more complex to implement Batch Apex, which requires three methods.
- Typically, the time taken to de-queue and execute can be several minutes or hours.
- Typically, the time taken to execute (depending on the number of items) can be hours.
- Up to 50 million database records or 50 thousand iterator items can be processed.
- Records or iterator items returned from the `start` method are cached by the platform and passed back via the `execute` method as opposed to being the latest records at that time from the database. Depending on how long the job takes to execute, such information might have changed on the database in the meantime.
- Consider re-reading record data in each execute method for the latest record state.
- You can track Batch Apex progress via its Apex job ID.
- Executing from an Apex Trigger is not advised from a bulkification perspective, especially if you are expecting users to utilize bulk data load tools.
- You can start another Batch Apex job from another (from the finish method).
- Calibrate the default scope size (the number of records passed by the platform to each `execute` method call) to the optimum use of governors and throughput.
- Provide a subscriber org configuration (via a protected Custom Setting) to change the default scope size of 200.

> Note that the ability to start a Batch Apex job from another can be a very powerful feature in terms of processing large amounts of data through various stages or implementing a clean-up process. This is often referred to as **Batch Apex Chaining**. However, keep in mind that there is no guarantee the second job will start successfully, so ensure you have considered error handling and recovery situations carefully.

Performance of Batch Apex jobs

As stated previously, the platform ultimately controls when and how long your job can take. However, there are a few tips that you can use to improve things:

- **Getting off to a quick start**: Ensure that your `start` method returns as quickly as possible by leveraging indexes.

- **Calibrating**: Calibrate the scope size of the records passed to the `execute` method. This will be a balance between the maximum number of records that can be passed to each execute (which is currently 2000) and the governors required to process the records. The preceding example uses 2000 as the operation itself is fairly inexpensive. This means that only 50 chunks are required to execute the job (given the test volume data created in this chapter), which in general, allows the job to execute faster as each burst of activity gets more done at a time. Utilize the `Limits` class with some debug statements when volume testing to determine how much of the governors your code is using, and if you can afford to do so, increase the scope size applied. Note that if you get this wrong (as in the data complexity in the subscribers orgs is more than you calibrated for your test data), it can be adjusted further in the subscriber org via a protected Custom Setting.

- **Frequency of Batch Apex jobs**: If the use of your application results in the submission of more Batch Apex jobs more frequently, perhaps because they are executed from an Apex Trigger (not recommended) or a user interface feature used by many users, your application will quickly flood the org's Batch Apex queue and hit the concurrent limit of 5, leaving no room for your Batch Apex jobs or those from other applications. Consider carefully how often you need to submit a job and whether you can queue work up within your application to be consumed by a Batch Apex Scheduled job at a later time. The Summer'14 **Batch Apex Flex Queue** will help reduce this problem.

Using external references in Apex DML

The `RaceService.processData` service method demonstrates a great use of external ID fields when performing DML to associate records. Note that in the following code, it has not been necessary to query the `Contestant__c` records to determine the applicable record ID to place in the `RaceData__c.Contestants__c` field. Instead the `Contestants__r` relationship field is used to store an instance of the `Contestant__c` object with only the external ID field populated, as it is also unique and it can be used in this way instead of the ID.

```
public void processData(Set<Id> raceDataIds)
{
  fflib_SObjectUnitOfWork uow =
    Application.UnitOfWork.newInstance();
  for(RaceData__c raceData :
      (List<RaceData__c>)
        Application.Selector.selectById(raceDataIds))
  {
    raceData.Contestant__r =
      new Contestant__c(
        RaceDataId__c =
          Contestants.makeRaceDataId(
            raceData.Year__c,
            raceData.RaceName__c,
            raceData.DriverId__c));
    uow.registerDirty(raceData);
  }
  uow.commitWork();
}
```

If the lookup by external ID fails during the DML update (performed by the **Unit Of Work** in the preceding case), a DML exception is thrown, for example:

```
Foreign key external ID: 2014-suzuka-98 not found for field
RaceDataId__c in entity Contestant__c
```

This approach of relating records without using or looking up the Salesforce ID explicitly is also available in the Salesforce SOAP and REST APIs as well as through the various **Data Loader** tools. However, in a data loader scenario, the season, race, and driver ID values will have to be pre-concatenated within the CSV file.

Volume testing

In this chapter, we have used the Apex code to generate additional data to explore how the platform applies indexes and the use of Batch Apex. It is important to always perform some volume testing even if it is just with at least 200 records to ensure that your Triggers are bulkified. Testing with more than this gives you a better idea of other limitations in your software search, such as query performance and any Visualforce scalability issues.

One of the biggest pitfalls with volume testing is the quality of the test data. It is not often that easy to get hold of actual customer data, so we must emulate the spread of information by varying field values amongst the records to properly simulate how the software will not only behave under load with more records, but under load with a different dispersion of values. This will tease out further bugs that might only manifest if the data values change within a batch of records. For example, the Apex script used in this chapter could be updated to apply a different PitStop strategy across the drivers, varying those types of records per race per driver.

The second challenge is to understand how long a process will take, for example, a Batch Apex job. As it is a multitenant environment, this can vary a lot. This does not mean to say that you should not try a few times during different times of the day and get a rough guide on how long jobs take with different data volumes. You should also experiment with your Batch Apex scope size during your volume testing. The higher the scope size, the fewer chunks of work to perform and, typically, the jobs need to execute for a reduced elapsed time.

As we have seen in this chapter, it only takes 100,000 records to fill a Partner Developer Edition org near to a capacity of 250 MB. The Partner Portal test orgs offer an increase to 1 GB so that you can push the volume testing further. You should also encourage relationships with your larger customers to utilize Beta package versions of your application in their sandboxes.

Finally, consider other ways to generate volume data; bulk loading CSV files can work, but can lead to less varied data as CSV files are typically static and not so easy to edit. It can be well worth investing in some off-platform code that either generates dynamic CSV files or directly invokes the Salesforce API or Bulk API to push data into an org directly. Also, remember that, while you're doing this, you're also testing your Apex Trigger code.

Summary

In this chapter, we have learned that understanding not just the volume of records, but also how data within them is dispersed can affect the need for indexes to ensure that queries perform without having to resort to expensive table scans or, in the case of Apex Trigger, runtime exceptions. Ensuring that you and your customers understand the best way to apply indexes is critical to both interactive and batch performance.

Asynchronous execution contexts open up extended and flexible control over the governors available in the interactive context, but need to be designed from the beginning with careful consideration for the user experience, such that the user is always aware of what is and is not going on in the background. Messaging is the key when there is no immediate user interface to relay errors and resolve them. Don't depend on the **Apex Jobs** screen; instead, try to contextualize error information through custom log objects related to key records in your application that drive background processes, allowing related lists to help relay information in context about the state and result of jobs.

Execution of background processes is not scoped to your application but affects the whole subscriber org, so the frequency in which your application submits processes to the background needs to be carefully considered. Understand the difference between application and end user jobs; the latter are more likely to flood an org and cause delays or, worse, result in end users having to retry requests. Consider leveraging Apex Scheduler to implement your own application queue to stage different work items for later processing. Upcoming features in Salesforce will allow a certain amount of queue and subscriber control over priority.

In the next chapter, we will be moving out of the packaging org as the primary development environment and moving into a place that supports multiple developers and an application development life cycle backed by Source Control and Continuous Integration to ensure that you have a real-time view on test execution and auditability over your application's source code.

11
Source Control and Continuous Integration

So far we have been making changes in the packaging org for the **FormulaForce** application. This has worked well enough, as you're the sole developer in this case. However, when you add more developers and teams other considerations comes into play, mainly traceability of code changes and also the practical implications of conflicts when more than one developer is working in a development org at a time.

This chapter sees the packaging org take on more of a **warehouse**-only role, accessed only when there is a need to create a beta or release package and no longer for day-to-day development as we have been doing. This principle can become quite important to you and your customers if they desire that you demonstrate compliance and auditability with respect to controls around your software development process and life cycle.

As the code base grows and the number of contributions to it at any given time increases, it's important to monitor the quality of the code more frequently. Finding out that your Apex tests are failing prior to an upload is frustrating and costly when you're trying to release the software to your customers. **Continuous Integration** works with a **Source Control** system to validate the integrity and quality (through your tests) of your application on an automated basis, often triggered by developers committing changes to Source Control.

In this chapter, you will learn the following:

- Developer workflow
- Developing with Source Control
- Hooking up to Continuous Integration
- Releasing from Source Control
- Automated regression testing

Development workflow and infrastructure

A development workflow describes the day-to-day activities of a developer in order to obtain the latest build, make changes, and submit them back to a repository that maintains the current overall state of the source code. Having a solid well-defined developer workflow, supporting tools, and infrastructure is critical to the efficiency of any development team.

The first thing a developer will want to know is where the source code is — typically in a common Source Control system such as SVN or Git. The next would be how to get it into a form so that they can start executing it. Salesforce provides a toolkit known as the **Migration Toolkit** that helps write scripts to deploy to a Salesforce org using the popular developer scripting language known as **Ant**. We will be building such a script in this chapter. Such scripts are also used by Continuous Integration build servers described later in this chapter.

The Migration Toolkit also provides a means to extract from Salesforce org source files that has all the components needed to represent your application, not just the Apex and Visualforce source files, but XML files describing Custom Objects, fields, tabs, and practically any other component that can be packaged. We will use this facility to extract the current state of our packaging org in order to initially populate a Git repository with all the component files needed to maintain further changes to the source code outside of the packaging org that we have been developing within so far.

Packaging org versus sandbox versus developer org

As mentioned previously, it can rapidly become impractical to have a number of developers within one org. They might accidently overwrite each other's changes, make Custom Object or setup changes that others might not want to see, and consume daily API limits for that org more rapidly, eventually blocking everyone from making changes.

When it comes to the packaging org there is another more important reason, and that is the ability to know exactly what changes have been applied to your application code between one version and the next. This is something you and your customers want to have confidence in being able to know at any given time.

There is also the ability to be able to control the release of features or rollback changes, which becomes harder if those changes have already been made in the packaging org. For these reasons, it is typically a good idea to limit access to your packaging org to those responsible for making releases of your packages, thus treating your packaging org conceptually as a warehouse only.

Sandbox orgs are often attributed to development of custom solutions within an Enterprise organization, where the sandbox has been initialized with a copy of the production org. This can include data, installed packages, and other customizations. At the time of writing, sandbox orgs are available from Partner Portal-provisioned Enterprise Edition orgs (maximum of five). A sandbox can be used as an alternative to a developer org. One advantage is the ability to configure the parent org to a default blank state and then leverage the sandbox refresh process to effectively clean the org ready for a new build deployment. Note that if you are using Field Sets, sandbox orgs do not currently allow the definition of **Available Fields**.

Creating and preparing your developer orgs

In the *Required and recommended organizations* section of *Chapter 1, Building, Publishing, and Supporting Your Application,* I recommended you create a developer org. If you have not done already, visit the Partner Portal or `https://developer.salesforce.com/` and obtain a new developer org (or DE org for short).

Once you have this, you might want to take some time to further clean out any sample packages, Apex code, or configuration that Salesforce has put in such orgs, as these components will be merged with your own components later in the developer workflow process and you would want to avoid committing them to Source Control, or worse, getting them added to your package.

Cleaning DE orgs is not something that Salesforce natively supports, yet most developers are familiar with the ability to clean their working environment (their DE orgs in the case of Force.com development) before taking new builds from Source Control. This avoids unwanted classes, objects, and fields building up during the course of development, for example when implementation strategies change or functionality is redefined, causing previously committed components to be renamed or deleted. This can leak back into your code base accidentally. Fortunately, there is an open source solution that leverages the Migration Toolkit to clean a DE org, which we will explore later.

Due to the overhead of creating and managing installation of packages, typically DE orgs are also used by test engineers and other members of the team to test or preview features being developed. That being said, it can be worth considering the creation of a beta package from a stable build of your code at various intervals throughout your release development cycles, for additional sanity and smoke testing ahead of your final upload process.

In this chapter, we are going to extract our application's components from the packaging org as files that we can later upload into a GitHub repository, to allow tracking and auditability of changes in a more robust way than is permitted within a Salesforce org. We will then use this repository to populate the DE org created, make some changes, and commit those changes back to the repository. This is known as **developer workflow**.

The developer workflow

There are many options when it comes to choosing an appropriate Source Control system to store your application code within. In this book we will use GitHub as a remote Source Control store and local Source Control repository.

The aim here is not to prescribe which tools to use but to give a general walk-through of a Force.com developer flow that you can adapt and explore different options within later. The following diagram illustrates the developer workflow that we will be walking through in this chapter:

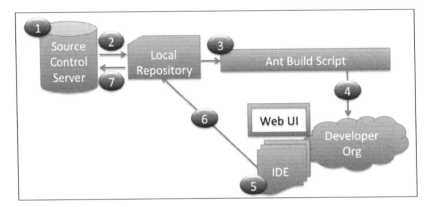

The following points relate to the preceding diagram:

1. Choosing a Source Control product and server is an important decision in which you should consider security, accessibility, and durability. The source code to your application needs to be securely managed for only authorized personnel, which is managed ideally through clear processes in your business when employees arrive and leave. Where you choose to store your Source Control server also adds further importance to this, if for accessibility reasons you choose to use one of the many cloud-based Source Control hosting services or indeed manage your own, for example via **Amazon EC2**. Perform durability tests from each location, ensuring that the server operates efficiently (developers hate waiting!). Finally, make sure that you have a backup and recovery process that is defined and tested, focusing on minimizing the downtime of your developers should the worst happen. The next section in this chapter will walk through populating a GitHub repository from the contents of our packaging org.

2. Populating a local repository with files stored in your Source Control server is the initial activity that most developers will perform. As described previously, this should be as efficient as possible. If you are using a cloud-based server, the amount of bandwidth needed to synchronize the remote and local repository is important. Some Source Control products offer more efficient implementations in this regard than others. Git is especially tailored for this kind of scenario, giving the ability to clone the whole or specific branches of the repository locally, complete with file history, followed by incrementally updating it as desired. Most common Source Control products offer excellent choices for GUI as well as the standard command-line interfaces. In this chapter we will use GitHub's GUI to clone the repository to a local folder ready for the next step in the developer flow.

3. The **Apache Ant** open source tool offers a good OS platform-neutral solution to making a standard build (deploy) script and other custom development tools you might want to build.

4. In its most basic form, an Ant build script simply leverages the Salesforce Migration Toolkit Ant task, `sf:deploy`, to deploy the contents of the local repository to a designated developer org. However, as we will discuss in a later section, it also forms a part of your Continuous Integration solution.

5. Once deployed to a developer org, the tools used to develop on Force.com range from using combinations of the **Setup** menu, **Schema Builder** (often overlooked), **Developer Console**, Force.com IDE (Eclipse) to newer third-party solutions such as MavensMate (my personal preference at the moment).

6. The key requirement is that once the developer is ready to submit to Source Control, there is an ability to synchronize the component files stored locally with the contents of the developer org. Most of the aforementioned IDEs provide a means to do this, though you can also leverage an Ant build script via the `sf:retrieve` Ant Task supplied with the Migration Toolkit. I will cover how I do this with MavensMate later in this chapter.

7. Once files have been synchronized from the developer org, the developer can use standard Source Control commit processes to review their changes and commit changes to the Source Control server (Git requires developers to commit to their local repository first). We will use the GitHub GUI for this. Later in this chapter, we will see how this action can be used to automatically trigger a build that confirms that the integration of the developer's changes with the current state of Source Control has not broken anything, by automatically executing all Apex unit tests.

More advanced developer flows can also utilize Continuous Integration to pre-validate commits before ultimately allowing developer changes (made to so-called feature branches) to be propagated or merged with the main branch. One such advanced flow is known as **GitFlow**, describing a staged processing for code flowing from developer/feature branches to release branches. Search via Google for this term to read about this more advanced developer flow.

Note that it is only after step 4 that a developer can actually start being productive, so it's worth ensuring that you check regularly with your developers that this part of the developer flow is working well for them. Likewise, step 5 is where most of their time is spent. Try to allow as much freedom for developers as possible to choose the tools that make each of them the most efficient but still work within the boundaries of your agreed development flow.

Debugging still remains one of the most time-consuming aspects of developing on Force.com. Make sure that all developers are fully up to date with all the latest tools and approaches from Salesforce as well as your chosen IDE environment. Making effective use of the **debug log filters** can also save a lot of time sorting through a large debug log, as debug logs are capped at 2 MB. Often, developers resort to System.debug to gain the insight they need. Do ensure that these are removed before **Security Review**. Though genuine supporting debug entries can be discussed and permitted (it is recommended that you utilize the appropriate debug levels), ad hoc debug entries should be removed as a part of general practice anyway.

Developing with Source Control

Now that we understand the general developer flow a bit more, let's take a deeper dive into using some of the tools and approaches that you can use.

In this case, we will be using the following tools to populate and manage the content of our chosen Source Control repository, in this case, Git. To provide an easy means to explore the benefits of a more distributed solution, we will use GitHub as a hosted instance of Git (others are available, including broader developer flow features):

- **GitHub**: Ensure that you have a GitHub account. Public accounts are free, but you can also use a private account for purposes of this chapter. Download the excellent GitHub GUI from either `https://windows.github.com/` or `https://mac.github.com/`. This chapter will use the Mac edition, though not to the level that it will not be possible find and perform equivalent operations in the Windows edition; both clients are really easy to use!

- **Apache Ant v1.6 or greater**: If you are on a Mac, you probably have this already installed; type in `ant -version` at the terminal prompt to confirm. If not or you are on a Windows machine, you can download it from `http://ant.apache.org/`.

- **Force.com Migration Toolkit**: This can be downloaded from within your developer org. Navigate to the **Tools** menu option under the **Setup** menu. The instructions in the read me file recommend that you copy the `ant-salesforce.jar` file into your Apache Ant installation folder. I do not recommend this and instead prefer to capture build tools like this in a `/lib` folder located within the source code. This makes it easier to upgrade for all developers in a seamless way, without having to perform the download each time.

- **MavensMate**: As stated previously, there are many tools, including those provided by Salesforce for developing on Force.com. In this chapter I will use MavensMate. Having used the Force.com IDE for several years, I find it a refreshing change, generally a little faster (though both ultimately use the same Salesforce APIs), and has some nice features such as improved code completion and a nice template engine.

 Summer'14 Salesforce released the Force.com IDE as an open source project, which now uses the **Tooling API** as opposed to the original metadata API, which should improve its performance and features. At the time of writing this book I have not had a chance to explore this new release further, but I am pleased to see the future looking brighter for this tool. It is certainly one to watch.

Populating your Source Control repository

A key decision when populating your Source Control repository is the folder structure. There are many conventions for this, some aligned more closely to the chosen Source Control product, for example SVN uses root folders such as /trunk, /branches, and so on.

Git repositories are less bound by this convention, regardless of the root-level structure used. The following table shows one structure that you might want to consider:

Folder	Purpose
/	Keep the content of the root as clean as possible, and typically, the only file here will be the Ant build.xml file. You might also have a README.md file, which is a common Git convention to provide important usage and documentation links. This is a simple text file that uses a simple notation syntax (known as **MarkDown**) to represent sections, bold, italics, and so on.
/lib	This folder contains any binary, configuration, or script files that represent build tools and dependencies needed to run the Ant build script, typically placed in the root. This is an optional folder but is used in this chapter to store the ant-salesforce.jar file, as opposed to having developers install it.
/src	This folder contains Force.com source files, structured in alignment with the folder structure returned by the Ant sf:retrieve task and expected by IDEs such as Force.com IDE and MavensMate.

Folder	Purpose
/source (alternative)	Note that if your application contains other Source Control artifacts from other platforms, you might want to consider having a more general /source folder, permitting paths such as /source/salesforce/src and then /source/heroku.

 If you want to follow through the steps in this chapter, follow on from the source code as contained within the chapter-10 branch. If you would rather review the end result, skip to the chapter-11 branch in the sample code repository to review the build.xml and package.xml files.

Perform the following steps to create the new repository and clone it, in order to create a local repository on your computer to populate with initial content:

1. Log in to your GitHub account from your web browser and select the option from the dropdown next to your user to create a new repository. Also select the option to create a default README file.

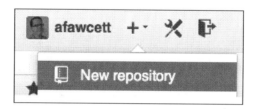

 If you plan to try out the Continuous Integration steps later in this chapter, the easiest option with respect to configuration at this point is to create a **Public repository**. An in-depth walk-through on how to configure Jenkins authentication with GitHub is outside the scope of this chapter.

2. From the web browser project page for the new repository, locate the **Clone in Desktop** button on the right-hand side bar towards the bottom of the page. Click on it to open the GitHub desktop client and begin cloning the repository, or open the GitHub desktop client manually and select the **Clone to Computer** option.

3. The preceding clone process should have prompted you for a location on your hard drive in which the local repository is to be stored. Make a note of this location, as we will be populating this location in the following steps.

4. Create a `/lib` folder in the root of the repository folder.

5. Copy the following files from the `/lib` sample code folder into the new `/lib` folder created in the previous step:

   ○ Copy the `ant-salesforce.jar` file

   ○ Copy the `ant-salesforce.xml` file

   ○ Copy the `ant-contrib-1.0b3.jar` file

6. Create a `/src` folder in the root of the repository folder.

7. Copy the `build.xml` file that you have been using from the previous chapters into the root of the repository folder.

In this chapter, we will update the Ant `build.xml` script file to allow it to deploy the application source code into new Developer Edition orgs as needed. Before this, we will use the Ant `sf:retrieve` task provided by the `salesforce-ant.jar` file to retrieve the latest content of our FormulaForce package, which you have been developing so far, in the form of component source files, which we will migrate to Source Control.

Note that we are performing this step due to the approach we have taken in this book, which is starting with development in the packaging org. If you are not starting from this point, you can create a `/src` folder and the `package.xml` file as described manually. That being said, you might want to make some initial inroads within the packaging org to establish a package and namespace with some initial objects.

The following `build.xml` target retrieves the content of the package defined in the packaging org and populates the `/src` folder. Make sure that your **Package** name is called **FormulaForce**. If not, update the `packageNames` attribute as follows:.

```
<target name="retrieve.package">
    <sf:retrieve
        username="${sf.username}"
        password="${sf.password}"
        retrieveTarget="${basedir}/src"
        packageNames="FormulaForce"/>
</target>
```

You can see the name of your package shown in the black banner in the top-right corner of the Salesforce page header when logged into the packaging org.

Perform the following command (all on one command line) with your own username, password, and token to execute the `retrieve` target. Ensure that you have changed the location to the root folder of your local repository first:

```
ant retrieve.package
    -Dsf.username=yourusername
    -Dsf.password=yourpasswordyourtoken
```

You should see something like the following in your local repository folder:

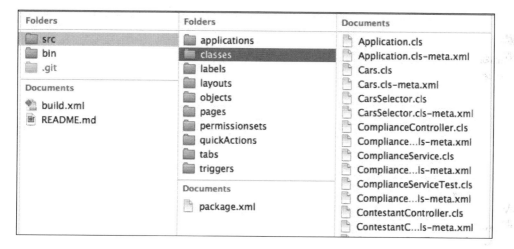

 You might find references to the package namespace present in the code and metadata files retrieved. These should be removed, otherwise the files might not deploy or execute within an unmanaged developer org. You can use file search utilities to find such references. For example, open the `/layouts/Contestant__c-Contestant Layout.layout` file and search for `QuickActionName`, then remove the namespace reference.

Before we are ready to commit this to your local repository (required before you can upload or push to the GitHub remote repository), open the `package.xml` file created by the retrieve operation and convert it to a more generic form. The one created by the preceding process contains explicit lists of each of the components in the package, such as classes.

This means that if developers add new component files within the subfolders such as /classes, /pages, and /objects for example, they will not be subsequently deployed automatically without first having to update the package.xml file.

To avoid the developer from having to remember to do this, the package.xml file can be updated to use wildcards instead:

```xml
<?xml version="1.0" encoding="UTF-8"?>
<Package xmlns="http://soap.sforce.com/2006/04/metadata">
    <types>
        <members>*</members>
        <name>ApexClass</name>
    </types>
    <types>
        <members>*</members>
        <name>ApexPage</name>
    </types>
    <types>
        <members>*</members>
        <name>ApexTrigger</name>
    </types>
    <types>
        <members>*</members>
        <name>CustomApplication</name>
    </types>
    <types>
        <members>CustomLabels</members>
        <name>CustomLabels</name>
    </types>
    <types>
        <members>*</members>
        <name>Layout</name>
    </types>
    <types>
        <members>*</members>
        <name>CustomObject</name>
    </types>
    <types>
        <members>*</members>
        <name>CustomTab</name>
    </types>
    <types>
        <members>*</members>
        <name>PermissionSet</name>
```

```
    </types>
    <types>
        <members>*</members>
        <name>QuickAction</name>
    </types>
    <version>30.0</version>
</Package>
```

> If you compare the above with the `package.xml` file created previously, you will note that some of the components in the original `package.xml` file are child components of the `CustomObject` component, such as `CustomField` and `ListView`. Thus, they don't need wildcard entries at all as they will be deployed through their parent, for example via the `CustomObject` component's `.object` file, which contains fields and layouts. As such, the preceding `package.xml` file is focused on the component types used. Thus, later in the FormulaForce application, if you utilize other component types, for example `Dashboard` or `Report`, you will need to edit this file to add a new wildcard.

Note that the actual list of components contained within the FormulaForce package still resides in the packaging org. The role and purpose of the `package.xml` file within Source Control is different and is more optimized for developer org deployments.

Finally, commit and sync the preceding changes to your local repository using the GitHub UI tool and upload or push (to use the correct Git term). If you run the tool, you should see it is already reporting that new files have been detected in the repository folder on your hard disk, as shown in the following screenshot of the Mac version of the tool. Simply enter a summary and description and click on **Commit & Sync**.

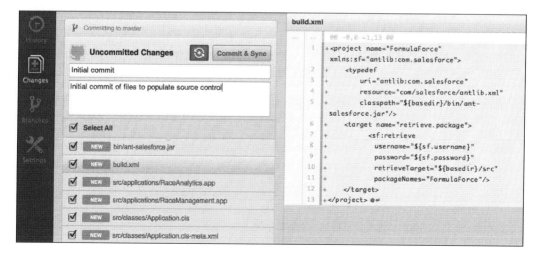

Note that this will both commit to the local repository and be pushed to the remote repository in one operation. Typically, developers would work on a set of changes and commit locally in increments, before deciding to push all changes as one operation to the remote repository.

 If your not familiar with Git, this might seem a bit confusing, as you have already physically copied or updated files in the repository folder. However, in order to push to the remote Git repository stored on the GitHub servers, you must first update a local copy of the state of the repository held in the `.git` folder, which is a hidden folder in the root of your repository folder. You should never edit or view this folder as it is entirely managed by Git.

The Ant build script to clean and build your application

Now that we have our initial Source Control content for the application created, let's deploy it to a developer org. To do this, we will update the `build.xml` file to clean the org (in case it has been used to develop an earlier build of the application) and then deploy to the org.

Salesforce does not provide an Ant task to completely clean a developer org of any previously deployed or created components. However, it does provide a means via its Force.com Migration Toolkit to deploy what is know as a `desctructivePackage.xml` file, which has a list of components to delete. Unfortunately, this needs a little help when there are component dependencies present in the org. **FinancialForce.com** has provided an open source solution to this via an `undeploy.xml` Ant script, which wraps this process and resolves the dependency shortcomings.

Download the following files from the `/lib` folder of the FinancialForce.com repository (`https://github.com/financialforcedev/df12-deployment-tools`), and place them in the `/lib` folder created earlier, along with the `ant-salesforce.jar` file:

- `exec_anon.xml`
- `undeploy.xml`
- `xmltask.jar`
- `ml-ant-http-1.1.3.jar`
- `ant-contrib-1.0b3.jar`

Next, the Ant script is updated to default by executing the existing `deploy` target (used to deploy the sample source code from previous chapters). Then, by importing the preceding tasks into the build file, the `undeploy` target becomes available as a dependent target to the `deploy` target, which means that it will be called before that target is executed. The following sample build script highlights these changes:

```
<project name="FormulaForce"
   xmlns:sf="antlib:com.salesforce" default="deploy">
  <property name="sf.server"
    value="https://login.salesforce.com"/>
  <import file="${basedir}/lib/exec_anon.xml"/>
  <import file="${basedir}/lib/undeploy.xml"/>

  <target name="deploy" depends="undeploy">
    <sf:deploy
        username="${sf.username}"
        password="${sf.password}"
        serverurl="${sf.server}"
        runAllTests="true"
        deployRoot="${basedir}/src"/>
  </target>

</project>
```

Execute the following command (all on one command line) to run the preceding script (make sure that you use your developer org username, password, and token):

```
ant
  -Dsf.username=yourdevusername
  -Dsf.password=yourdevpasswordyourdevtoken
```

 It appears to output quite a lot of messages to the console due to the complexity of the `undeploy` target being executed. After a few moments, it will begin executing the `deploy` target. Once you receive confirmation that the entire script is successfully complete, you can confirm that the application has been deployed by logging into the org.

Once you're happy that the `build.xml` file is working fine, go back to the GitHub UI application and, as before, use the **Commit and Sync** button to commit your changes and push to the GitHub server's remote repository.

Congratulations! You have now left home (the packaging org) and moved out into your own brand new developer org. This also means that you can now allow other developers to start work independently on your code base by following the same developer flow using their own developer orgs.

Starting from Spring'14, Salesforce no longer automatically grants access to applications, tabs, pages, objects, and fields deployed using the Migration Toolkit. So, you will find that before you can see these components, you need to assign your Permission Sets to your developer org user. Doing this is a good way to ensure that these are kept up to date with new components and are valid. In general, testing as a **system administrator** is not a reliable confirmation of your application working in an end-user scenario. This is why Salesforce has adopted this policy — to make the developer think about which permissions need to be applied, even in a developer org.

Developing in developer orgs versus packaging orgs

Now that you have moved out of the packaging org and into a developer org, you will no longer be developing or executing code within the associated namespace context that it provides. If you recall back to the chapter around execution contexts, remember that the debug logs from Apex code executed in the packaging org had two namespaces referenced: the packaging org one and the default one. While everything runs in this namespace implicitly in the packaging org, nothing would ever run in the default namespace.

As you will have noticed, when writing the Apex code in the packaging org, you don't have to prefix Custom Objects or fields with that namespace the way you would have to in a subscriber org where your package was installed. Instead, in the packaging org, this is done implicitly on the whole, which made it easier to export into Source Control, as the target developer org environments do not have the namespace assigned to them (because it can only be assigned once).

When developing and executing code in a developer org, everything runs in the default namespace. Keep in mind the following differences when developing in a developer org:

- Apex features that can help implement Application Apex APIs such as the `@depricated` annotation and the `Version` class that are not supported outside of the packaging org and results in compilation failures in the developer org. The main downside here is the lack of ability to use the `@depricated` attribute as you want to retire old Apex APIs. Behavior versioning using the `Version` class is not something I would recommend for the reasons outlined in *Chapter 9, Providing Integration and Extensibility*.

- Apex tests that utilize Dynamic Apex to create and populate SObject instances and fields will need to dynamically apply the namespace prefix by autosensing, whether the Apex test is running in a namespace context or not. The following code snippet is a good way to determine whether the code is running in a namespace context or not. You can place this in a test utility class:

```
DescribeSObjectResult seasonDescribe =
    Season__c.SObjectType.getDescribe();
String namespace =
    seasonDescribe.getName().
    removeEnd(seasonDescribe.getLocalName()).
    removeEnd('__');
```

- Apex tests that utilize `Type.forName` to create instances of Apex classes (for example, a test written for an application plugin feature) will also need to dynamically apply the namespace prefix to the class name given to the plugin configuration (such as the custom setting featured in *Chapter 9, Providing Integration and Extensibility*).

Later in this chapter, we will discuss Continuous Integration. This process will automatically perform a test deployment and execution of Apex tests in the packaging org and thus continue to ensure that your tests run successfully in the namespace context.

Leveraging the Metadata API and Tooling APIs from Ant

The Migration Toolkit actually wraps the Metadata API with some handy Ant tasks that we have been using in the preceding Ant scripts. The toolkit itself is written in Java and complies with the necessary interfaces and base classes that the Ant framework requires, to allow XML elements representing the tasks to be injected into the build scripts such as the `sf:retrieve` and `sf:deploy` tasks.

While you can apply the same approach as Salesforce to develop your own Ant tasks for more custom tasks relating to your application and/or automation of common tasks during setup or deployment, you will need to be a Java programmer to do so. As an alternative and with the addition of a few supporting Ant tasks (those copied into your `/lib` folder), you can actually call these APIs directly from the Ant scripting language.

In a previous chapter, we saw how Ant macros can be written to call the Metadata API's package install and uninstall capabilities, this was achieved without Java code. This capability from Ant can be quite useful if you are developing an application that extends another package, as you can easily automate installation/upgrade of the package(s) ahead of the deployment by extending the deploy script we ran earlier.

The open source exec_anon.xml file from FinancialForce.com imported earlier into the build.xml file actually contains within it an Ant macro that leverages the Tooling API's ability to call the Apex code anonymously, much like the Force.com IDE and developer console tools offer.

In previous chapters, we leveraged the SeasonService.createTestSeason method to create test record data in the application's Custom Objects. Using the Ant executeApex task, this can now be called from the Ant script in order to autocreate some useful data in a developer org. This approach will help developers, testers, or business analysts to easily try out or demonstrate the new features from the latest builds with the manual data setup as follows:.

```
<target name="deploy" depends="undeploy">

  <sf:deploy
      username="${sf.username}"
      password="${sf.password}"
      serverurl="${sf.server}"
      deployRoot="${basedir}/src"/>

  <executeApex
      username="${sf.username}"
      password="${sf.password}">
    SeasonService.createTestSeason();
  </executeApex>

</target>
```

Updating your Source Control repository

Once the application is deployed to a developer org, you have a number of options and tools to choose from as you then proceed in developing on Force.com. Your choices impact the way in which your changes find their way back into your Source Control repository. Making sure that everyone in the development team is crystal clear on this aspect of the development workflow is not only important to their efficiency, but also helps prevent work being lost or rogue files finding their way into Source Control.

Browser-based tools such as the **Setup** menu and **Schema Builder** provide an easier way of editing **Custom Objects, Fields, Layouts,**and **Permission Sets** than their XML-based formats. However, for other aspects of development the browser-based developer console is not to everyone's liking when it comes to editing Apex and Visualforce code. I personally prefer a desktop tool such as Force.com IDE or my current favorite, MavensMate, to edit these types of files.

You can use either the browser- or desktop-based approaches exclusively or in combination. It is important to keep in mind which approach is automatically keeping your local repository files in sync with the org and which is not.

- **Browser-based development**: Any changes that you make via the browser-based tools (including developer console) will remain in the developer org and will not automatically find their way to your local repository folder, and thus, they are not visible to the Git tools for you to commit to Source Control.

- **Desktop-based development**: If you're using a desktop tool such as MavensMate or Force.com IDE mapped to your repository local folder location, edits you make here will automatically sync between your local repository folder and your developer org by such tools.

- **Browser and desktop-based development**: This option allows the developer to make the best use of the tools at their disposal, all be it at the cost of some complexity and additional consideration when it comes to gathering all the changes to commit to Source Control.

Browser-based development and Source Control

To download the changes that you have made using the browser-based development tools to your local repository folder, an Ant script and the Migration Toolkit can once again be used by applying a similar approach to that used when initially downloading the contents of the package from the packaging org using the `sf:retrieve` Ant task earlier.

The following Ant script will refresh the contents of the `/src` folder based on the component types listed in the `package.xml` file (again you might need to add new component types to this file from time to time as you make use of new platform features):

```
<target name="retrieve">
  <sf:retrieve
      username="${sf.username}"
      password="${sf.password}"
      serverurl="${sf.server}"
      retrieveTarget="${basedir}/src"
      unpackaged="${basedir}/src/package.xml"/>
</target>
```

To run the preceding target, use the following command (all on one command line):

```
ant retrieve
  -Dsf.username=yourdevusername
  -Dsf.password=yourdevpasswordyourdevtoken
```

Once this command completes, you can use the Git tools to review changed files, accepting, ignoring, or discarding (reverting back to the last committed version) accordingly. These are some use cases you might encounter with this approach and ways to handle them:

- **Additional files downloaded**: Wildcards are used in the `package.xml` file, as described earlier, to make it easier to add and remove files. The downside is that for some components such as **application** and **layout**, you might find that some of the standard files for these get created in your repository folders as well. One solution is to drop using wildcards for these metadata types, and the other is to leverage the `.gitingore` file to prevent these files from being candidates for commits. With the GitHub UI tool, you can right-click on these files and select **Ignore**. This will create a `.gitignore` file if one does not already exist and add the appropriate file to it. As this file is also committed into the repository, you only have to do this once.

- **Differences in file content order or additional elements**: Sometimes file changes are flagged up by the Git tools when you have not directly made modifications to the corresponding component in the browser tools. This can be the case after a platform upgrade when new features arise or an org-wide configuration change is made (such as switching on the Multi-Currency support), or on occasions when the order of the XML elements have changed, but the overall effect on the object is the same. If you experience these changes often and they result in a change that you're happy to accept, it can be worth initially accepting them, such that less false differences appear in the future. However, don't let such browser-based development such differences go unexplained, the root cause could be quite important! Use of different org types or org templates between developers can also result in this type of issue, ensure that all developers are sourcing their developer orgs from the same sign-up page and are of the same type.

Desktop-based development and Source Control

The key benefit with desktop-based tools and Source Control is that they allow you to edit Force.com source files while synchronizing with both Source Control and an attached Salesforce Developer Edition org. In either Force.com IDE or MavensMate, the default is to automatically upload to the attached developer org each time a file is saved. So long as these tools are editing files from the local repository folder location, file edits are automatically seen by the Source Control system, which in our case is Git.

MavensMate provides a means to easily associate Git repository folders with MavensMate projects. Simply open MavensMate and drag the folder into an empty edit window. The folder will appear on the sidebar. Right-click and select **Create MavensMate Project** from the context menu. You will be prompted for your developer org login details. MavensMate will use the `package.xml` file to configure the components editable via the project.

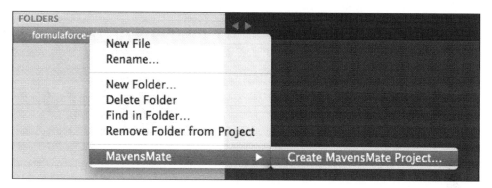

MavensMate relocates the repository folder under its `/MMWorkspace` folder once this process completes. You might need to close the GitHub UI application and re-open it for it to recognize the new location. In addition, it creates a `/.config` folder and project files in the repository's root folder. You can use the `.gitignore` facility to omit these from Source Control visibility unless everyone in your team is using MavensMate. This screenshot shows how the project looks after creation, allowing you to begin editing your Apex code immediately:

You are also able to edit files that represent Custom Objects and fields:

If you choose to combine this development approach with the browser-based approach, both Force.com IDE and MavensMate offer a way to refresh the files from within the desktop tool. Simply right-click on the folder and select the appropriate option. These facilities effectively perform a retrieve operation similar to that described in the earlier section via the Ant `build.xml` script. As such, watch out for similar side-effects in terms of additional files or file changes.

Hooking up Continuous Integration

So far we have been depending on the developer to ensure that the changes they push up to the GitHub remote repository do not cause regressions elsewhere in the application, by running Apex tests before making their commits. This is always a good practice!

However, this is not always a fully reliable means of determining the quality of the code, as the main code base will likely have moved on due to other developers also pushing their changes. When integrated together, they might cause tests or even code to fail to compile. Continuous Integration monitors changes to the Source Control repository and automatically starts its own build over the fully integrated source code base. Failures are reported back to the developers who last pushed code to the repository.

In this part of the chapter, we are going to explore this process using the popular Jenkins Continuous Integration server that uses the Ant script to perform the build step. Before we get into setting this up, let's take a moment to review the CI process that we are going to use.

The Continuous Integration process

The following diagram shows the CI process that we will be setting up over the course of the next few sections. Once you have a basic CI setup like this, you can start to add other features such as code documentation generation, static code analysis, security code scanner, and automated regression testing (something we will discuss briefly later on).

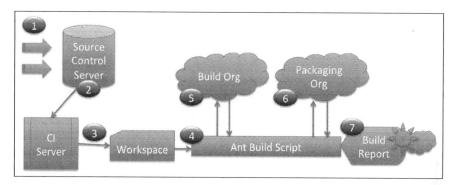

The following is the CI process:

1. Developers make multiple contributions to Source Control, just as we did earlier in this chapter via the GitHub UI desktop client.

2. The CI server is able to poll (configurable) the Source Control server (in our case, the GitHub remote repository) for changes.

3. Once changes are detected, it downloads the latest source code into a local workspace folder.

4. A part of the configuration of the CI server is to inform it of the location of the Ant `build.xml` script to execute after the workspace is set up.

5. A build org is simply a designated developer org set aside solely for the use of the CI process. We will create one of these shortly. As with the deploy process, the same Ant script is used to deploy the code to the build org (thus confirming code compilation) and run Apex tests.

6. As described earlier, developer orgs are used to develop the changes that are unmanaged environments as opposed to managed. Some of the constraints, such as the ability to change a previously released `global` Apex class, that would normally apply are not enforced. In this step, a verification check-only deployment is performed against the packaging org to confirm that the code would, when needed, still deploy to the packaging org for release. This step can also help validate code and tests continue to execute in a managed namespace context. This deployment is only a check, no changes are made to the packaging org regardless of the outcome.

7. Finally, the CI server will record the log and results of the build for analysis and the number of success versus failed builds and provide reports and notifications on the overall health of the source code in Source Control. If there are failures, there are options to e-mail certain team members as well as specific targets (those who made the most recent changes). Making sure a team stops what they are doing and attends to a broken build is very important. The longer the broken builds exist, the harder they are to solve, especially when further changes occur.

Updating the Ant build script for CI

Before we can set up our CI server, we need to ensure that our Ant script has an appropriate entry point for it. This is similar to that used by the developer in the steps described earlier. The following is a new target designed as an entry point for a CI server. More complex scripts might involve some reuse between developer usage and CI usage.

The following target will clean the build org (by virtue of the dependency on the undeploy target) and then deploy to it. It will then perform a second deploy to perform a check-only deployment to the packaging org. If you are following along, commit the changes to the build.xml file so that the Jenkins server can see the new target when it downloads the latest source code from GitHub.

```
<target name="deploy.jenkins" depends="undeploy">
  <sf:deploy
      username="${sf.username}"
      password="${sf.password}"
      serverurl="${sf.server}"
      runAllTests="true"
      deployRoot="${basedir}/src"/>
  <sf:deploy
      username="${sf.package.username}"
      password="${sf.package.password}"
      serverurl="${sf.server}"
      checkOnly="true"
      runAllTests="true"
      deployRoot="${basedir}/src"/>
</target>
```

Installing, configuring, and testing the Jenkins CI server

Setting up a Jenkins server is a broad topic beyond the scope of this chapter. A good way, however, to get started is to go to `http://jenkins-ci.org/` and download one of the prebuilt installations for your operating system. In this case I used the Mac download. After installation, I was able to navigate to `http://localhost:8080` to find Jenkins waiting for me!

Jenkins has a plugin system that permits many custom extensions to its base functionality, by clicking on **Manage Jenkins** and then **Manage Plugins** to locate a **GitHub Plugin**:

Once this plugin is installed, you can create a Jenkins job that points to your GitHub repository and Ant script to execute the `deploy.jenkins` target defined earlier. On the Jenkins main page, click on **New Item** and select the **Build a free-style software project** option. Complete the following steps to create a build project:

1. Complete the **Project Name** field with an appropriate name such as `FormulaForce Build`.

2. In the **GitHub project** field, enter the full URL to your GitHub repository, for example `https://github.com/afawcett/formulaforce-chapter11`.

3. Under the **Source Control Management** section, select **Git**.

4. In the **Repository URL** field, enter your GitHub repository URL, which is different from the preceding URL and takes the format of `https://github.com:githubuser/repositoryname.git`, for example, `https://github.com:afawcett/formulaforce-chapter11.git`.

5. If your repository is private and not public, you will need to ensure that you have exchanged deployment keys between Jenkins and your GitHub account. This involves generating a key and copying and pasting it to the **Deploy** keys section in your GitHub repository settings. For the purposes of this book, it is recommended that you use a public GitHub repository.

6. Although not recommended for a production Jenkins server, let's set it to poll every minute for changes to the repository. In the **Build Triggers** section, select **Poll SCM** and enter `*/1 * * * *` in the **Schedule** field.

7. Scroll further down the project setup page to the **Build** section, and from the **Add build** step drop-down select **Invoke Ant**.

8. In the **Targets** field, enter `deploy.jenkins` (as per the name of the Ant target created in the `build.xml` file).

9. Click on the **Advanced** button, then click on the black down arrow icon to the right of the **Properties** field to expand it so that you are able to enter multiple properties. The `deploy.jenkins` Ant target that we created earlier requires the `username` and `password` parameters to deploy to the build org and perform the check deploy to the packaging org. Enter the property name-value pairs on separate lines as follows:

   ```
   sf.username=buildorgusername
   sf.password=buildorgpasswordbuildorgtoken
   sf.package.username=packagingorgusername
   sf.package.password=packagingorgpasswordpackagingorgtoken
   ```

10. Click on the **Save** button at the bottom of the page.

After a minute, Jenkins realizes that there has not been a build yet and starts one. However, you can also click on the project and click on the **Build Now** button if you cannot wait!

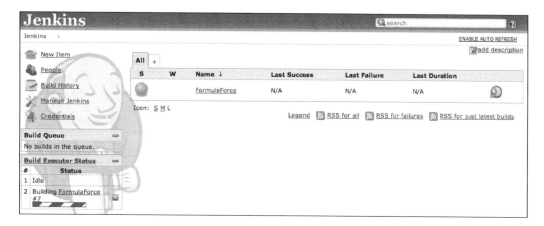

If you click on the hyperlink to the build itself (shown in the sidebar), you can monitor in real time the Ant script log just as if you had run it manually:

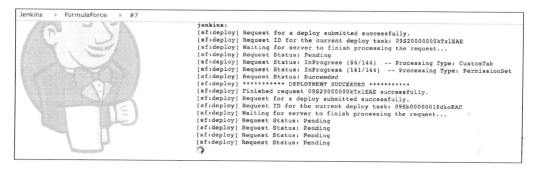

After this build completes, Jenkins will resume monitoring the GitHub repository for changes and automatically start a new build when it detects one.

Exploring Jenkins and CI further

This section has barely scratched the surface of what is possible with Jenkins and Ant scripts. You can either extend your Ant scripts to perform additional checks as described earlier and/or even custom logic to write back statistics to your own Salesforce production environment. Continue to explore this process a bit further by making some minor and some major changes to the repository to see the effects.

For example, try changing the method name of one of the global Apex methods (for example, `ComplianceService.report` to `ComplianceService.reportX`) as well as the methods in `ComplianceResource` and `ComplianceResource_1_0` calling it. While this compiles in the developer and build orgs, it eventually results in the following error from the Jenkins build, as the check deployment to the packaging org failed because published global methods cannot be removed or renamed. In this case, the following build failure will be reported by Jenkins:

```
classes/ComplianceService.cls -- Error: Global/WebService identifiers
cannot be removed from managed application: Method: LIST<fforce.
ComplianceService.VerifyResult> report(SET<Id>) (line 1, column 8)
```

The dashboard on Jenkins shows the project with a dark cloud as one out of the last two builds have now failed. It is time to fix the build:

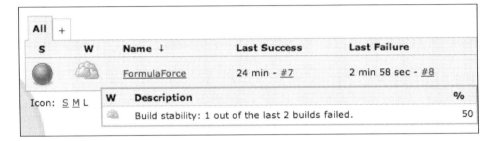

Once a new build completes successfully, Jenkins rewards you with some sunshine:

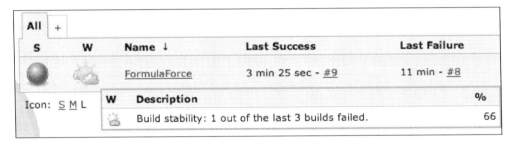

Releasing from Source Control

When you're ready to release a beta or release version of the package for your application, you will transfer the source code from Source Control into your packaging org. Thankfully, this can also be achieved with the help of the following Ant script target. Note that unlike the `deploy` Ant target, this does not attempt to clean the target org!

```
<target name="deploy.package">
  <sf:deploy
      username="${sf.username}"
      password="${sf.password}"
      serverurl="${sf.server}"
      runAllTests="true"
      deployRoot="${basedir}/src"/>
</target>
```

The process of updating the packaging org can only be partially automated by running the preceding Ant target, as you still need to log in to the packaging org to add brand new components that are not automatically added through a relationship with components already in the package.

The following is a list of recommended steps to update and confirm that the content of your packaging org matches the content of Source Control:

1. Run the following command (all on one command line):

    ```
    ant deploy.package
      -Dsf.username=packagingusername
      -Dsf.password=packagingpasswordpackagingtoken
    ```

2. Log in to the packaging org and review the contents of the package. You can utilize the **Add Component** page to determine whether components now reside in the packaging org that are not presently included in the package.

3. Rename the `/src` folder to `/src.fromsc` and create a new `/src` folder. Then, run the `retrieve.package` Ant target as per the command line you used to download files from the packaging org at the beginning of this chapter.

4. Compare the `/src` and `/src.fromsc` folders using your favorite file comparison tool. Review differences to determine whether changes exist either in the packaging org or in the Source Control system that do not belong to the application being packaged!

5. As per best practice, confirm that your package dependencies are still as expected. Then, perform an upload in the usual way as discussed in the previous chapters.

Automated regression testing

While Apex tests are very much a key tool in monitoring regressions in your application, the limitations and scope of functionality they can test is small, particularly to perform volume or user interface testing (clients using JavaScript for example).

 You might wonder why the Ant script used by Jenkins deploys twice, as the check deploy to the packaging org will confirm whether the Apex code compiles and that all Apex tests complete successfully. The reason is that having the build org deployed with the latest build allows for it go on to be used for other purposes, such as executing further regression testing steps.

Here are some considerations to implement further testing approaches:

- It is possible to execute the Apex code from the Ant scripts using the approach described earlier in this chapter, when we populated the developer org with sample data by calling the `SeasonService.createTestSeason` method. You can extend this approach by using loop constructs within Ant to create volume data or start more Batch Apex jobs (Apex tests only permit a single chunk of 200 records to be processed), pause for completion, and assert the results.

- The Salesforce data loader tool is actually a Java program with a command-line interface. Thus, you could consider using it to load data into a build org to test against different datasets, used in combination with the preceding Apex code executed to clean records between tests.

- Once you have the data loaded into the build org, you can execute tests using a number of Salesforce testing tools. For example, the **Selenium WebDriver** tool is an excellent choice, as it provides a headless mode (no need for a physical screen) and can be run on multiple operating systems. This tool allows you to test Visualforce pages with large amounts of JavaScript (`http://docs.seleniumhq.org/projects/webdriver/`).

Summary

In this final chapter of the book, we have seen how to scale developer resources to the development of your Enterprise application using industry strength Source Control tools, development processes, and servers such as Jenkins.

Some of the steps described in this chapter might initially seem excessive and overly complex compared to developing within a single packaging org or using other manual approaches to export and merge changes between developer orgs. Ultimately, more time is lost in resolving conflicts manually and not to mention the increased risk of losing changes.

Certainly, if your business is aiming to be audited for its development processes, adopting a more controlled approach with tighter controls over who has access to not only the source code but also your mechanism to release it (your packaging org) is a must.

Opening up your Force.com development process to tools such as Git for example allows for a much better developer interaction for aspects such as code reviews and carefully staging features in development to release. Such tools also give a greater insight into statistics around your development process that allow you optimize your development standards and productivity further over time.

Index

Symbols

@Depreciated annotation 281
@Depricated flag 282
/ folder
  purpose 338
@future
  utilizing 322
/lib folder
  purpose 338
.NET
  URL 277
/source (alternative) folder
  purpose 339
/src folder
  purpose 338
@TestVisible annotation 220

A

action attribute
  used, for executing code on page load 237
action methods
  versus JavaScript Remoting 252
Advanced Encryption Standard (AES) 46
Aggregate SOQL queries 214
Aloha 30
AngularJS 258
Ant
  about 332
  Metadata API, leveraging from 347, 348
  Tooling API, leveraging from 347, 348

Ant build script
  developing, in developer org 346, 347
  updating, for CI 354
  used, for building application 344-346
  used, for cleaning application 344-346
Apache Ant open source tool 335
Apache Ant v1.6
  URL 337
Apex
  about 43
  Anonymous Apex 103
  Apex Controller action method 103
  Apex Controller remote action 104
  Apex REST API 105
  Apex scheduler 105
  Apex Trigger 104
  Apex web service 105
  Batch Apex 105
  Flow plugin 105
  Inbound messaging 105
  need for 103
  running, in asynchronous mode 321
  Separation of Concerns (SOC) 107
Apex application APIs
  behavior, versioning 285, 286
  calling 279, 280
  depreciating 281
  modifying 281
  providing 277-279
  versioning 282-284
Apex classes 194

Apex Commons library,
     FinancialForce.com 114
Apex compiler 158
Apex data types
  combining, with SObject types 213
Apex Debug log 94
Apex Describe facility 56
Apex DML
  external references, using 327, 328
Apex Domain classes
  comparing, to other platforms 158, 159
Apex Enum types
  JavaScript Remoting, applying to 257
Apex exception class 270
Apex governors
  deterministic governors 101
  namespaces 99
  non-deterministic governors 101
  scope 99-101
Apex inheritance 158
Apex Interface
  application logic, extending with 295-297
  using 171
Apex Interface example
  about 171
  compliance framework implementation,
       summarizing 179, 180
  Domain class factory pattern 175
  Domain class interface,
       implementing 173, 174
  generic service, defining 172, 173
  generic service, implementing 176, 177
  generic service, using from generic
       controller 177, 178
Apex Metadata API library
  URL 44
Apex property syntax 127
Apex REST APIs
  versioning, need for 294
Apex, running in asynchronous mode
  @future, utilizing 322
  about 321
  Batch Apex, utilizing 323-325
Apex Scheduled job 84

Apex script
  used, for creating Race Data object 301, 302
Apex Trigger event handling
  about 166
  field values, defaulting on insert 167
  validation, on insert 167, 168
  validation, on update 168, 169
Apex Trigger events 158
Apex Trigger execution 230
Apex Triggers 79, 294
Apex Visualforce Controller 219
Apex wrapper
  URL 44
API definition
  versioning 267, 268
API functionality
  versioning 269
API governors 235, 236
AppExchange package 23, 24
AppExchange Publishing Org (APO) 11, 23
AppExchange solutions
  bulk API 91
  outbound messaging 90
  replication API 90
application
  extensibility needs 275
  integration needs 272, 273
  logic, extending with Apex
       interfaces 295-297
application access
  versioning, through Salesforce APIs 268
Application Cache 79
application component 350
application integration APIs 277
application logic concerns
  versus execution context logic
       versus 108-110
application resources 287-289
Application.Selector.setMock
  used, for writing test 222
application vocabulary of terms 122
aspects, for developing libraries
  developer flow 259
  security 259
  testing frameworks 259

async design considerations
  background work, types 319
  concurrency 321
  error recovery 321
  logging 320
  messaging 320
  user experience 320
asynchronous execution contexts
  about 318, 319
  Apex, running in asynchronous
     mode 321, 322
  async design considerations 319
Aura
  about 259
  URL 259
automated regression testing
  about 360
  implementing, considerations 360
Auto Number Display Format
  customizing, by subscribers 85
Auto Number fields
  about 82-84
  Display Format, customizing 85

B

background work, types
  application 319
  end user 319
Batch Apex
  about 323
  external references, using in Apex
     DML 327, 328
  implementing 324
  job performances 326
  utilizing, implementation guidelines 325
Batch Apex Chaining 325
Batch Apex Flex Queue 326
Batch Apex jobs performances
  calibrating 326
  frequency 326
  start method, using 326
benefits, security review
  bypass subscriber org setup limits 30
  licensing 30

  push upgrade 30
  subscriber support 30
beta packages 20, 21
browser-based development
  using, with Source Control
     repository 349, 350
Bulk API 62, 91
bulkification 125
bulkified implementations 159

C

cache attribute
  used, for caching content 238
Chatter
  about 79
  enabling 68-72
Chatter feed 261
Chatter Files 81
Chatter post 79
CheckMarx
  URL 30
CI
  about 30, 353
  Ant build script, updating for 354
  exploring 358
  hooking up 352
  Jenkins CI server, configuring 355-357
  Jenkins CI server, installing 355-357
  Jenkins CI server, updating 355-357
  process 353
CI process
  steps 353, 354
class names 122
client communication layers
  about 233
  API governors 235
  availability 235
  client calls 236
  database transaction scope 236
  options 233
client communication options
  AJAX Toolkit 234
  Analytics API 235
  Salesforce REST/SOAP API's 234
  Salesforce Streaming API 234

Visualforce Components 234
Visualforce JavaScript Remote Objects 234
Visualforce JavaScript Remoting 234
client-managed state
    versus server-managed state 251
client-side logic
    considerations 256, 257
columns
    versus rows 76, 77
common Apex Interface 215
compliance application framework
    creating 170, 171
compliance framework implementation
    summarizing 179, 180
ComplianceService.verify method 279
components
    adding, to package 18
component tree
    demonstrating 248-250
    managing, considerations 250
composition approach 158
compound services 129, 130
concrete type 158
considerations, Platform APIs
    Apex Triggers bulkification 63
    API name consistency 62
    Custom Objects, naming 62
    fields, naming 62
    label consistency 62
    Naming Relationships 62
constructor 163
contentType attribute
    used, for creating Download
        button 239, 240
Contestant object 76
contexts, of Domain class callers
    Apex Triggers 185
    Domain layer 185
    Service layer 185
Continuous Integration. See CI
Contract Driven Development 146, 148
Cross-site Request Forgery (CSRF) security
    about 238
    URL 238
CRUD and FLS Enforcement
    testing, URL 56
    URL 56

CRUD and FLS security 98
CRUD (Create, Read, Update,
        and Delete) operations 166, 233
Custom Button
    about 230
    creating 231, 232
custom data set
    using, with custom Selector
        method 210-212
customer licenses
    managing 33
customer metrics 38
customer support
    providing 36, 37
Custom Field label 233
custom fields, features
    about 45
    default field values 45, 46
    encrypted fields 47
    filters 47-50
    layouts 47-50
    lookup options 47-50
custom indexes 303, 304
customizable user interfaces
    building 65, 66
    layouts 66
    Visualforce pages 66
Custom Labels
    about 233
    creating 65
Custom Objects 12, 160
Custom Publisher Actions 260
custom query logic
    Aggregate SOQL queries 214
    custom Selector method 206
    custom Selector method, using with
        custom data set 210
    custom Selector method, using with
        related fields 209
    custom Selector method, using with
        sub-select 207
    implementing 205
    SOSL queries 214
Custom Reporting 261
custom Selector method
    about 206
    using, with custom data set 210-212

using, with related fields 209, 210

using, with sub-select 207, 208

custom Selector method, using with custom data set

Apex data types, combining with SObject types 213, 214

custom settings

creating 80

D

data

archiving, options 90

defining 126, 127

exporting 87, 89

importing 87, 89

passing 126, 128

replicating, options 90

data consistency 194

Data Loader tools 328

Data Mapper (Selector) layer, Enterprise Application Architecture patterns

about 114

Apex Commons library, FinancialForce.com 114

URL 114

data security

about 53, 57-59

code review considerations 60

security review considerations 60

data storage

about 76

columns 76, 77

custom settings storage 79

object model, visualizing 78, 79

rows 76, 77

Data Transformation Objects (DTO) 114

debugging aspect 337

debug log filters 337

default field values 45, 46

default order, selectSObjectsById method 202

delete event 157

DELETE method 289

design guidelines implementation, Domain layer

about 159

bulkification 161

data, defining 162

data, passing 162

naming conventions 159, 160

transaction management 162

design guidelines implementation, Selector layer

bulkification 196

fields, querying 197, 198

implementing 195

naming conventions 195

record order consistency 196

design guidelines implementations, Service layer pattern

about 121

bulkification 125

checklist 131

compound services 130

data, defining 126

data, passing 126

naming conventions 122

transaction management 129

desktop-based development

using, with Source Control repository 351, 352

Detail Pages 170

deterministic governors 101, 102

Developer Console 248

Developer Console Preview feature 248

Developer Mode 248

developer org

creating 333, 334

preparing 333

URL 333

versus packaging org 332-347

versus sandbox orgs 332

Developer Workbench tool 308

developer workflow

about 334

diagrammatic representation 335, 336

Developer X
  about 266
  calling, APIs off-platform 274
  calling, APIs on-platform 273
development tools, Source Control
  Apache Ant v1.6 or greater 337
  Force.com Migration Toolkit 337
  GitHub 337
  MavensMate 338
development workflow
  about 332
  developer org, versus packaging org 332
  packaging org, versus developer org 332
  sandbox orgs, versus developer
      org 332, 333
DML
  handling, with Unit of Work
      pattern 132, 133
  used, for Apex Trigger method testing 181
DNF (Did not Finish) object 260
docType attribute 241
Domain class factory pattern, Apex
      Interface example 175
Domain class interface, Apex Interface
      example
  defining 173
Domain class methods
  testing 183, 184
Domain class template 162, 163
Domain Custom logic
  implementing 169, 170
Domain layer
  Apex Trigger methods, testing
      with DML 181, 182
  Apex Trigger methods, testing
      with SOQL 181, 182
  calling 184
  custom Domain class methods,
      testing with 183
  design guidelines, implementing 159
  Domain class methods, using 183, 184
  interpreting, in Force.com 157, 158
  testing 180
  unit testing 181
  URL 156
Domain layer interactions 187-189

Domain layer logic 230
Domain layer pattern
  about 156
  Apex Domain classes, comparing with
      other platforms 158, 159
  interpreting, in Force.com 157
  object's behavior, encapsulating
      in code 157
Domain Model layer, Enterprise
      Application Architecture patterns
  about 113
  URL 113
Domain Trigger logic implementation
  Apex Trigger event handling 166
  object security, enforcing 166
  trigger events, routing to Domain class
      methods 164, 165
Download button
  creating, with contentType
      attribute 239, 240
dummy implementation 146
Dynamic Apex 22
Dynamic Apex type
  creating 295
Dynamic SOQL 199

E

e-mail templates
  used, for e-mail customization 66, 67
encrypted fields 47
end user storage requirements
  mapping 74
Enterprise and Developer Edition orgs 260
Enterprise API 61
Enterprise Application Architecture
      patterns
  about 93, 112
  Data Mapper (Selector) layer 114
  Domain Model layer 113
  Service layer 113
  URL 112
Enterprise applications software 12
Entity Relationship Diagram (ERD) 78
enum 270
Execute Anonymous prompt 301

execution context logic
  versus application logic
    concerns 108-110
execution contexts
  about 94
  error handling 108
  exploring 94-96
  number of records 109
  security 109
  security features 97
  state 96
  state management 109
  transaction management 98, 99, 108
Execution Governors and Limits
  URL 319
expires attributes
  used, for caching content 238
extensibility, Force.com
  features 294, 295
extensibility needs
  about 275
  reviewing 266
Extension Controller 228
extension packages 13, 19
extensions 275
external data sources 91
external identifiers 82
external ID fields
  adding 82

F

Factory pattern
  about 175
  URL 175
features, managed packages
  governor scope 14
  Intellectual Property (IP) protection 14
  naming scope 14
  upgrades 14
  versioning 14
fflib_SObjectSelector class 206
FIA Super License 170
field-level security (FLS) 56, 242-246
Field Sets fields, selectSObjectsById
    method 203

file storage 81
filter criteria 305
filters, custom filed 47-50
FinancialForce Apex Enterprise Pattern
    library 136, 162, 198
FinancialForce.com
  about 344
  URL 344
Flow. *See* **Visual Flow**
fly-by reviews approach 125
Force.com
  about 9, 260
  Domain layer, interpreting in 157, 158
Force.com Migration Toolkit 337
Force.com platform APIs
  for integration 276, 277
Force.com Web Service Connector
    (WSC) 276
Formula fields 77
FormulaForce package, Domain layer
  updating 190
FormulaForce package, Selector layer
  implementing 223
FormulaForce package, Service layer
  updating 152
FormulaForce package, User Interface
  updating 262
functional security
  about 53
  code review considerations 56, 57
  Permission Sets, creating 53-56
  Permission Sets, designing 54
  profiles, creating 53-56
  security review considerations 56, 57

G

generic service, Apex Interface example
  defining 172, 173
  implementing 176, 177
  using, from generic controller 177, 178
GET method 289
GitFlow 336
GitHub
  about 337
  URL 337

GitHub Salesforce Deployment Tool
  URL 14
global components, release package 21

H

heap 96, 198
heap governor 314
HTTP GET 233
HTTP methods
  mapping 289, 290
HTTP POST 233
HTTP protocol 233
hybrid mobile application 241
hybrid standard
  creating 228, 229

I

Idempotent 289
Independent Software Vendor (ISV) 28
indexes
  about 303
  custom indexes 303
  queries leverage indexes, ensuring 305
  queries, profiling 307
  references 306
  standard indexes 303
  using, factors 305, 307
inner class names 124
integration needs
  reviewing 266
internal view state 247
Internet of Things (IoT) 266
ISVForce Guide (Packaging Guide)
  about 14
  URL 14

J

JavaScript Remote Objects
  using 257
JavaScript Remoting
  about 25, 235
  applying, to Service layer 256
  combining, with action methods 255
  using 318
  versus action methods 252-254

Jenkins CI server
  configuring 355-357
  exploring 357, 358
  installing 355-357
  testing 355-357
  URL 355
JQuery Mobile 255

L

language attribute
  used, for overriding page language 240
layouts, custom filed 47-50
layouts, customizable user interfaces
  actions 66
  Custom Buttons 66
  report chart, embedding 66
  Visualforce pages, embedding 66
Leads tab 39
License Management Application(LMA) 31
License Management Org (LMO) 11
Licenses tab 33, 34
licensing
  about 31-33
  customer licenses, managing 33, 34
  enforcing, in subscriber org 36
  Licenses tab 33, 34
  Subscriber Overview page 35
  Subscribers tab 34
List View layouts 228
localization 63, 270, 271
logging solutions 79
log table 110
Lookup field 187
lookup filters 48
lookup options, custom fields 47-50

M

managed package
  about 13
  assigning, to namespace 17
  benefits 14
  components, adding to 18
  creating 15-17
  extension packages 19
  features 14
  package namespace, setting 15, 16

manifest attribute
  about 241
  used, for offline web pages 241
Master-Detail relationships, Salesforce 85
MavensMate 259, 338
messaging and logging, considerations
  Custom Object logging 320
  notifications 321
  unhandled exceptions 321
Metadata API
  about 61
  leveraging, from Ant 347, 348
method names 123
Migration Toolkit 332
mobile strategy 261
mocking 150
mock Selector class
  creating 221
Model View Controller (MVC) 258
Multi-Currency feature, selectSObjectsById
    method 204

N

namespaces
  assigning 16
  managed package, setting up 17
naming conventions, Domain layer design
    guidelines
  acronyms, avoiding 159
  class names 160
  inner classes 160
  interfaces 160
  method names 160
  parameter names 160
  parameter types 160
naming conventions, Service layer design
    guidelines implementations
  about 122
  acronyms, avoiding 122
  class names 122
  compound services 129
  data, defining 127
  data, passing 127
  inner class names 124
  method names 123

  parameter names 123
  parameter types 123
  SObjects, using 128
naming conventions, Selector layer design
    guidelines
  class names 195
  method names 196
  method signatures 196
newInstance method
  caching 217
  mocking 217
  usage 216, 217
non-deterministic governors 101, 102
nonselective query 305
non-upgradable components 42

O

object-orientated programming (OOP) 106
  about 157, 170
  Apex Interface example 171
  compliance application framework,
    creating 170, 171
Object Read Security 202
Object Relational Mapping (ORM) 156
object's behavior
  encapsulating, in code 157
object security
  enforcing 166
outbound messaging 90

P

package
  about 13
  beta packages 20
  beta packages 21
  dependencies 19, 20
  installing 24
  release packages 21
  release, uploading 20
  testing 24
package Apex developers
  key governors 102
package dependencies
  options 22

package dependencies, options
  Dynamic Apex 22
  extension packages 22
  Visualforce 22
package installation
  Approve Package API Access step 25
  automating 26-28
  Connected App and Remote Access 25
  package overview step 25
  security configuration step 25
package namespace
  setting up 15, 16
packaging code
  about 116, 117
  Apex classes 116, 117
packaging components 42, 43
packaging org
  about 12, 15, 223
  versus developer org 332-347
  versus sandbox orgs 332, 333
PageReference.getContentAsPDF
    method 242
page response time
  about 247, 248
  component tree, demonstrating 248, 249
Partner Account Manager 236
Partner API 61
Partner Community
  URL 28
Partner Developer Edition orgs 29
Partner Portal Developer Edition org 314
Partner Portal website 10
PATCH method 289
PDF content
  generating, with renderAs attribute 241
Permission Sets
  creating 53
  designing, requisites 54, 55
  FormulaForce - Race Analytics 55
  FormulaForce - Race Management 55
  FormulaForce - Race Management - Update
    DNF Status 55
personas 74
picklist values 43
PitStop Time 310
Plain Old Java Object (POJO) approach 194

platform alignment 272
platform APIs
  about 60, 61
  Bulk API 62
  Enterprise API 61
  field naming, considerations 62
  Metadata API 61
  object naming, considerations 62
  Partner API 61
  Replication API 62
  REST API 61
  Streaming API 62
  Tooling API 61
POST method
  versus PUT method 289
private listing 23, 24
Production / CRM Org 11
production implementation 146
Professional Edition 236
profiles 53
protected keyword 145
public methods 157
Publisher Actions 261
PUT method
  versus POST method 289

Q

Qualification Lap child object 76
queries
  profiling 307-312
queries leverage indexes
  ensuring 305
QueryLocator 223
query optimization 303
Queue 59

R

Race Data object
  creating, Apex script used 301, 302
RaceDataSelector class 323
race object layout 230
RaceService.processData method 323
readOnly attribute 242
Recycle Bin 317
referential integrity rule 47

Related lists 230
relationships, Salesforce
  limits 85
  Lookup 85
  Master-Detail 85
  referential integrity features 85
release packages 21
release upload 20
Remote Objects 235, 236
renderAs attribute
  used, for generating PDF content 241
Replication API 62
report charts 66
Report Designer 262
REST
  versus SOAP 274
REST APIs
  about 61, 261
  versioning 292, 293
REST application APIs
  about 290, 291
  calling 291
result sets, Apex
  50k maximum results, processing 314
  Apex read-only mode 317, 318
  handling 313
  processing, with Salesforce APIs 315-318
  Race Data, generating 317
  Visualforce, leveraging 317, 318
role hierarchy 59
Rollup summary option 50, 52
rows
  versus columns 76, 77

S

Salesforce
  URL 265
Salesforce Analytics API 261
Salesforce APIs
  application access, versioning through 268
  used, for processing unlimited result
    sets 318
Salesforce Aura. *See* Aura
Salesforce Data Loaders 136

Salesforce Metadata API
  about 26
  URL 26
  used, for upgrade automation 44
Salesforce Migration Toolkit 26
Salesforce Mobile Packs
  URL 261
Salesforce Object Search Language
  (SOSL queries) 214
Salesforce organizations
  about 10
  URL 10
Salesforce partner
  becoming 28, 29
Salesforce Reporting engine 261
Salesforce REST API 261
Salesforce standard UI
  Custom Buttons 230
  hybrid standard 228
  leveraging 226, 227
  overriding 227, 228
  Related lists 230
  rendering, within Visualforce page 232
  Visualforce UIs 228, 229
Salesforce Translation Workbench tool 43
sandbox 21
sandbox orgs
  versus developer org 332, 333
  versus packaging org 332, 333
Savepoints 99
Schema Builder 78
Seat based licensing 26
security compliance 194
security features
  about 53
  CRUD and FLS security 98
  data security 53
  functional security 53
  sharing security 98
security review
  about 29, 31
  benefits 30
Selector 142
Selector class template 198-200

Selector factory
   about 215
   methods 216
   Selectors, mocking 219
SelectorFactory methods
   about 216
   newInstance method 216
   tests, writing 218
Selector layer
   about **194**
   design guidelines, implementing 195
   URL 194
Selectors, mocking
   @TestVisible annotation, applying 220
   about 219
   Application.Selector.newInstance
      approach 219
   mock Selector class, creating 221
   Selector methods, identifying 223
   test, writing with
      Application.Selector.setMock 222
   virtual keyword, applying 220
selectSObjectsById method, features
   default order 202
   FieldSet fields 203
   Multi-Currency 204
   security 202
Selenium WebDriver tool
   about 360
   URL 360
Sencha **241**
Sencha ExtJS **258**
Sencha Touch **255**
Separation of Concerns (SOC)
   about 93
   benefits 106
   code evolution 106, 107
   code reuse, improving 110-112
   execution context logic, versus application
      logic concerns 108, 109
   in Apex 107
server-managed state
   versus client-managed state 251
Service code **171**
Service layer **158**
   calling 150, 151
   FormulaForce package, updating 152

JavaScript Remoting, applying to 256
   mocking 150
   testing 149
Service layer, Enterprise Application
      Architecture patterns
   about 113
   URL 113
Service layer interactions **185**
Service layer logic
   considerations 256
Service layer pattern
   about 120
   URL 120
service methods
   implementing 141-145
sharing rules **59**
sharing security **98**
Signup Request API **38**
Single Developer Editions orgs **29**
Sites.com **260**
skinny tables **313**
SLA **319**
SOAP
   versus REST 274
SObject
   about **194**
   using, in Service layer interface 128
social features
   Chatter 68-72
SOQL
   about 308
   used, for Apex Trigger method
      testing 181, 182
SOQL FOR LOOP **314**
Source Control repository
   Ant build script, using 344
   content, releasing from 359
   developing with 337, 338
   populating 338-344
   repository, populating 338
   repository, updating 348
   updating 348, 349
   using, with browser and desktop-based
      development option 349
   using, with browser-based
      development 349, 350

using, with browser-based
        development 349
using, with desktop-based
        development 349-352
special considerations, Unit of Work pattern
    e-mails, sending 140
    granular DML operations 140
    self and recursive referencing 140
standard indexes
    about 303, 304
    fields 303
standard objects
    reusing 87
standard query logic
    implementing 201
    selectSObjectsById method, features 201
standardStylesheets attribute 242
state management 97
storage types
    about 75, 76
    auto numbering 81
    data storage 76
    file storage 81
    record, identifying 81
    uniqueness feature 81
Streaming API 62
subscriber org 14
    licensing, enforcing 36
Subscriber Overview page 35
Subscribers tab 34
Subscriber Support feature 307
sub-select
    using, with custom Selector
        method 207, 208
system administrator 346
system testing
    versus unit testing 115

T

target devices
    determining 226
team principle 54
Technical Account Manager (TAM) 57
template method pattern
    URL 165
test data
    creating, for volume testing 300, 301

Test Drive button 38, 39
test-driven development (TDD) 115
Tooling API
    about 61, 338
    leveraging, from Ant 347, 348
transaction management 129
translation 64, 270, 271
Trialforce Management Org (TMO) 11
Trialforce Source Org (TSO) 11
trigger events
    routing, to Domain class methods 164
Type.forName method 295

U

Uniform Resource Identifier (URI) 287
Unique Id field
    adding 82
Unit of Work pattern
    about 99, 162, 170
    avoiding 134-136
    scope 140
    special considerations 140, 141
    URL 132
    used, for handling DML 132, 133
    using 136-139
unit testing
    about 181
    definition, URL 181
    versus system testing 115
unmanaged packages 13, 14
update event 157
upgradable components
    about 42
    picklist values 43
    upgrades, automating with Salesforce
        Metadata API 44
Usage Metrics Visualization application 38
use cases, browser-based development
    additional downloaded files 350
    file content order or additional elements,
        differences 350
user experience, considerations
    background work start 320
    monitoring process 320
    progress bar indicators 320
user profile 63

V

versioning
about 267
Apex REST APIs 294
API definition 267, 268
API functionality 269
application access, through Salesforce
  APIs 268
REST APIs 293
View State debugger tool 248
Viewstate limits 251
viewstate size 198
virtual keyword, Selectors 220
Visual Flow 67
Visualforce
about 236
action methods, versus JavaScript
  Remoting 252-255
client-managed state, versus
  server-managed state 251
client-side alternatives, Visualforce
  UI components 258
code execution, on page load with action
  attribute 237
content caching, with cache attributes 238
content caching, with expires attributes 238
docType attribute 241
Download button, creating with
  contentType attribute 239, 240
field-level security 242
HTML5 241
iterator limits 242
JavaScript Remote Objects, using 257
JavaScript Remoting, applying to Service
  layer 256
manifest attribute, using for offline web
  pages 241
page language, overriding with language
  attribute 240
page response time 247
PDF content generation, renderAs attribute
  used 241
platform areas 236
readOnly attribute 242
Visualforce SOQL 242
working with 237

Visualforce client developer 149
Visualforce components 295
Visualforce Controller 171
Visualforce pages
about 13, 22, 63
embedding 66
Salesforce standard UI, rendering 232
Visualforce SOQL 242
volume testing
about 328
pitfalls 328
Race Data object, creating with
  Apex script 301, 302
test data, creating for 300, 301

W

**Web Application Definition Language
  (WADL) 274**
Web Service Connector (WSC) 276
**Web Service Definition Language
  (WSDL) 90**
websites, creating
ways 260
Workflow 67
wrapper class approach 158

X

XML metadata 19

Thank you for buying
Force.com Enterprise Architecture

About Packt Publishing

Packt, pronounced 'packed', published its first book "Mastering phpMyAdmin for Effective MySQL Management" in April 2004 and subsequently continued to specialize in publishing highly focused books on specific technologies and solutions.

Our books and publications share the experiences of your fellow IT professionals in adapting and customizing today's systems, applications, and frameworks. Our solution based books give you the knowledge and power to customize the software and technologies you're using to get the job done. Packt books are more specific and less general than the IT books you have seen in the past. Our unique business model allows us to bring you more focused information, giving you more of what you need to know, and less of what you don't.

Packt is a modern, yet unique publishing company, which focuses on producing quality, cutting-edge books for communities of developers, administrators, and newbies alike. For more information, please visit our website: www.packtpub.com.

About Packt Enterprise

In 2010, Packt launched two new brands, Packt Enterprise and Packt Open Source, in order to continue its focus on specialization. This book is part of the Packt Enterprise brand, home to books published on enterprise software – software created by major vendors, including (but not limited to) IBM, Microsoft and Oracle, often for use in other corporations. Its titles will offer information relevant to a range of users of this software, including administrators, developers, architects, and end users.

Writing for Packt

We welcome all inquiries from people who are interested in authoring. Book proposals should be sent to author@packtpub.com. If your book idea is still at an early stage and you would like to discuss it first before writing a formal book proposal, contact us; one of our commissioning editors will get in touch with you.

We're not just looking for published authors; if you have strong technical skills but no writing experience, our experienced editors can help you develop a writing career, or simply get some additional reward for your expertise.

Salesforce CRM: The Definitive Admin Handbook

ISBN: 978-1-84968-306-7   Paperback: 376 pages

A comprehensive, power-packed guide for all Salesforce Administrators covering everything from setup and configuration, to the customization of Salesforce CRM

1. Get to grips with tips, tricks, best-practice administration principles, and critical design considerations for setting up and customizing Salesforce CRM with this book and e-book.

2. Master the mechanisms for controlling access to, and the quality of, data and information sharing.

3. Take advantage of the only guide with real-world business scenarios for Salesforce CRM.

Force.com Tips and Tricks

ISBN: 978-1-84968-474-3   Paperback: 224 pages

A quick reference guide for administrators and developers to get more productive with Force.com

1. Tips and tricks for topics ranging from point-and-click administration, to fine development techniques with Apex and Visualforce.

2. Avoids technical jargon, and expresses concepts in a clear and simple manner.

3. A pocket guide for experienced Force.com developers.

Please check **www.PacktPub.com** for information on our titles

Force.com Development Blueprints

Stephen Moss

[PACKT] enterprise

Force.com Development Blueprints

ISBN: 978-1-78217-245-1   Paperback: 350 pages

Design and develop real-world, cutting-edge cloud applications using the powerful Force.com development framework

1. Create advanced cloud applications using the best Force.com technologies.

2. Bring your cloud application ideas to market faster using the proven Force.com infrastructure.

3. Step-by-step tutorials show you how to quickly develop real-world cloud applications.

Salesforce CRM: The Definitive Admin Handbook
Second Edition

Paul Goodey

[PACKT] enterprise

Salesforce CRM: The Definitive Admin Handbook
Second Edition

ISBN: 978-1-78217-052-5   Paperback: 426 pages

A comprehensive guide for the setup, configuration, and customization of Salesforce CRM

1. Updated for Spring '13, this book covers best practice administration principles, real-world experience, and critical design considerations for setting up and customizing Salesforce CRM.

2. Analyze data within Salesforce by using reports, dashboards, custom reports, and report builder.

3. A step-by-step guide offering clear guidance for the customization and administration of the Salesforce CRM application.

Please check **www.PacktPub.com** for information on our titles

Made in the USA
Lexington, KY
10 January 2015